THE CAMBRIDGE COMP...

PARADISE LOST

This *Companion* presents fifteen short, accessibl... ...ost important topics and themes in John Milton's mas... ...*radise Lost*. The essays invite readers to begin their own independent exploration of the poem by equipping them with useful background knowledge, introducing them to key passages, and acquainting them with the current state of critical debates. Chapters are arranged to mirror the way the poem itself unfolds, offering exactly what readers need as they approach each movement of its grand design. Essays in Part I introduce the characters who frame the poem's story and set its plot and theological dynamics in motion. Part II deals with contextual issues raised by the early books, while Part III examines the epic's central and final episodes. The volume concludes with a meditation on the history of the poem's reception and a detailed guide to further reading, offering students and teachers of Milton fresh critical insights and resources for continuing scholarship.

Louis Schwartz is Professor of English at the University of Richmond, Virginia. His essays and book reviews on Milton and early modern English literature and culture have been published in journals such as *Milton Quarterly*, *Milton Studies*, *Reformation*, *The Comparatist*, and *The Lancet*. His book, *Milton and Maternal Morality* (Cambridge, 2009), is the winner of the Milton Society of America's James Holly Hanford Award for 2009.

A complete list of book in the series is at the back of this book.

THE CAMBRIDGE
COMPANION TO
PARADISE LOST

THE CAMBRIDGE COMPANION TO
PARADISE LOST

EDITED BY
LOUIS SCHWARTZ
University of Richmond

CAMBRIDGE
UNIVERSITY PRESS

CAMBRIDGE
UNIVERSITY PRESS

32 Avenue of the Americas, New York NY 10013-2473, USA

Cambridge University Press is part of the University of Cambridge.

It furthers the University's mission by disseminating knowledge in the pursuit of education, learning and research at the highest international levels of excellence.

www.cambridge.org
Information on this title: www.cambridge.org/9781107664401

© Cambridge University Press 2014

First published 2014

A catalogue record for this publication is available from the British Library

Library of Congress Cataloguing in Publication data
The Cambridge Companion to *Paradise Lost* / edited by Louis Schwartz.
pages   cm. – (Cambridge Companions to Literature)
Includes bibliographical references and index.
ISBN 978-1-107-02946-0 (hardback) – ISBN 978-1-107-66440-1 (paperback)
1. Milton, John, 1608–1674. Paradise lost.   I. Schwartz, Louis, 1962– editor of compilation.
PR3562.C336   2014
821′.4–dc23   2013046191

ISBN 978-1-107-02946-0 Hardback
ISBN 978-1-107-66440-1 Paperback

CONTENTS

CONTENTS

CONTRIBUTORS

W. GARDNER CAMPBELL, Virginia Commonwealth University

JOHN CREASER, University of London

KAREN L. EDWARDS, University of Exeter

STEPHEN M. FALLON, University of Notre Dame

MARY C. FENTON, Western Carolina University

NEIL FORSYTH, Université de Lausanne

MAGGIE KILGOUR, McGill University

WILLIAM KOLBRENER, Bar Ilan University

SHANNON MILLER, Temple University

JOAD RAYMOND, Queen Mary, University of London

JOHN RUMRICH, University of Texas, Austin

JEFFREY SHOULSON, University of Connecticut

WILLIAM SHULLENBERGER, Sarah Lawrence College

VICTORIA SILVER, University of California, Irvine

PAUL STEVENS, University of Toronto

PREFACE

Milton's *Paradise Lost* makes enormous demands on a reader who tries to meet it on its own lofty and ambitious terms. Few texts, however, are as intensely rewarding to those willing to open themselves to its peculiar power and to the surprisingly open-ended trains of thought and feeling it can provoke. A reader is constantly pulled in various directions at once. Beneath the surface of the poem's expressed allegiance to a rational theology, images proliferate and double in ways that seem hardly rational at all. The poem is suffused with tremendous energies, presenting images of vast, cosmic spaces, angelic warfare, intense discussions on topics ranging from theology and politics to gender relations, astronomy, gardening, the nature of the erotic, and beyond. It also invites us to confuse things, to fuse seemingly incompatible concepts together in our minds and imaginations, and yet also to make surprisingly subtle distinctions that then lead to more confusions and then to even finer distinctions.

Each response and act of interpretation, each confusion and act of distinguishing, is like a choice made by a gardener: we allow one thing to grow, cut another, train something else along a trellis. But the work is never done. The thing we let grow today has to be cut tomorrow, the things we cut today grow back more abundantly, and the things we train need continual care, continual watch against their tending to wild. As W. Gardner Campbell observes in the essay on temptation in this volume, the temptation of the tree of knowledge, which is of course the central episode of the poem, is merely a paradigmatic and extreme example of what we face as readers throughout. "Reason is but choosing," Milton says in *Areopagitica*, and he has God the Father echo the phrase in Book 3 of the epic (3.108). And what is at stake in the choosing is nothing less than the question of whether or not existence as we know it can be said to have any meaning – and if so, what sources that meaning might have. Choosing is also meaning, therefore, and in the poem choices proliferate, a garden of forking paths, each one inviting us.

Part of what both disciplines our choosing and licenses our roving minds and feelings along each path is contextual knowledge and an awareness of what others have thought and felt as they have made their way through the vast cosmological spaces, the intimate bowers, and the mazes and mirrors of the poem. There are accessible beauties throughout, but readers are often discouraged by the poem's many allusions to and echoes of previous literary works. We are constantly aware, as we read, of the Hebrew scriptures, the New Testament, and a wide range of mythological and literary traditions. Their pressure is always felt, and we are asked to compare what we read to images and verbal patterns that we (hopefully) recall from our previous reading. We also always feel the poem's deep and complex engagement with the political, theological, and aesthetic debates of its time, as well as those stretching back through the history of Western European culture. These pressures and engagements are both tantalizing and daunting. If we only knew more, we often think, the poem would open itself more fully, reveal more of what we have been told is there.

The purpose of this *Companion* is to help new readers understand more of this vast scope of reference and context, providing advice and guidance about how to begin thinking about the poem and apprehending what so many readers of all kinds have found so richly compelling about it. To that end, the collection presents fifteen short, accessible essays, each by a recognized Milton scholar who is also a gifted teacher. The essays are designed to invite readers to begin their own independent exploration of the poem by equipping them with useful background knowledge, introducing them to key passages, and acquainting them with the current state of critical debates. They are arranged, moreover, to mirror the way the poem itself unfolds, offering exactly what readers need as they approach each movement of its grand design. The essays of Part I acquaint us with the characters we encounter first in the poem, the agents who frame its story and set its plot and its theological dynamics in motion. Stephen M. Fallon begins the collection by introducing us to the narrator who tells us the tale, a fictionalized version of Milton himself, who prays for the authority and inspiration to accomplish his unprecedented task, then sets out to accomplish it, turning the telling itself into an uncertain heroic drama. Neil Forsyth then introduces us to Satan, who is named near the start as the story's primary cause. He is also famously the character to whom Milton gave his best lines, and to some he is the hero of the poem in his indignant resistance to a God he sees as a tyrant. John Rumrich then helps us navigate our encounter with Sin, Death, and Chaos, a strange set of allegorical personae who suggest some of the darker aspects of human experience and some of the stranger aspects of Milton's ontology. Finally, Victoria Silver introduces us to the ironic poetic power of Milton's difficult God, whose goodness, despite all the darkness we have witnessed already, the poem means to defend.

The essays of Part II deal with the key contextual issues raised by the early books, matters most readers will need to understand before they continue on to the episodes at its center. The first, by Maggie Kilgour, introduces readers to what is at stake in reading the poem as an epic against the backdrop of its great classical models. Jeffrey Shoulson's essay on Milton's treatment of his biblical sources follows, explaining how Milton both adhered to and altered his scriptural precedents. John Creaser then introduces readers to the principle features and originality of Milton's verse style, with special attention to the way Milton's innovations help express and embody key themes of the poem. Paul Stevens then discusses the poem's intense interest in politics – a "pre-secular" politics that grounds its values of freedom and responsibility in Christian faith and action. Karen L. Edwards, finally, puts the poem's cosmology into its proper historical and intellectual contexts, helping unravel for us Milton's poetic treatment of the astronomical debates of his day.

Part III introduces the key conceptual issues of the epic's central and final episodes. The first essay, by William Shullenberger, explores the bewildering beauty of Milton's Eden, into which we are invited in Book 4, a place of great natural beauty and sensual delight, but also a place that tends to "wild," creating unexpected challenges both for its two inhabitants and for the reader. Next, Joad Raymond provides an introduction to Milton's angels, suggesting how important it is that we grasp their difference from us if we are to understand what the poem ultimately has to say about humanity. The third essay, by Shannon Miller, examines the centrality of gender difference to Milton's conception of human (as opposed to angelic) existence and introduces us to the historical contexts that help make sense of Milton's depiction of gender hierarchy. She shows just how conflicted Milton sometimes was about such hierarchy, at times reinforcing the assumptions that underpin early modern conceptions of male superiority, and at other times undermining them. The fourth essay offers W. Gardner Campbell's account of the dynamics of temptation at the heart of the poem, offering an answer to a key question: Why did Milton write his justification of God's goodness in the form of a poem at all? Campbell suggests that he did so to make use of the peculiar power that symbol has to express the tension between discipline and liberty that Milton felt was central to reality, and in an important sense constitutive of its value. The final essay, by Mary C. Fenton, guides readers through the poem's final books with their introduction of the counterdynamics of regeneration and consolation in the midst of ongoing sorrow and loss. The collection then concludes with a summary essay by William Kolbrener on the reception history of the poem, tracing the way aspects of its poetic and intellectual dynamics have driven readers to opposed positions. He also surveys the current state of Milton studies and offers a list of works for further reading.

It has been a pleasure and a privilege to commission the essays collected here and to work with each of their authors. I want to thank them all for being gracious and flexible about taking direction from me when I offered it and for working hard in the "narrow room" of a very tight word count. Each essay, I hope, has grown luxuriant by restrain. Several colleagues – some included in this collection, some not – offered welcome advice, encouragement, and sometimes solace along the way. I especially wish to thank Peter Herman, Stephen Buhler (I'm sorry we had to turn off the music), Mary C. Fenton, W. Gardner Campbell, and Anthony Russell. In addition, I want to thank Ray Ryan at Cambridge University Press for proposing this project to me and for being so patient with my slow delivery. The anonymous readers at the Press also offered important suggestions and encouragement, and Louis Gulino and everyone else in the New York office were unfailingly supportive and helpful with all the details on the Press's side of things. Thanks also, finally, to the English Department and the School of Arts and Sciences at the University of Richmond, to Emily Tarchokov for helping with logistics and communication, and to my family for coping with my frequent periods of grumpy inattention.

I dedicate this volume to the memory of my grandmother, Ella Ash, who left this earth after somewhere between 98 and 101 years while I was preparing the manuscript for the Press. Although she thought I should have been a "real doctor" instead of getting a PhD in literature, and although she would never have actually read the book – "eh," she would have said with a wave of her hand – still, she would have been proud, as she always was, that her grandson was publishing something again. It is a long way from the shtetl to Cambridge University Press, and no one could see all the way across that "vast abrupt" better than she could. Even if she did not always understand what she saw, knowing her and loving her (and being loved by her) helped *me* to see and, in part at least, to understand.

Louis Schwartz

NOTE ON THE TEXT AND LIST OF ABBREVIATIONS

References to works quoted or mentioned are given in parentheses in the text. Full bibliographical details can be found in the lists for "Further Reading" that conclude each essay. All biblical quotations, unless otherwise noted, are from the Authorized (King James) Version. All references to Milton's poetry are keyed to and quoted from the Modern Library Edition of *The Complete Poetry and Essential Prose of John Milton*, edited by William Kerrigan, John Rumrich, and Stephen M. Fallon (New York, 2007), abbreviated *MLM*.

CW	*The Works of John Milton*, 18 vols., ed. Frank Allen Patterson *et al.* (New York, 1931–8)
DDC	*De Doctrina Christiana*
MQ	*Milton Quarterly*
MS	*Milton Studies*
OED	*The Oxford English Dictionary, Online* (Oxford, 2013) http://www.oed.com
PL	*Paradise Lost*
PR	*Paradise Regained*
YP	*Complete Prose Works of John Milton*, 8 vols., ed. Don M. Wolfe *et al.* (New Haven, 1953–82)

PART I

I

STEPHEN M. FALLON

Milton as Narrator in *Paradise Lost*

Milton, as the narrator of *Paradise Lost*, rises out of a sea of relatively anonymous European epic narrators. In the poem's several invocations, Milton revises the definition of heroism to mean telling rather than acting, bringing order to the world not by arms but, to borrow from his later epic, *Paradise Regained*, "By winning words to conquer willing hearts" (*PR* 1.223). The narrator's description of his experience and situation, moreover, suggests that there is little demarcation between narrator and author. The line we are used to drawing between poet and narrator, between author and speaker, is difficult if not impossible to find in *Paradise Lost*. ~~boundary~~

At the front of the epic tradition stands the anonymous, composite "Homer." While both Homeric epics contain apostrophes to characters, the narrator himself otherwise remains impersonal, with the *Odyssey*'s invocation "Sing in me [lit. Tell me], Muse" (1.1) marking a minute step beyond the *Iliad*'s "Anger be now your song, immortal one [lit. Sing, Goddess]" (1.1). Aristotle turned to Homer for his model of excellence in epic, not least for the near-anonymity of his narration. In his *Poetics*, he praises Homer for saying "very little *in propria persona*" and letting the narrative unfold primarily in the words of his characters (1460a5–12). Virgil follows Homer's practice and Aristotle's prescription. His self-references in the *Aeneid* are limited to the poem's first line ("*Armum virumque cano*/ Arms and the man I sing") and to a handful of brief apostrophes.

Milton rejects Aristotle's prescription. He employs first-person singular pronouns five times in his first twenty-six lines. And it is not only the frequency with which Milton's narrator refers to himself that sets him apart, but also his taking on the role of hero and the increasing convergence, as the epic proceeds, of the narrator's self-descriptions and the facts of the author's life. Milton suspends the narration of the feats of the nominal hero, the "one greater man" who will "Restore us, and regain the blissful seat" (1.4–5), until the end of the epic, where it takes up a mere 105 lines (12.359–463). Among the candidates to fill the intervening void is Milton himself, who

3

begins *Paradise Lost* by invoking God to inspire his "advent'rous song,/ That with no middle flight intends to soar/ Above th'Aonian mount," turning his "justify[ing] the ways of God to men" into a heroic act (1.13–15, 26). He fashions himself as second only (if second at all) to Moses, the "shepherd, who first taught the chosen seed" (1.8). He inserts himself also into the two other major invocations, in Books 3 and 7, and into the near-invocation in Book 9, turning his narrator and himself into an epic character in his own right. In these invocations he wrestles with doubts about the authenticity of the very inspiration that makes his audacious song possible. If those doubts are warranted, Milton risks the fate of Satan, who aspires above his place. The recurring danger of falling from prophetic election to Satanic presumption thus becomes a key subplot. When in Book 9 Milton explicitly redefines true heroism as involving "patience and heroic martyrdom" (9.32), he is pointing in part to the arduous and potentially dangerous labor of invention required by his chosen subject: "... long choosing, and beginning late" (9.25–26).

Begin late he did. His nephew Edward Phillips reports that Milton wrote *Paradise Lost* in his early fifties, starting around 1658 ("two years before the king came in") and finishing four or five years later (Darbishire 13). He most likely reached the midpoint of the poem around the time of the restoration of Charles II, when Milton, who had good reason to fear for his life, first went into hiding and then was jailed for months. Writing between the autumn and spring equinoxes, Milton composed between ten and thirty lines per day. Intriguingly, Phillips relates in his biography that the subject of the "heroic poem, entitled *Paradise Lost* ... was first designed a tragedy," and that Milton had shown him several years earlier ten lines designed to be its beginning (these now begin Satan's soliloquy to the sun [Darbishire 72–3; *PL* 4.32–41]). Fortunately, four early plans for that tragedy survive in Milton's Trinity Manuscript, a notebook in Milton's hand.

With their choruses and allegorical figures, the first three plans show the influence of the Italian *dramma per musica*, or oratorio; Milton probably composed these not long after August 1639, when he returned from Italy. Adam, Eve, Michael, Moses, and Lucifer share the stage with Heavenly Love; Conscience; the theological virtues Faith, Hope, and Charity; and a melancholy crowd including Death, Labor, Sickness, Discontent, and Ignorance, among others. While the first plans contain only character lists, the third, titled "Paradise Lost," begins to fill in what will become the shape of Milton's epic, with choral songs describing creation, paradise, and the marriage of Adam and Eve (*YP* 8:554–55, 559–60). Significantly, the audience is to see Adam and Eve directly only after their fall, because, as Moses "prologuizes," fallen spectators "cannot se Adam in the state of innocence by reason of thire sin." This plan presents Lucifer "contriving Adam's ruine" and moves directly to the fallen Adam and Eve, as they are exhorted by Conscience and presented by an angel with the evils listed above (8:554–55).

The fourth plan, "Adam unparadiz'd," contains still more of the elements of *Paradise Lost*: an angel visits earth to see the new created man (Gabriel here, Satan in the future epic), the chorus sings the War in Heaven, and, foreshadowing *Paradise Lost* 10, "Adam then & Eve ... accuse one another but especially Adam layes the blame to his wife, is stubborn in his offence" (8:560). Mercy, in the role later played by Michael, relates the future and the promise of the Messiah. Once again, however, the audience is not to see Adam and Eve before their fall, presumably owing in part to the impossibility of actors performing nude. In turning from stage to page, Milton will leave behind this constraint and present Adam and Eve "with native honor clad/ In naked majesty" (*PL* 4.289–90). Milton will be allowed to see, and to share with his audience, what his Moses in early drafts hid behind a veil.

At the same time that he was projecting a tragedy of the Fall, Milton was casting about for a subject for an epic poem. In his 1639 *Epitaphium Damonis* he promises an Arthurian epic, as he had months earlier in *Manso*, a poem dedicated to the patron of Tasso, author of the great Italian epic *Gerusalemme Liberata*. And he alludes to this ambition again in 1642, wondering aloud, in an autobiographical digression in *The Reason of Church-Government*, "what K[ing] or Knight before the conquest might be chosen in whom to lay the pattern of a Christian *Heroe*" (*YP* 1:813–14). For the next fifteen or sixteen years, however, political events prevented Milton, occupied first as a pamphleteer and then as spokesperson for Commonwealth and Protectorate, from doing more with this last plan than composing the Satanic verses that Phillips saw. During this time Milton abandoned plans for an Arthurian epic. He decided to repurpose his plans for a Genesis tragedy as the foundation of a great biblical epic.

In ultimately choosing a narrated over a dramatic form, Milton, notwithstanding Aristotle's rule, opened a door for himself to enter the poem in his own voice and person. Milton, in my view, is not creating a character/narrator such as Joseph Conrad's Marlowe or Dickens' David Copperfield, or an impersonal narrator of the kind familiar to us from the novels of Jane Austen or Thomas Hardy (for an opposing view, see Coiro). Going out of his way to identify the narrator with himself, Milton makes the telling of the story itself into a dramatic story. What the narrator in *Paradise Lost* says about himself fits not only the stories that Milton tells about himself elsewhere but also objective biographical facts available to us, down to repeating in the invocation to Book 3 his doctors' diagnosis of the cause of his becoming blind in 1652 (3.23–26).

Consequently, early readers did not hesitate to identify Milton with his narrator. In 1695, Patrick Hume pointed to the passage just mentioned as an example of Milton writing about himself, as did the Jonathan Richardsons, father and son, in 1734 (Richardson 94). The Richardsons regard the narrator's lament in Book 7 that he is "fall'n on evil days,/ ... and evil tongues;/ In darkness, and with dangers compassed round/ And solitude" (7.25–28) and his taking comfort in the muse's nightly visits as matching precisely what they had learned of Milton's life. According to "a piece of Secret History" for which they had "Good Authority," Milton dictated his poem at a time when he "Apprehended himself to be in Danger of his Life ... (having been very Deeply engag'd against the Royal Party) and, when Safe by a Pardon, from Private Malice and Resentment[,] He was Always in Fear; Much Alone, and Slept Ill" (Richardson 291). In 1749, Thomas Newton echoed Hume's and the Richardsons' comments. His annotation to 9.1 not only identifies the narrator as Milton, but also defends Milton for violating epic precedent (and Aristotle's prescription) by speaking about himself:

> These prologues or prefaces of Milton to some of his books, speaking of his own person, lamenting his blindness, and preferring his subject to those of Homer and Virgil and the greatest poets before him, are condemn'd by some critics: and it must be allow'd that we find no such digression in the Iliad or Æneid; it is a liberty that can be taken only by such a genius as Milton.... As Monsieur Voltaire says upon the occasion, I cannot but own that an author is generally guilty of an unpardonable self-love, when he lays aside his subject to descant upon his own person: but that human frailty is to be forgiven in Milton; nay I am pleased with it. He gratifies the curiosity he has raised in me about his person; when I admire the author, I desire to know something of the man; and he, whom all readers would be glad to know, is allow'd to speak of himself. (Newton, 2:123)

In several prose works Milton encourages us to expect him to speak in his poetry in his own voice about himself, rather than to work through the intermediary of a fictionalized narrator. In *The Reason of Church Government* he indicates that poets may speak directly of themselves, freed from the constraints of prose:

> although a Poet soaring in the high region of his fancies with his garland and singing robes about him might without apology speak more of himself then I mean to do, yet for me sitting here below in the cool element of prose, a mortall thing among many readers of no Empyreall conceit, to venture and divulge unusual things of my selfe, I shall petition to the gentler sort, it may not be envy to me. (*YP* 1:808)

Milton then launches into an extended autobiographical account. Several months later, in April 1642, he comes near to equating the poet not merely with the narrator but with the poem:

> he who would not be frustrate of his hope to write well hereafter in laudable things, ought him selfe to bee a true Poem, that is, a composition, and patterne of the best and honourablest things; not presuming to sing high praises of heroick men or famous Cities, unlesse he have in himselfe the experience and the practice of all that which is praise-worthy. (*Apology for Smectymnuus*, YP 1:890)

The poet's life, character, and actions merge seamlessly, Milton insists, into heroic poetry. An immoral poet cannot write of a virtuous hero, and a true poem reveals the virtue of its poet. In July 1657, about the time that he began composing *Paradise Lost*, Milton writes to a correspondent that "he who would write worthily of worthy deeds ought to write with no less largeness of spirit and experience of the world than he who did them" (7:501). A book is intimately connected to its author; it is, he asserts in *Areopagitica* (1644), "the pretious life-blood of a master spirit, imbalm'd and treasur'd up on purpose to a life beyond life" (2:493).

Given Milton's understanding of the relation between poet and poem and of the qualities necessary for the heroic poet, and given that *Paradise Lost* is the fulfillment of his promise in the *Reason of Church Government* to write a work "doctrinal and exemplary to a Nation" (1:815), his approach to epic narration makes sense. To convince his readers (and himself?) that he is equal to his ambition, he must assert his virtue and his capacity for heroism. This, as I intimated earlier, is the work of the opening invocation, where he stakes his narrator's claim to be poet and prophet. Near the end of that invocation, Milton petitions God's spirit, asking for illumination and support and linking the creation of the epic with the creation of the universe:

> thou from the first
> Wast present, and with mighty wings outspread
> Dove-like sat'st brooding on the vast abyss
> And mad'st it pregnant: what in me is dark
> Illumine, what is low raise and support ... (*PL* 1.19–23)

While this is the least personal of the poem's proems, the allusive moment opens a window on what will be an increasingly intimate portrait. The *dark* of line 22 registers Milton's (conventional) modesty and, implicitly, the particular affliction – blindness – that will turn out to be a mark of divine favor.

What is implicit at the end of the first invocation becomes the central theme in the second, the great invocation to light in Book 3. This invocation, which, as we have seen, has long been cited as evidence of the autobiographical aspects of Milton's narrator, is twice as long as the first, and Milton devotes nearly four-fifths of it (13–55) to a meditation on his blindness, his inspiration, and the paradoxical but necessary link between them. Modeling himself on epic heroes, he claims, either boastfully or with relief (or both), to have "Escaped the Stygian pool, though long detained/ In that obscure sojourn," as Odysseus had escaped detention on Kirke's and Kalypso's islands and as Aeneas had escaped Carthage. Like each of those heroes, he has also journeyed to the underworld, and he marks his re-ascent in terms borrowed from Virgil's Sybil, who tells Aeneas that "the way downward is easy from Avernus,/ .../ But to retrace your steps to heaven's air/ There is trouble, there is toil (*hoc opus/ hic labor est*)" (*Aeneid* 6.126–29). Milton echoes these words when he tells us, with triumphant concision, that his muse taught him "to venture down/ The dark decent, and up to reascend,/ Though hard and rare" (*PL* 3.19–21).

Precisely at this point the narrating Milton turns to pathos-laden self-representation. Having returned from his "dark descent," he complains to the sun: "thou/ Revisit'st not these eyes, that roll in vain/ To find thy piercing ray, and find no dawn" (3.22–24). The second half and more of this invocation is a meditation on blindness and inner sight by turns anguished and triumphant. Milton associates himself with the inner vision of blind bards and prophets, hoping to be "equaled … in renown" with Thamyris and Homer ("blind Maeonides") and with "Tiresias and Phineus prophets old," a fate dependent on an inspiration that enables "harmonious numbers" (3.34–38). Loss of eyesight is momentarily compensated by literary fame and prophetic insight, but immediately the anguish of blindness returns:

> Thus with the year
> Seasons return, but not to me returns
> Day, or the sweet approach of ev'n or morn,
> Or sight of vernal bloom, or summer's rose,
> Or flocks, or herds, or human face divine;
> But cloud instead, and ever-during dark
> Surrounds me, from the cheerful ways of men
> Cut off, and for the book of knowledge fair
> Presented with a universal blank
> Of Nature's works to me expunged and razed,
> And wisdom at one entrance quite shut out. (3.40–50)

In this brilliant passage Milton truncates the heartbreaking catalog of sights never to be seen again as abruptly as the caesura isolating the heavily stressed "Cut off" at the beginning of line 47, and he evokes the finality of blindness in another series of stressed monosyllables, "quite shut out." This cry from the heart is again particularized to Milton's experience. As he wrote to Leonard Philaras in 1654, the blind Milton saw not black darkness but a milky whiteness (*YP* 4.2:869–70), "a universal blank" (a pun more obvious in the spelling – "blanc" – in the earliest editions).

The narrator's oscillation between confident assertion and defensive anxiety echoes a similar oscillation in Milton's prose. In his *Second Defense of the English People* (1654), Milton dismissed royalist claims that God blinded him for supporting the execution of Charles I:

> Divine law and divine favor have rendered us not only safe from the injuries of men, but almost sacred, nor do these shadows around us seem to have been created so much by the dullness of our eyes as by the shade of angels' wings. And divine favor not infrequently is wont to lighten these shadows again, once made, by an inner and far more enduring light. (4.1:590).

In similar fashion, at the moment of deepest pathos in Book 3's invocation, unable to see the beauties of nature, Milton returns to the expectation of inner light with confidence warranted by the poem he is composing:

> So much the rather thou celestial light
> Shine inward, and the mind through all her powers
> Irradiate, there plant eyes, all mist from thence
> Purge and disperse, that I may see and tell
> Of things invisible to mortal sight. (*PL* 3.51–55)

Nevertheless, the invocation that ends with such confidence also betrays anxiety. Milton asked at the beginning if he can "express" holy light "unblamed" (3.3), which suggests concern lest he violate canons of secrecy. This invocation does not move steadily from doubt to confidence, but twice interrupts its confidence with anguished evocations of blindness. Although it ends hopefully, the impression is of Milton grappling with blindness, finding it both barely tolerable and a sign of election (Fallon 210–33).

In the third invocation, at the beginning of Book 7, the grappling continues. As the Richardsons recognized, Milton's narrator describes himself as in the precise historical position of Milton shortly after the Restoration, when he probably wrote this section of the poem and when he was vulnerable to both legal and extralegal violence for his literary labors on behalf of the interregnum governments. The elegant chiasmus of "fall'n on evil days,/ On evil days though fall'n, and evil tongues" circles and encloses the narrator, an uneasy sense made explicit in the next line, "In darkness, and with dangers compassed round" (*PL* 7.25–28). Milton then raises the pathos with the phrase "And solitude," caught alone at the beginning of the next line after a strong pause.

The anxiety in lines 25–28 colors the whole invocation. After calling again on the divine muse, now under the name of Urania ("The meaning, not the name I call" [7.5]), Milton spends most of the invocation warding off dangers external and internal. Where he boasted in Book 1 that his song "intends to soar/ Above th'Aonian mount" 1.14–15), he now, having been drawn by the muse to possibly dangerous heights ("Up led by thee/ Into the Heav'n of Heav'ns I have presumed,/ An earthly guest"), asks to be returned to the safety of earth, his "native element" (7.12–14, 7.16). If a guest, Milton is authorized; if uninvited, he has crossed a forbidden boundary. In the midst of poetic flight, Milton worries that he will plunge to Earth, "Erroneous there to wander and forlorn" (7.20). The vivid term "forlorn" is associated in the poem with alienation from God. Up to this point it has been used only about or by devils (1.180, 2.615, and 4.374). If Milton fails, he risks ending up like them, forlorn and eternally wandering. Milton's safety lies in authentic inspiration. He must be, as William Kerrigan writes, "both author and amanuensis" (Kerrigan 138). His inspiration must come from the divine muse that, unlike the "empty dream" that is the pagan muse, can protect the poet from the fate of the dismembered Orpheus, a fate that haunted Milton (*Lycidas* 58–63), and one that could have seemed far from unlikely in the days following the restoration, when angry mobs searched for those who, like Milton, had punished one Stuart king and opposed the crowning of another. Homer has Athena protect Odysseus, and Virgil has Venus protect her son Aeneas; in calling on divine protection, Milton once again places himself in the position of hero as well as narrator.

Milton opens Book 9 with another proem about inspiration, poetry, and heroism, but now without an invocation of a muse. Instead he reflects again on the authenticity of his inspiration and the implications of its withdrawal. Changing his "notes to tragic" (*PL* 9.6), he will write about the alienation of Adam and Eve from angels and God. The easy intercourse between Adam and Raphael, now ended, parallels the easy intercourse of Milton and his muse, or Milton and God; if the former can be lost, why not the latter? Milton is confident that his story is more heroic than those of pagan epic, of "Neptune's ire or Juno's, that so long/ Perplexed the Greek and Cytherea's son" (9.18–19), and that true heroism lies in "the better fortitude/ Of patience and heroic martyrdom" (9.31–32), but his confidence is again shadowed by anxiety. The closing lines of the proem to Book 9 mark the end of a trajectory that began with the epic's first lines, as Milton the poet and narrator has focused increasingly on the danger of making strong claims for inspiration and his own heroism. At the end of this last proem, Milton registers once more the very real worry that he has imagined rather than received divine inspiration:

> higher argument
> Remains, sufficient of itself to raise
> That name, unless an age too late, or cold

Climate, or years damp my intended wing
Depressed, and much they may, if all be mine,
Not hers who brings it nightly to my ear. (9.42–47)

Perhaps, living far from the Mediterranean home of epic ("cold/ Climate")
and a century after its last great poems, time and place will thwart epic
composition. And perhaps he is simply too old. Virgil began the *Aeneid*
at forty-one and completed it at fifty-one. Ariosto published his massive *Orlando Furioso* at forty-two, and Tasso his Virgilian epic at thirty.
Edmund Spenser published the first three books of *The Faerie Queene* at
thirty-seven or thirty-eight, and the fourth through sixth and the fragmentary seventh at forty-four, before his early death at forty-six – a precedent
that must have weighed on Milton, who as we have seen was approach-
ing fifty when he began *Paradise Lost*. These lines mark the last moment
in which the narrator directly shares with us his anxieties about his task.
The fact that Milton finished his tale suggests that in one sense, as heroic
singer, he overcame those anxieties. Nevertheless, anxieties remained for
a poet marked by the fallen human condition; these anxieties haunt the
more indirect ways, to which I now turn, in which Milton shares with us
his experience.

The speaker of the proems of Books 1, 3, 7, and 9 shares the task of narration in different ways and to different degrees with two angels: Raphael in
Books 5–7, before the fall, and Michael in Book 12, after the fall. I begin with
Michael, whose narration, more than Raphael's, is colored by Milton's anxieties. For the second half of Book 11, Michael serves as interpreter, though
not the narrator, of the visions granted to Adam of the future providential
history from Cain and Abel to Noah's flood; "both," the narrator tells us,
"ascend/ In the visions of God" (11.376–77). Significantly, it is *Adam*'s eyes
that are "purged" and opened to visions by Michael, as the narrator's had
been by God. Milton had asked God to "Purge and disperse" from his eyes
"all mist," so that he could "see and tell/ of things invisible to mortal sight"
(3.53–55). In Book 11, "Michael from Adam's eyes the film removed/ .../ ...;
then purged with euphrasy and rue/ The visual nerve" (11.412–15). Milton's
eyes, purged by God (at least as he claims), are clearer than Adam's, cleared
as they are by an angel. And the Miltonic narrator himself continues the narration of Book 11, bracketing Michael's extended speeches. Even in Book
12, as Adam's eyes fail and as Michael must narrate to Adam the rest of
providential history, the Miltonic narrator frames Michael's speeches and
Adam's replies. Michael's comments are mediated, themselves spoken by
the narrator, who prefaces each of the angel's speeches with "To whom thus
Michael" (12.79, 386) or some variation of the same. As fallen readers, we
receive Michael's lessons at a remove, through the voice of the narrator.

In the failure of Adam's eyes and in the layers of mediation, we can trace the outlines of anxieties more explicitly addressed in the invocations.

With Raphael's narration we have at least the illusion of bypassing the narrator, who, having had Adam ask Raphael in the middle of Book 5 to explain how sin and rebellion could have arisen in heaven, disappears for more than a thousand lines (a full tenth of the epic). Raphael in this large interim tells the story of the rebellion and War in Heaven without framing reminders of the Miltonic narrator's presence. The narrator returns at the beginning of Book 7, invoking the spirit muse for the third time and framing a brief exchange in which Adam asks Raphael to explain how the world began, after which point the narrator again disappears for more than five hundred lines, as we listen with Adam to the angel's paraphrase of Genesis. Significantly, the two questions that invite these long passages free of the narrators' comments are the two questions with which the narrator begins the epic: How did sin enter the world, and how did the world begin? And each of these long passages begins with a feature of Milton's invocations, an acknowledgment of the difficulty of relating things beyond human sense and experience.[1] In Book 5, Raphael asks, "how shall I relate/ To human sense th'invisible exploits/ Of warring spirits," before resolving that "what surmounts the reach/ Of human sense, I shall delineate so,/ By lik'ning spiritual to corporeal forms,/ As may express them best" (5.564–66, 571–74). Raphael prefaces his long narration of creation in similar fashion:

> to recount almighty works
> What words or tongue of Seraph can suffice,
> Or heart of man suffice to comprehend?
> Yet what thou canst attain, which best may serve
> To glorify the Maker, and infer
> Thee also happier, shall not be withheld
> Thy hearing, such commission from above
> I have received. (7.112–19)

As Milton is to his reading audience, so Raphael is to Adam and Eve (Reisner 207). To disclose matters not only outside the experience but also beyond the natural capacities of his audience, both have received "commission from above."

In addition to these large episodes in which the angels' narration indirectly echoes his own, there are moments when Milton's narrator addresses us no less directly, though more briefly, than he does in his proems to 1, 3, 7, and 9. As often as not, they are marked by a failure to control the meaning of speeches or the actions to which they refer. In one variation, the narrator points out hidden vices or laments a character's moral weakness. Belial in the Council in Hell might seem reasonable, but the narrator prefaces his speech by warning us that in Belial, though he seems "graceful and humane," "all was false and hollow," and that he "could make the worse appear/ The better reason" (*PL* 2.109–14). Lest we be moved by Belial's speech, the narrator comments again at the end, "Thus Belial with words clothed in reason's garb/ Counseled ignoble ease, and peaceful sloth,/ Not peace" (2.226–28). The narrator in important respects is right. Belial's suggestion that, in time, "Our supreme foe in time may much remit/ His anger, and .../ Not mind us not offending" glosses over the fact that the devils continue to offend as long as they see God as enemy (2.210–12). The dismissal, however, seems a particularly blunt tool to counter this extraordinary speech. Few readers are immune to Belial's soaring rhetoric:

> who would lose,
> Though full of pain, this intellectual being,
> Those thoughts that wander through eternity,
> To perish rather, swallowed up and lost
> In the wide womb of uncreated Night,
> Devoid of sense and motion. (2.146–51)

While the narrator may correctly read the moral landscape, it is difficult to fault Belial for arguing that, given their predicament, it is better for the devils not to antagonize God further but to make the best they can of their infernal home. Belial embodies a species of flawed nobility; Mammon's counsel to begin mining gems beneath Hell's soil is by comparison crassly materialist, and Moloch's counsel of renewed war futilely belligerent. Significantly, the narrator does not step in at the end of Moloch's and Mammon's speeches with a critical review. Milton's harsh reaction to Belial's rhetoric may point to an obscure intimation that its soaring language and aspiration at some level resembles his own. Through Belial's speech Milton dramatizes the creative power of even morally compromised creatures as well as our (and his) susceptibility to evil.

The most poignant and revealing of the narrator's intrusions betray Milton's frustrated inability to intervene and protect the poem's vulnerable characters. Here he follows the practice of Homer's *Iliad*, in which in seventeen of nineteen instances characters directly addressed by the narrator "exhibit," according to Elizabeth Block, "characteristic traits of vulnerability, loyalty, and a vague but poetically essential weakness" (16). Milton, who is narrating the tragic tale of disobedience (which precedes the comedy of regeneration), captures the pathos of the fall by voicing his inability to change the direction of the story. A privileged seer, he knows the impending catastrophe but is unable to prevent it. At the beginning of Book 4, as Satan steers toward Earth, he cries:

> O for that warning voice, which he who saw
> Th' Apocalypse, heard cry in Heav'n aloud,
> Then when the Dragon, put to second rout,
> Came furious down to be revenged on men,
> "Woe to the inhabitants on Earth!" That now,
> While time was, our first parents had been warned
> The coming of their secret foe, and scaped
> Haply so scaped his mortal snare. (*PL* 4.1–8)

God will send Raphael as a "warning voice," but Milton, writing a poem "doctrinal and exemplary to a Nation," is himself a warning voice to his contemporaries. The inefficacy of another warning voice – for Adam and Eve will fall – sent by God must weigh on him. Here the distance that Milton had closed between narrator and the heroes of Homeric and especially Virgilian epic reopens. Odysseus and Aeneas, favored by sponsoring goddesses, endure trials before reaching home, the native Ithakan home for Odysseus and a new Italian home for Aeneas and his Trojans. Milton arguably succeeds in the heroic task of justifying God's ways to men, but he cannot lead his people to safety – a role reserved for the "one greater man." The regaining of paradise, the equivalent of Homer's Ithaka or Virgil's Rome, must unfold internally and individually, as Adam learns in his dialogue with Michael, and as Milton poignantly figures in the epic's closing pages. An exemplary poem *can* participate in this effort, but that depends on something beyond Milton's control – the wills of individual readers. The limit of the narrator's assumed heroic role echoes another, the limit of the poet-author, as Milton the spokesperson for the interregnum governments had failed to rally the English to republican liberty, which also, in Milton's view, depended on the individual regeneration of his compatriots.

Perhaps the most pathetic moment in the poem comes at the next moment of failed warning, after Eve has, by separating from Adam in Book 9, become more vulnerable to Satan. The narrator is overcome:

> O much deceived, much failing, hapless Eve,
> Of thy presumed return! Event perverse!
> Thou never from that hour in Paradise
> Found'st either sweet repast, or sound repose. (9.404–07)

The narrator who has aspired to heroism, and the author who has achieved heroism by a literary labor unsurpassed by any in English, is powerless to intervene to save Eve or us. Awareness of the sources for this moment in the *Iliad* and the *Aeneid*, identified by Thomas Newton in 1749, sharpens the irony of Milton's position. In the *Iliad*'s seventeenth book, the Trojans Khromíos and Arêtos, confident of victory over the Greeks, challenge Alkimédon and Automédôn; Homer remarks on their confidence, "But they were/ fooled in this: from Automédôn's strike they would not come unbloodied" (*Iliad* 17.497). A moment later Automédôn kills the hapless Arêtos. In the *Aeneid*'s tenth book, as Turnus glories over the body of Pallas, Virgil's narrator comments ruefully, "*Nescia mens hominum fati:*"

> The minds of men are ignorant of fate
> And of their future lot, unskilled to keep
> Due measure when some triumph sets them high.
> For Turnus there will come a time
> When he would give the world to see again
> An untouched Pallas, and will hate this day. (10.501–05)

Homer knows that Arêtos will die, and Virgil knows that Turnus will die (just as we know that Turnus *must* die), and their warnings are therefore futile. Their narrators write from the perspective of the Greek enemies of Arêtos and the Trojan enemies of Turnus. However tragic their deaths, the pathos is tempered by their being on the wrong side of history, especially in Virgil's poem. In his passage on Eve, Milton writes from the side of the soon-to-be-vanquished. The consolations available to Homer and Virgil and to their audiences are not available to Milton or to us, for Eve is not our enemy but our mother.

The dissonance between Milton's epic heroic ambitions and his failure to save his race is inevitable, for Milton has redefined heroism in the proem to Book 9. "Patience and heroic martyrdom" (9.32) are the new epic virtues, and victories are won by the obedience and moral heroism of individuals. It is fitting, then, that Milton – who believed that one must work out one's beliefs for oneself by reading the Bible under the influence of the Spirit – takes on himself the role of narrator and presents his own struggles as heroic, despite the fact that, unlike Aeneas', his heroism cannot save his characters and his race. In the end he leaves it to each reader to participate in, and to fulfill the promise of, that heroism.

NOTES

1 I am indebted to Garrett Jansen, who in an unpublished essay has demonstrated manifold resonances between Milton's invocations and Raphael's brief proems.

Further Reading

Aristotle, *Poetics*, tr. Ingram Bywater, in *The Basic Works of Aristotle*, ed. Richard McKeon (New York, 1941).

Block, Elizabeth, "The Narrator Speaks: Apostrophe in Homer and Vergil," *Transactions of the American Philological Association* 112 (1982), 7–22.

Coiro, Ann Baynes, "Drama in the Epic Style: Narrator, Muse, and Audience in *Paradise Lost*," *MS* 51 (2010), 63–100.

Darbishire, Helen, ed., *The Early Lives of Milton* (1932; New York, 1965).

Fallon, Stephen M., *Milton's Peculiar Grace: Self-Representation and Authority* (Ithaca, NY, 2007).

Ferry, Anne, *Milton's Epic Voice: The Narrator in "Paradise Lost"* (1963; Chicago, 1983).

Hume, Patrick, *Annotations on Milton "Paradise Lost"* (London, 1695).

Homer, *The Iliad*, tr. Robert Fitzgerald (New York, 1974).

The Odyssey, tr. Robert Fitzgerald (1961; New York, 1990).

Kerrigan, William, *The Prophetic Milton* (Charlottesville, VA, 1974).

Newton, Thomas, ed., *Milton, "Paradise Lost."* 2 vols. (1749; rpt. London, 1770).

Reisner, Noam, *Milton and the Ineffable* (Oxford, 2009).

Richardson, Jonathan, *Explanatory Notes and Remarks on Milton's "Paradise Lost"* (London, 1734).

Riggs, William G., *The Christian Poet in "Paradise Lost"* (Berkeley, CA, 1972).

Virgil, *The Aeneid*, tr. Robert Fitzgerald (New York, 1984).

2

NEIL FORSYTH

Satan

Readers of *Paradise Lost* are often surprised to find that there is no mention of Satan, only a talking snake, in the book of Genesis. Indeed Satan's appearances in the Bible are decidedly few and inconsistent. In Job he is a sneaky member of the Heavenly Court, in the Gospels he is the opponent of Jesus in the wilderness, and in Revelation he appears as a "great dragon" to fight a cosmic battle with the angel Michael. One could not reconstruct Milton's magnificent creation from such sparse hints.

By Milton's time, however, many other poets and theologians had developed the story of God's adversary. Milton knew many of the apocryphal and patristic sources and also the works of immediate predecessors like Du Bartas and Grotius (whom he met in Paris). Yet even if he knew the remarkable Old English poem "Genesis B," as has been argued (Evans 255; Revard 143), little among all that background literature suggests the way Satan became the most memorable character of *Paradise Lost*. Indeed he has often been taken to be its hero (Steadman 1976). The author of an anonymous 1750 poem imagined meeting Milton in Hell (where he is condemned for his politics): he there admits that "the Devil really was my Hero" (Shawcross). One of the pleasures of *Paradise Lost* is that readers have to decide the question for themselves. A sign of Satan's power is the way some editors fill their commentaries with anxious notes warning us against deciding it in his favor.

Satan dominates the first two books, and frequently returns. That splendid antithesis he proclaims in an early speech, "Better to reign in Hell, than serve in Heav'n" (1.263) is one of the best-known lines in English poetry. Satan evokes many readers' sympathy both because of what he says himself and of what the narrator, perhaps not quite intentionally, reveals about him. We are told he is capable of love and jealousy, despair and remorse. He even sheds "Tears such as angels weep" (1.620). True, he is the accomplished seducer of Eve in his guise of a cunning serpent. Indeed we first meet him as the "infernal serpent" (1.34). True, he is the "first grand thief" (4.192), who leaps too easily into Paradise like the wolves of John 10:12 whom Milton had earlier (in "Lycidas" and in his polemical prose) likened to the hireling and ignorant priests of the corrupt Church of England. True, the angel Gabriel reminds him, in an angry speech, of what he had been like in Heaven, a toady to God who "Once fawned, and cringed, and servilely adored/ Heav'n's awful Monarch" (4.959–60). But that is not the Satan we remember. Rather what sticks in the mind is the figure who drives the poem into motion by his reaction to finding himself in the Hell God has made for him and his fellow angels; who embodies the classical epic tradition and so calls it into question (as Milton does explicitly at the beginning of Book 9); who rebels against what he regards as tyranny and fights a heroic war; who devises the plot to colonize Eden; who undertakes a bold and dramatic voyage through Chaos to get to Paradise; who invents a clever plan to corrupt Adam and Eve by noticing how they love each other; who imagines himself into the serpent so thoroughly that we may even forget he is lying about having wound himself around "the mossy trunk" of the forbidden tree (9.589) or eaten its fruit; who returns to Hell like a conquering hero and there finds his speech become a hiss – and his angels returning "hiss for hiss … with forkèd tongue/ To forkèd tongue" (10.518–19). The cruel irony is complete. Anticipated "bliss" (503) becomes a "din/ Of hissing" (521–22). The great, defiant, and once beautiful angel is humiliated in the form he had himself chosen to adopt. And with that he disappears from the poem.

It is especially those speeches to his fellow devils, and later to himself, in the first quarter of the poem that make Satan such a compelling character. As in Shakespeare's tragedies with a villain as hero (*Richard III* and *Macbeth*), we meet and get close to him early. As soon as the poem gets going, the narrative describes Hell, and it does so almost entirely as Satan perceives it. We are told that Satan and his crew "Lay vanquished, rolling in the fiery gulf" (1.52) nine days after their fall from Heaven, and we quickly get to his thoughts, and then his perceptions:

> for now the thought
> Both of lost happiness and lasting pain
> Torments him; round he throws his baleful eyes
> That witnessed huge affliction and dismay
> Mixed with obdurate pride and steadfast hate:
> At once as far as angels ken he views
> The dismal situation waste and wild … (1.54–60)

The effect of the mingling of Satan's thought and perception here is to render the Hell he perceives the product of that thought. Hell, as we gradually become aware, like Paradise later in the poem, is both a place and a state of mind.

What Satan actually sees, however, with those "baleful eyes" is notoriously uncertain:

> A dungeon horrible, on all sides round
> As one great furnace flamed, yet from those flames
> No light, but rather darkness visible
> Served only to discover sights of woe … (1.61–64)

"Darkness visible" has become a famous phrase (and the title of at least four books) since T. S. Eliot made it the focus of his attacks on Milton for his blindness (Thorpe 327). In fact the curious phrase picks up centuries of interesting speculation about whether the flames of Hell give any light (Fowler 63–64), and sets up a contrast that is further explored throughout the poem between what may be seen in Hell and, paradoxically, not seen in Heaven. There, we learn later, God speaks from "a flaming mount, whose top/ Brightness had made invisible" (5.598–99).

The light in Hell, or lack of it, also reinforces through allusion Milton's challenge to the whole epic tradition from which he draws the heroic aspect of Satan's character. As often, the lines allude to Virgil's *Aeneid*, especially, in this case, to the uncertain luminosity that Aeneas perceives as he starts his journey through the underworld (*Aeneid* 6.267–70), a famous passage beginning "Ibant oscuri …" that Milton and many contemporaries would have known by heart. It is characteristic of Milton, however, that he can echo Virgil and at the same time, without apparent contradiction, allude to widely known paradoxes of the Judeo-Christian idea of Hell. Job 10:22, for example, says that in the land of the dead, Sheol, "the light is as darkness." This enigma was of some philosophical and scientific interest, especially for a blind man, but it also has obvious symbolic resonance (Steadman 1984). Imagery of light and darkness pervades the poem. Cumulatively the paradoxes, like the burning lake or the fiery deluge, show the difficulty of imagining Hell, and invite the readers to experience that difficulty for themselves.

Milton's text explores such difficulties not only through what Satan sees or does not see around him, but through his first words in the poem. Like "darkness visible" they also contain a double allusion to the Bible and to Virgil. As Satan looks around him, and before he speaks, the narrator exclaims as if he had become Satan's consciousness:

> O how unlike the place from whence they fell!
> There the companions of his fall, o'erwhelmed
> With floods and whirlwinds of tempestuous fire,
> He soon discerns, and welt'ring by his side
> One next himself in power, and next in crime,
> Long after known in Palestine, and named

> Beëlzebub. To whom th' Arch-Enemy,
> And thence in Heav'n called Satan, with bold words
> Breaking the horrid silence thus began.
>   "If thou beest he; but O how fall'n! how changed
> From him, who in the happy realms of light
> Clothed with transcendent brightness didst outshine
> Myriads though bright ..." (1.75–87)

Both the place and the person are immediately contrasted with Heaven. And Satan's explicit reaction to what he sees of his fallen comrade reiterates those words of the narrator: "O how fall'n! how changed."

Milton is here recalling Aeneas's account of a dream in which the dead Hector appeared to him as he was when he had been dragged behind Achilles' chariot, covered in blood and dust:

> ei mihi, qualis erat, quantum mutatus ab illo
> Hectore qui redit exuvias indutus Achilli
> vel Danaum Phrygios iaculatus pubbibus ignis! (2.274–76)

[Ah me, what a sight he was, how changed from that Hector who came back wearing the trophies of Achilles, or after hurling Phrygian firebrands onto the Greek ships!] [translation mine]

The parallels are important. Hector appears to tell Aeneas Troy will be utterly lost and he must prepare to flee to a new home across the sea. Satan speaks for the first time at a moment when he too comes to the consciousness of his new state, now that Heaven is lost. Soon he too will have to escape the place he finds himself in. But note the difference. Hector is changed but still Hector, and his deeds are still in Aeneas' memory. That indeed is one of the classic functions of epic poetry, to preserve heroes in the memory of others. But who this comrade is, Satan cannot quite say: he used to be ...? Who? We never in fact learn the name he used to have in Heaven. And he is not yet Beëlzebub, as he will be called "long after." Not only can Satan not name his companion, he is not sure at first he even recognizes him. Thus the Virgilian allusion both establishes a parallel between the heroes of the two epics and invites us to consider the differences.

The classical allusion overlaps with the biblical: "How art thou fallen from heaven, O Lucifer, son of the morning" (Isaiah 14:12). That text is one of the most important for the identification of the devil as the agent of evil in history, as the so-called Fathers of the Christian Church constructed him, and especially for the story of his fall from Heaven. Satan "trusted to have equaled the Most High" (1.40), as we have just heard, an allusion to the same passage. The words in Isaiah are actually spoken to the king of Babylon, whom they address ironically in language borrowed from an ancient myth about an ambitious god who had tried to enthrone himself among the stars, the divine assembly, but had been cast down to Sheol, to the pit, where he now finds himself, just as Satan does. The Isaiah allusion, taken alone, might well appear to place the poem's language firmly in the tradition of Judeo-Christian reading of the Bible. In the New Testament, Jesus says to the disciples that he saw "Satan fall like lightning from Heaven. Behold I have given you power to tread on snakes and scorpions, upon every power of the enemy" (Luke 10:18–20). But the simultaneous presence of Virgilian epic, especially the language of the great and good hero, *pius Aeneas*, loosens the relation between Milton's Satan and the role eventually given the devil by the Church Fathers as they ran together all those biblical texts. We may wonder at least just what story is being told or retold here, and feel uncertain how we are to evaluate it.

This first grand speech of Satan's (1.84–124), in which he drags himself into consciousness, at first in a shambling uncertain syntax, and virtually reinvents himself after the disastrous fall from Heaven, gradually shifts its tone and is latterly full of passion, defiance, and grandeur. It is no surprise that it raises the spirits of his second-in-command through its (oddly) passionate stoicism. The language is splendidly heroic – "bold words" at last, as the narrator had said they would be. But at the end of the speech the narrator again comments:

> So spake th' apostate angel, though in pain,
> Vaunting aloud, but racked with deep despair ... (125–26)

The comment is at odds with what our first reading of the speech will have told us, and invites us to go back and look again, to hear the inner despair within the outward pride that boasts of his "unconquerable will,/ And study of revenge, immortal hate,/ And courage never to submit or yield" (106–08). If we do so listen the second time, and hear the despair, we will also note curious contradictions. How, for example, we might ask Satan, can you expect a more successful outcome to the war when at the same time you insist it will be eternal?

> We may with more successful hope resolve
> To wage by force or guile eternal war
> Irreconcilable, to our grand foe ... (120–22)

At a first reading we also may not notice that Satan sees everything in physical terms: God's power, like that of pagan gods, is simply his Thunder. Satan is discovering himself in Hell, and Hell in himself. To be in Hell, as his great soliloquy in Book 4 will later reveal, is to be incapable of repentance, and so to be beyond redemption. The "fixed mind" (97) of which he here boasts, the refusal to "repent or change" (96), is grand from the point of view of an epic hero, but also desperately tragic. The speech itself is all about "hope" (88, 120), but the narrator has already told us, alluding to Dante, that here in Hell "hope never comes/ That comes to all" (66–67), and the comment of the narrator after the speech suggests that the real emotion driving it is "despair."

The contradiction between the willful grandeur of the speech and the narrator's subsequent comment has been a valuable site of critical discussion. Some readers have complained that Milton's method is flawed given that what is shown, the speech, and what is told, the comment, work against each other (Waldock 77–8). Some have argued this is deliberate: Milton expects the reader to be overwhelmed by Satan's rhetoric and then invites us to check or correct our (presumably sinful) reaction (Fish 1997). Others have attributed the contradiction to a conflict not in Satan's but in Milton's nature. One of the best-known comments on *Paradise Lost* is William Blake's 1790 aphorism: "Milton wrote in fetters when he wrote of Angels and God, and at liberty when of Devils and Hell, ... because he was a true poet and of the Devils party without knowing it" (Blake 35; Steadman 1976). It was the "true poet" who wrote Satan's speeches, so this reading would have it, and the Christian theologian, a stern moralist, who made the narrator's comment.

Opinion among Milton critics has often divided as to which side of Milton to support (for a survey, see Carey or Forsyth 2003, 1–17, 62–76), and this may be partly because the two are not so easy to distinguish. For there is a further allusion in the narrator's words. Following the great speech in the *Aeneid* when the hero talks his tired and draggled men back to courage, Virgil adds:

> Talia voce refert, curisque ingentibus aeger
> spem vultu simulat, premit altum corde dolorem. (1.208–09)

> [Such things he says aloud, and while sick with great cares simulates hope in his face and suppresses his deep grief within his heart.] [translation mine]

Virgil's "altum dolorem" is not quite Satan's despair, but a similar conflict is signaled in the pagan hero. Virgil's reader is clearly asked to sympathize with Aeneas, and arguably the intensification in Milton's language may increase our sympathy for a being in such stifled pain. The heroic public persona becomes a troubled private self. The sudden glimpse of that personal, intimate interior increases the closeness of the reader to Satan. The narrator's comment about despair is not simply a theologian's gloss.

Satan soon recovers himself. In his second speech ("Fallen Cherub, to be weak is miserable") he already begins to develop a plan, and resolves to reverse God's plot for the world and the poem, and "out of good still to find means of evil" (1.165). The speech also extends and answers the phrases of the narrator. The paradox of "darkness visible" is picked up in Satan's more explicit:

> Seest thou yon dreary plain, forlorn and wild,
> The seat of desolation, void of light,
> Save what the glimmering of these livid flames
> Casts pale and dreadful? (180–83)

And at the end of the speech he actively takes on the despair of which the narrator had covertly accused him. We should, he says, when we get over to that shore, consider

> What reinforcement we may gain from hope,
> If not what resolution from despair. (190–91)

Satan thus accepts openly what had in the narrator's comment been a probing and apparently damning insight into the Satanic self. We may be reading the words of a devil, but also of a self-conscious tragic hero.

This tragic dimension becomes even more explicit in the great soliloquy of self-exploration and self-accusation that Satan makes on Mt. Niphates, once he has landed on the new Earth. According to Edward Phillips, Milton's nephew, the first ten lines (4.32–41) of the speech were "designed for the very beginning" of the tragedy in which the concept of *Paradise Lost* originated (Darbishire 72). Although these lines echo the openings of two Greek tragedies (Aeschylus's *Prometheus Bound* and Euripides' *Phoenissae*), it seems clear that the most important influence in the speech was not Greek but English drama (Gardner). Shakespeare and his contemporaries had learned new ways to represent inwardness and now Milton extends their techniques. Marlowe's Mephistopheles had said, "Why, this is hell, nor am I out of it … being deprived of everlasting bliss" (*Dr Faustus* 1.3.77–81): Milton's Satan, as the narrator insists has

> … Hell within him, for within him Hell
> He brings, and round about him, nor from Hell
> One step no more than from himself can fly
> By change of place … (4.20–23)

We have seen that the early speeches in Book 1 already reveal a Satan who experiences Hell as a state of mind. Now Satan confirms this in his own words: "Which way I fly is Hell; myself am Hell;/ And in the lowest deep a lower deep/ Still threat'ning to devour me opens wide" (4.75–77). Narrator and Satan both equate the inner depth of the Satanic self with Hell. After his heroic performance at the beginning of the poem it is especially the reproachful, tortured, Baroque quality of this Hamlet-like introspection that shows the link with English drama, and which, in spite of his free choice of evil, leads many readers to find some kinship with Satan. In particular in this great soliloquy he recognizes that he was wrong to rebel, that God "deserved no such return/ From me" (4.42–43).

Satan further reveals himself as he begins to explore this new world. He has already learned "immortal hate" (1.107): now he turns that hatred on mankind. Hatred in fact is becoming his defining characteristic and Milton manages to make us understand this process, partly by showing how he turns it against himself, but above all by articulating his remarkable self-knowledge as he does so. He hates the sun's beams because they remind him of who he had been in Heaven, and he curses himself (4.71). Later, in his reactions to Adam and Eve, he recognizes how he could have loved them, but in practice their happiness makes them a "sight hateful, sight tormenting." He is now a jealous voyeur who sees them "Imparadised in one another's arms/ The happier Eden .../ ... while I to Hell am thrust." They are enjoying, he tells himself, "their fill/ Of bliss on bliss," a word that, we know, eventually turns its final hiss against him (4.505–08, cf. 10.503, 518–22). Torn between love and hate, Satan eventually has to admit that hate is what now defines him.

Yet, even in the temptation sequence, when he finds Eve alone, he wavers like a Macbeth afflicted by doubt. He speaks of "sweet/ Compulsion" (9.473–74) and says to himself that he feels she is "divinely fair, fit love for gods,/ Not terrible, though terror be in love/ And beauty" (9.489–91); but soon "Fierce hate he recollects" (9.471), so giving himself the strength to pursue his prey. He recovers the rhetorical skill that made him so formidable earlier and that makes him now an unequal match for the first lovely, innocent woman. Milton has him invent a convincing story about how he has already eaten the fruit, and so has learned, unusual for a snake, to speak. Satan then persuades Eve that the prohibition is unfair: it is an injurious withholding of knowledge, and so a test of her courage rather than of her obedience (Empson 159). The poem bends a little to try to counter this claim, but this is what many readers remember, and may well continue to think.

This complicated, private, deeply reflective Satan, who needs to talk himself back into hate, who can be so misled by his own thoughts as to be momentarily touched by innocent beauty and stricken "Stupidly good" (9.465), is a far more radical development than anything Milton found among his predecessors. The figure of Satan within the Christian tradition is a composite and contains ingredients from various sources, but one role above all characterizes him: he is what his Hebrew name implies, the Adversary (Forsyth 1987).

This was the most general, and so the most inclusive, of his many titles. When Milton's hero calls himself Satan, for the only time in the poem, at 10.386–87, the point is quite explicitly the meaning of his name: "for I glory in the name,/ Antagonist of Heav'n's Almighty King." *Satan* is the Hebrew for "adversary," and *devil* comes from its Greek equivalent, *diabolos,* which means "opponent" in the etymological sense of "obstruction," something placed in the way. So it is enmity itself that is signaled by the name of the Christian enemy. *Fiend* too comes from a Germanic word meaning "enemy."

Thus an important reason for the ambivalence that attaches to Satan, even before Milton, is that he is not really the personification of evil (or its *incarnation* – to use a loaded term that Milton himself exploits at 9.166). Historically speaking, he was first, and really always remained, a character in the myth of combat that informs the Christian story of Fall and Redemption. In *Paradise Lost*, Satan is the "Arch-Enemy" (1.81), he who opposes and rebels against the divine decree: to do ill will ever be his sole delight, he announces, because he is "contrary to his high will/ Whom we resist" (1.161–62), and he chooses evil in order to be different, because, or rather *if*, God is good. Satan explicitly rejects Michael's term *evil* for the War in Heaven, which "we style/ The strife of glory" (6.289–90). Only later, when Satan has arrived on Earth and seen the newly created physical world, the sun included ("How I hate thy beams" 4.37), does his initial choice become the famous and paradoxical cry, "Evil be thou my good" (4.110). Then the degree to which Milton complicates the picture can be seen by the way that, in the same passage in which Satan is struck "Stupidly good" by the sight of Eve, he is, for the only time, called "the evil one" (9.463–65). That is what we have seen him actively become.

The origin of evil, as Milton well knew, had been a favorite topic among the theologians of the early Church. The main story that came to be told was really about how the Arch-Enemy came to be, often through the rebellion of a hitherto subordinate god or hero. Traces of this mythic paradigm and its several variants are to be found in many places in the ancient world and in the sacred literature of the Judeo-Christian tradition. Such myths are not spelled out in full in the Bible, but several biblical passages were generally thought to tell parts of the story; these included descriptions of the monstrous Leviathan (in Job 41:1, for example), the passage in Ezekiel 28 about the Prince of Tyre that parallels Isaiah's apostrophe to the king of Babylon as Lucifer, as well as several New Testament texts. Milton makes some use of all these traces. The Briareos-Typhon-Leviathan simile for Satan near the opening of the poem (1.199–208) or Python nearer the end (10.530–31), and indeed the cataclysmic battle itself at the center, are all evidence of Milton's interest in these ancient tales, which he tried (like Origen and Augustine before him) to restore to their proper shape and place in the narrative. Yet because the story is nowhere told *in extenso* within the canon, Milton had much freedom to invent. An example is the allegory of the birth of Sin from Satan's head, another is the reason for Satan's rebellion itself – his envy of the Son's arbitrary promotion by God. In the extra-biblical precedents for this episode, it is Adam, not the Son, whom a jealous Satan feels has been unfairly magnified (Evans 226). Milton can also add the motive that animates Achilles in Homer. The *Iliad* and *Paradise Lost* both turn on the connection between "a sense of injured merit" (*PL* 1.98) and the hero's wrath.

One motive that guided Milton's invention was that like many of his apocalyptically minded contemporaries Milton saw the events of the Christian myth as paradigms or archetypes for the events of his own times (Revard 108–28). The cosmic struggle and the origins of human sin were the main subjects of the epic, but those events could be understood in the terms of contemporary politics. The comparison of Satan's original brightness, now dimmed, to an eclipse that (note the present tense) "with fear of change/ Perplexes monarchs" (1.598–99) almost led to the entire poem being censored. Satan has been likened to both Charles I and Cromwell (Bennett 33–58; Hill 367–73). In the pamphlet literature of this revolutionary period, as Peter Thomas has put it, "Sometimes the very layout of broadsheets confronts readers with conflict and choice, as when *The Two Incomparable Generalissimos of the World* (Satan and Christ) are drawn up facing us in two vertical columns of verse" (Thomas 127). The earliest Christians too had told versions of this combat myth because they felt themselves to be living through it. As one of Paul's letters puts it, eventually Christ will destroy "every principality and authority and power. For he must reign until he has put all his enemies under his feet" (1 Corinthians 15:24–27). It is the point of Paul's rhetoric that human empires and their rulers, like the Roman imperium, must also be seen in the cosmic perspective. The biblical book of Revelation offers the most elaborate vision of such cosmic combat in which a great dragon, Satan, "that old serpent," flings down a third of the stars (Yarbro-Collins). Michael, God's champion, does battle with and defeats him (each with a host of angels in support). Milton puts that battle at the center of his poem because it was central in the experience of the time. But he makes the ultimate victor not Michael but the Son of God, called in this episode the Messiah. And as if to insist on Satan's modernity, Milton has him invent gunpowder. Thus warfare itself passes from the heroic code of classical epic to the logistical battles of the modern world, where what wins is not courage but superior firepower, and where the enemy is always depersonalized, even demonized. This new sense of Satanic danger, of a world gotten out of hand, pervades the poem. It is a world that needs a Messiah.

The biblical passages also reflect a battle of ideas. Paul was writing his letters to dissuade his correspondents from mistaken interpretations, and Milton knew that Christianity had formed itself as a religion of controversy, indeed that many of its fundamental doctrines arose from the quarrel with what came to be called heresy. Milton was sympathetic to heresy, recognizing its views as often more original than those of the orthodox. That quarrel he partly dramatized in the figure of Satan and his opposition to God: for example, in the first stage of his rebellion, Satan has a revealing quarrel with Abdiel, a "fervent Angel" (5.849) that Milton invented, in the course of which Satan is made to claim not to have been created. "We know no time when we were not as now" (5.859), he says, and this idea echoes Manichaean myths about the eternal opposition of Light and Dark. Indeed Milton calls Satan at that moment "Th'Apostate" (5.852–63), just as Irenaeus and the other heresy-hunters of the early Church had done. But Milton also has Satan admit on Mt. Niphates that God had indeed created him (4.43). Even there, however, as Satan allows that it was God who made him what he was "in that bright eminence," Milton risks the heresy of laying responsibility for evil on God. In the rest of the speech Satan soon takes responsibility himself for his rebellion, and so absolves God. But such heresies were woven into the Christian tradition, and Milton often accentuates in this way the conflicts that arise from them. At every turn in the poem Satan's intelligence and his emotional intensity make the reader challenge easy orthodoxies, even the meanings of good and evil. He may not be a hero in the epic sense, but it is hard to deny him the status of a tragic hero. As the Romantic essayist William Hazlitt said, Milton "did not scruple to give the devil his due" (Hazlitt 385).

Further Reading

Bennett, Joan, *Reviving Liberty: Radical Christian Humanism in Milton's Great Poems* (Cambridge, MA, 1989).

Blake, William, "The Marriage of Heaven and Hell," in *The Complete Poetry and Prose of William Blake*, 2nd ed., ed. David V. Erdman (New York, 1988), 33–4.

Carey, John, "Milton's Satan" in *The Cambridge Companion to Milton*, ed. Dennis Danielson, (Cambridge, UK, 1999), 160–74.

Darbishire, Helen, ed., *The Early Lives of Milton* (Oxford, 1932).

Empson, William, *Milton's God* (London, 1961).

Evans, J. Martin, "*Paradise Lost*" and the Genesis Tradition (Oxford, 1968).

Fish, Stanley E. *Surprised by Sin* (London, [1967] 1997).

Forsyth, Neil, *The Satanic Epic* (Princeton, NJ, 2003).

The Old Enemy: Satan and the Combat Myth (Princeton, NJ, 1987).

Fowler, Alastair, ed., John Milton, *Paradise Lost*, 2nd ed. (London, 1998).

Gardner, Helen, "Milton's Satan and the Theme of Damnation in Elizabethan Tragedy," *English Studies*, N. S. I, 1948, 46–66, reprinted in *A Reading of "Paradise Lost"* (Oxford, 1965), 99–120.

Hazlitt, William, "Lectures on the English Poets, 'III: On Shakespeare and Milton,'" in *The Romantics on Milton*, ed. Joseph Wittreich (Cleveland, OH, 1970), 374–87.

Hill, Christopher, *Milton and the English Revolution* (New York, 1977).

Revard, Stella, *The War in Heaven: "Paradise Lost" and the Tradition of Satan's Rebellion* (Ithaca, NY, 1980).

Shawcross, John T., "An Early View of Satan as Hero of *Paradise Lost*," *Milton Quarterly* 32 (1998), 104–5.

Steadman, John M., "'Darkness Visible': The Quality of Hellfire," *Milton's Biblical and Classical Imagery* (Pittsburg, PA, 1984), 121–35.

"The Idea of Satan as the Hero of *Paradise Lost*," *Proceedings of the American Philosophical Society*, CXX (1976), 253–94.

Thomas, Peter, "The Impact on Literature," in *The Impact of the English Civil War*, ed. John Morrill (London, 1991), 123–42.

Thorpe, James, ed., *Milton Criticism: Selections from Four Centuries* (New York, 1950).

Virgil, *The Aeneid*, ed. R. D. Williams (London and Basingstoke, 1972).

Waldock, A. J. A., *Paradise Lost and Its Critics* (Cambridge, UK, [1947] 1964).

Yarbro-Collins, Adela, *The Combat Myth in the Book of Revelation* (Missoula, MT, 1976).

3

JOHN RUMRICH

Things of Darkness: Sin, Death, Chaos

It is often remarked that in Book 4 <u>Milton introduces the unfallen Adam</u> <u>and Eve from Satan's perspective</u>. The first place presented to us in the poem, Hell with its rebel angels, is also envisioned for the reader through Satan's "baleful eyes," as Neil Forsyth notes in the previous chapter (1.56). Indeed, for much of the <u>first third of the epic the narrator takes pains to tell us how</u> <u>things look and feel to Satan.</u> Our first glimpses of Sin, Death, and Chaos occur along that same long narrative march, which recounts what Satan – the damned, defeated, but undaunted adversary of God – meets, sees, and overcomes during his mission to pervert God's new creation.

Despite this basic continuity of narrative perspective, the episodes describing Satan's encounters in Eden and at Hell's Gate are easily distinguished. When Satan first comes upon the human couple, he has already completed the middle passage of his voyage, and the full narrative arc of his mission has been foreseen and assimilated into the Almighty's announcement of his salvation plan (3.80–343). When Satan encounters Sin and Death, however, God has not yet appeared in the epic narrative, which to this point has remained confined to Hell. Sin and Death recognize Satan before he recognizes them and put themselves athwart his path with the apparent intention of forbidding his departure. The unfallen Adam and Eve, by contrast, never detect Satan's presence in the Garden and unwittingly reveal themselves to him.

The impression we are given of Sin and Death and their blocking role is misleading, however, whether we regard it with respect to the episode's outcome or its poetic mode. The deceptiveness of the initial impression depends on two related causes: first, the unrecognized reunion of characters who, as we learn, have been violently sundered and transformed; second, the confusion of seemingly incompatible modes of literary representation – narrative history and allegory. Allegory differs from ordinary narrative because allegorical characters, unlike characters presented as real agents in a narrative, "are for the most part suffered only to do their natural office, and retire" (Johnson 74). They represent ideas or concepts, not agents in the action.

Yet Sin and Death do not initially appear as personifications of moral and existential concepts. Instead, they have their own history, to which Satan, although he originated it, is initially oblivious. Nor has the reader been prepared for the allegorical implications that will unfold as the history of Sin and Death is told and their characters named. This unsuspected allegorical freight rolls down the narrative line until gradually it becomes apparent that Sin and Death are not *meant* to hinder Satan's progress. Instead, these signifying monsters, although at first they seem like real and perhaps insuperable obstacles to his mission, provide the backstory for Satan's present intention and then take an active part in furthering his mission.

The effect of allegorical participation in the epic narrative, as Samuel Johnson observed, is to "shock the mind by ascribing effects to non-entity" (Johnson 74). The impact of this odd quasi-allegorical, quasi-narrative episode is similar to that of collage in visual art as pioneered by Picasso in the early twentieth century. Fascinated by what he took to be the recurring oxymoron of "the story and the abolition of the story," Picasso used collage as a formal means of expressing "the limits between abstraction and narrative."[1] What Picasso achieved by juxtaposing images from distinct media – a painted violin and a bottle with a clipped newspaper account of a suicide pasted between them – Milton manages in part by permitting allegorical abstractions to become narrative agents. This chapter offers an account of what Satan learns – and the reader learns with him – in his bid to comprehend the things of darkness that he meets during his escape from Hell: abstractions of his own history that intrude on his story and propel it forward. The rationale for the tight focus, especially at the beginning of this account, lies in two seemingly contradictory but equally valid clichés: God is in the details; the devil is in the details. That's where Milton's theodicy has them fight it out.

The shape that turns out to be Sin is first described to the reader as a monster similar to Ovid's Scylla (*Met.* 14.60–65), though with a significant difference. The dogs surrounding the classical Scylla sprout from her trunk in writhing appendages footed with clamorous dog heads. The Hellhounds vexing the Scylla-like monster that Satan sees are sometimes free of her and sometimes fully incorporated, repetitively born and unborn:

> when they list, would creep,
> If aught disturbed their noise, into her womb.
> And kennel there, yet there still barked and howled,
> Within unseen. (2.656–59)

These dogs, Milton says, are far more abhorrent than the ones that plagued Ovid's Scylla (2.659–60).

While Milton's physiological rendition of the deformed Scylla-like figure and her hounds engages and then horrifies a reader's imagination, the description of her companion at Hell's Gate begins by acknowledging that his shapelessness defies anatomization:

> The other shape,
> If shape it might be called that shape had none
> Distinguishable in member, joint, or limb,
> Or substance might be called that shadow seemed,
> For each seemed either. (2.666–70)

The description resembles references elsewhere in the epic to the flexible corporeality and comprehensive functionality of angels, "uncompounded .../ Nor tied or manacled with joint or limb" (1.425–26; cp. 6.350–53). Yet we are told that the unshape is "black ... as night,/ Fierce ... terrible," that it shakes "a dreadful dart," and that on what seems its head sits "the likeness of kingly crown" (2.670–73). These fragmentary incitements to imagination coalesce with angelic celerity as the quasi-regal terror expresses itself as a figure admirably capable of executing its still hostile purposes. As Satan approaches, it comes "as fast/ With horrid strides" (2.675–76).

In an early example of a pattern of prevented conflict that runs through the narrative of Satan's mission, the Scylla-like figure leaves her post at "Hell gate," to which we *now* learn she keeps "the fatal key," and intervenes between Satan and his challenger (2.725). We then learn the shocking news that Satan is her father, and his would-be opponent their child. Yet the full identities of these children are only incrementally revealed, in the course of a story that opens with a moment familiar from Greco-Roman mythology, the birth of Athena, virgin goddess of wisdom. The ominous nativity scene recounted by Satan's daughter is accompanied by the same dark explosive imagery and generative violence that is the signature effect of Satan's subsequent machinations, from his invention of gunpowder during the War in Heaven to the invasion of the sleeping Eve (6.470–91, 584–89; 4.800–19):

> All on a sudden miserable pain
> Surprised thee, dim thine eyes, and dizzy swum
> In darkness, while thy head flames thick and fast
> Threw forth, till on the left side op'ning wide,
> Likest to thee in shape and count'nance bright,
> Then shining heav'nly fair, a goddess armed
> Out of thy head I sprung: amazement seized
> All th' host of Heav'n; back they recoiled afraid
> At first, and called me Sin, and for a sign
> Portentous held me. (2.752–61)

The story of Sin's head-splitting origin recounted here serves as an allegorical preview of historical events that will be narrated by Raphael in Books 5 and 6: Satan's rebellion and subsequent fall into Hell. The moment of rebellious self-estrangement recounted as the birth of Sin may thus be understood as an allegorical rendition of the archetypal moment that Satan compulsively inhabits – his point of origin as God's determined adversary. It amounts to self-reformation, or re-creation through subtraction, and is in this respect equivalent to the other moment in the narrative described as Satan's first experience of pain – when Michael's sword "shared/ All his right side" (6.326–27).

One of Satan's followers, Nisroch, defines pain as the perfection of misery (6.462). And misery, an amazed Michael insists when he comes to confront Satan in battle, is a condition that Satan has discovered, "uncreated till the crime/ Of thy rebellion" (6.268–69). It is a self-begotten affliction to which a rebel who thinks himself "impaired" by the exaltation of the Son becomes subject (5.665). In the ensuing swordfight, Michael "with discontinuous wound," literally impairs Satan and, by inflicting pain, perfects his misery (6.329). Satan will invent gunpowder in response. But well before the larger epic narrative arrives at the point (chronologically earlier) where Michael expresses his amazement at what Satan has begotten and wounds him, Sin has already identified the original instance of "miserable pain" as the scene of her birth and naming (2.752). These narratives are incommensurate in form and content. They nevertheless account for the same occurrence. The extraordinary self-rendition by which Satan gives birth to Sin is followed by astonishment at and then passionate embrace of the idealization of what has been lost – "what [he] was/ In that bright eminence" (4.43–44).

After the expulsion from Heaven, cruel childbirth and incestuous rape ensue, and the procreative cycle accelerates with the compulsively repetitive birth and reincorporation of the Hellhounds. Louis Schwartz has detailed the anxiety and life-threatening ordeal that regularly accompanied maternity as experienced in seventeenth-century London and finds that such terrors inform these scenes of infernal reproduction:

> At last this odious offspring, whom thou seest
> ...
> Tore through my entrails, that with fear and pain
> Distorted, all my nether shape thus grew
> Transformed: but he my inbred enemy
> Forth issued, brandishing his fatal dart
> Made to destroy: I fled, and cried out "Death";

Hell trembled at the hideous name, and sighed
From all her caves, and back resounded "Death." (2.781–89)

Born in Heaven, Sin became pregnant when Satan "joy ... took'st/ With [her] in secret" (2.765–66). The subsequent embraces of Death, "forcible and foul" defy such euphemistic idiom as the Hell-born child attacks his mother immediately after tearing his way out of her, more "inflamed with lust than rage" (2.793, 791). The downward spiral of the generative process initiated by Satan in Heaven conforms to the insistently if perversely procreative constitution of Hell, "which God by curse/ Created evil, for evil only good,/ Where all life dies, death lives, and nature breeds,/ Perverse, all monstrous, all prodigious things" (2.622–25).

The account of the origin of Sin and Death culminates in compulsive reproductive seizures as Sin bears the children of Death's rape. As Schwartz suggests, what the rapist Death engenders in the mind and body of his victimized mother may be understood as an extreme version of the fallen experience of time as the incremental measure of mortality. The Hellhounds engendered by her first child, "of that rape begot," become the chronological index of an unremitting process of terror and sorrow, "hourly conceived/ And hourly born," howling and gnawing at her bowels in an etymologically literal image of remorse and then "bursting forth/ Afresh with conscious terrors vex [her] round/ That rest or intermission none [she] find[s]" (2.794, 796–97, 800–02). The milder but precedent imagery of Milton's early lyric "On Time" suggests the development of Milton's thought. In that genre-establishing short poem, "[to be] set on a clock-case," the womb of time is depicted as devouring successive generations, anticipating what Milton here renders in Sin's allegorical flesh and ultimately in his account of Death as an insatiable maw. Yet the action of Sin's womb is nonetheless clocklike, chronically spasmodic – with the Hellhounds hourly kenneling, hourly bursting forth, and circling round her – a hideous organic variation on the mechanism of a cuckoo clock. The mood of "On Time" with its evocation of the "leaden stepping hours" suggests the melancholy impact of time's passage. But that lyric ends with a promise of salvation and ultimate triumph over time. Sin has no such hope. The operation of death for the unregenerate, sunk in sin, boils down to a waiting game, one experienced most onerously by the divinely cursed mothers of every sinful human generation.

Insofar as Sin occurs in the narrative as a developing character with a backstory rather than as a static personification, readers may pity her as a passive victim, more sinned against than sinning. Soon after giving birth to her in Heaven, her father recognizes himself in her and then couples with her. The joy of that embrace, however, leads to her being cast down to Hell, where she is seized by birth pangs, viscerally mutilated, raped by her child, and tormented in darkness by the monstrous litter of that rape. The allegorical point of having "Sin" suffer as she does and be given the key to Hell, the realm of "Death," is intelligible from a doctrinal standpoint. "Sin" signifies violation of divine law, and Hell is the place where such violations are punished spiritually and bodily.

Yet the allegory seems irreconcilably at odds with the narrative, as Daniel Defoe was the first commentator to observe: "Mr. Milton has indeed made a fine Poem, but it is *the Devil of a History*" (71). Defoe argues that once the poet settles on a "local Hell," as if it were a torture dungeon divinely established by God, one must wonder how it is that the prison is so poorly kept: "I demand then, how [Satan] got out" (81)? It is in consideration of the role and character of Sin that Defoe's demand becomes inescapable. When Satan and his daughter are somehow separated during the "general fall" – yet before she undergoes the disfiguring birth of Death – God intervenes to assert his authority over her. At that point, noted but not narrated, the theodicy becomes subtly, but unavoidably complicated.

At first Sin speaks in the passive voice of the duty divinely imposed on her, as if mention of her taskmaster were to be avoided: "this powerful key/ Into my hand was giv'n, with charge to keep/ These gates for ever shut" (2.774–76). Yet later she explicitly acknowledges that it was "Heav'n's all-powerful King" who entrusted her with the key to Hell, that she was "by him forbidden to unlock/ These adamantine gates" (2.851–53). The slow reveal seems designed to soft-pedal God's role. As a Defoe-like Satan will later insist of Hell's security, "Let him surer bar/ His iron gates, if he intends our stay/ In that dark durance" (4.897–99). It is difficult not to concede, as Gabriel later seems to, that the "facile" Gates of Hell are "too slightly barred" (4.967).

Christianity construes Sin as that which qualifies or fits creatures for entrance into Hell. But Sin appears to oppose Satan's exit from Hell, not permit his entrance. Judging her as a character in a narrative, we can hardly blame Sin for choosing instead to defy God and cooperate with Satan:

> But what owe I to his commands above
> Who hates me, and hath hither thrust me down
> Into this gloom of Tartarus profound,
> To sit in hateful office here confined,
> Inhabitant of Heav'n, and heav'nly-born,
> Here in perpetual agony and pain,

> With terrors and with clamors compassed round
> Of my own brood, that on my bowels feed. (2.856–63)

Rather than blame the personification of disobedience for disobeying, readers may wonder if God intends for Sin to obey his command when he entrusts her with the key, or if, as would be consistent with the Calvinist concept of Sin, his secret will is that she violate his ostensible command and actively abet Satan's exit. Milton will later echo Sin's lament in detailing his own fearful situation at the Restoration: "though fall'n on evil days,/ On evil days though fall'n, and evil tongues;/ In darkness, and with dangers compassed round,/ And solitude" (7.25–28). Milton suffers not because he was, like Sin, a pliant manifestation or a passive receptacle of Satanic defiance, but on account of what he deemed to be obedient devotion to a righteous antimonarchical rebellion. He still looks to Heaven for protection. Sin cites her suffering, on the other hand, as a rationale for disobeying the heavenly monarch's command.

The echo between Sin's response to her situation and the epic narrator to his nevertheless suggests a doctrinal problem pertinent to the theodicy. As a poet and a theologian Milton insists on human freedom and rejects the unsettling implication of Calvinist theology that God is responsible for sin (Treip 241). At the same time that Milton insists on rational creatures' responsibility for their own destinies, however, he also insists on God's perfect control of events. Upholding both of these propositions generates logical problems that John Calvin avoids by declaring for a thorough determinism. Milton's flirtation with this theological paradox has its consequences for the epic narrative. In *Christian Doctrine*, specifically the chapter devoted to divine providence (1.8), or God's control over the course of human events, Milton, writing as a theologian, inserts a long discussion of sin, though he acknowledges he has "not yet reached the place where [he] deal[s] with that subject" (*MLM* 1210). The topic of sin is untimely born into the midst of his exposition on divine providence because, Milton claims, "even in sin ... we see God's providence at work, not only in permitting it or withdrawing his grace, but often in inciting sinners to commit sin, hardening their hearts, and blinding them" (*MLM* 1210–11). God is not responsible for sin, says Milton, but he does push sinners to sin in the manner that he providentially intends, and indeed pushes and blinds hardened sinners in ways that would seem to infringe upon their freedom, a freedom that, Milton argues, they have as confirmed sinners already surrendered (Pharaoh is the most relevant scriptural example; see, e.g., Exodus 7:2–5).

In the standard English translation, Milton's justification for apparently straying off topic in a chapter devoted to divine providence begins with the observation that he is not writing for those "wholly ignorant of

Christian doctrine." Instead, he says, he writes to the already indoctrinated ("*communi ... disserentes*") – that is, to Protestants already familiar with the debates over free will that raged with peculiar force and consequence in England during the first half of the seventeenth century. In the Latin original, however, the justification begins not with characterization of Milton's intended audience but with explicit reference to the topic that is cropping up out of its proper place – "*In peccatis*" or "about sin." Then, after identifying those to whom he is addressing his argument, Milton repeats the phrase "*in peccatis*" to remind his "fairly well informed" readers of the reason for the digression. Repeatedly obtruding itself in Milton's chapter on divine providence, the concept of sin demands an accounting even in a theological situation where the uninformed reader might think it does not belong.

In terms apt for Satan's epic encounter with Sin and Death, the theological Milton explains that God assumes control of sin after the would-be sinner "had conceived sin, when [the heart] is heavy with it, and already giving birth to it; then God as the supreme arbiter of all things turns and points it in this or that direction or towards this or that object" (*MLM* 1211).[2] From this perspective, awarding Sin possession of the key that unlocks Hell may be considered an allegorical expression of God leaving Satan "at large to his own dark designs/ That with reiterated crimes he might/ Heap on himself damnation, while he sought/ Evil to others" (1.213–16). Although Satan may be said to have conceived Sin and Death on his own, by the time he meets them at Hell's Gate, God has already appropriated them, "My Hell-hounds," to accomplish his providential plan, part of which is to have them "lick up the draff and filth/ Which man's polluting sin with taint hath shed/ On what was pure" (10.630–32). Contrary to the classic argument of Stanley Fish, Sin surprises us not because we – like certain Romantic readers – tend to find her father sympathetic but because God works out his will in such an advantageous manner by providentially managing her intrusion into the narrative.

The alignment of Sin and Death with God, an alignment acknowledged and quickly disavowed by Sin – but later insisted upon again by God himself – should perhaps come as no surprise despite the rising complications of allegiance, morality, and authority that surface during the meeting between Satan and his children, who are both allegorical and yet active in the narrative. As Milton explains in his theological treatise, God ultimately controls what Sin, Death, and Satan accomplish. God begins his first speech of the epic, at the opening of Book 3, ostensibly quite impressed by the grit of Satan, "whom no bounds/ Prescribed, no bars of Hell, nor all the chains/ Heaped on him there, nor yet the main abyss/ Wide interrupt can hold" (3.81–84). Yet this statement, to the extent that it suggests that Satan has heroically managed to overcome barriers that God had presumed adequate to contain him, exemplifies the derisively ironic posture that he consistently adopts toward Satan and that the fallen angels attribute to him, with scriptural authority that lies at the heart of *Paradise Lost* (5.735–37; cp. Psalm 2:4). The narrator too informs us from the first moment we witness Satan "chained on the burning lake" that however much he credits his own intrepid power he could not have so much as lifted his head without divine permission (1.209–15).

Over the long arc from the initial report of Satan's utterly abject condition – supine and in chains on the infernal lake of torment – various forms and degrees of providential permission, incitement, turning, hardening, and blinding occur, to point him in the direction of his divinely sanctioned targets: Adam and Eve. The difficulty of perceiving divine providence in Satan's encounter with Sin and Death is reflected in the slow narrative pace at which Satan, and the reader with him, comes to recognize Satan's own children. Although they derive from him, once put into God's service, they are obscured from their father, an obscurity that is imposed when Satan is thrown from Heaven. At that point in the narrative he is separated from these rebellious expressions of his own psychology, and in that interval God intervenes to assert his control. The cross currents of Sin's divided loyalty are deftly summarized in the conflicted allegorical object of the key, which the narrator first brings into view well after Sin first appears in Satan's path, and which is not explained to Satan or the reader until well after that. The key is a concentrated expression of the dark side of the narrative, dark to Satan and dark to the reader. The story behind the key suggests on the one hand that God would prefer that Sin and all the fallen remain confined to Hell, but on the other hand that God intends for Satanic disobedience to proceed in precisely the direction he has chosen.

There is an exception to this providential rule. Chaos too plays a part in advancing Satan's mission, so much so that Regina Schwartz, citing mythological antecedents involving a hostile Chaos and the insistence of Milton's Chaos that "Havoc and spoil and ruin are [his] gain" (2.1009), concludes that Chaos represents a greater threat than Satan and his progeny do (Schwartz 8–39). Yet unlike Sin, who represents a moral condition of creatures endowed by God with free will, Milton's personification of Chaos represents a material precondition of creatures. He does not defiantly open a gate that he has been commanded by God to leave locked. Instead, he orients Satan toward his destination – "if that way be your walk, you have not far" (2.1007) – and encourages the rebel angel in his declared intention to "reduce/ To her original darkness" the new creation, which formerly was part of Chaos (2.983–84). As the personification of his realm, he seems interested in Satan's resistance to God's creative initiatives, or, as Satan puts it, "usurpation" on Chaos's "region lost" (2.982–83). But his declaration of interest in destruction is balanced by the narrator's observation that the "pregnant causes" of Chaos are biddable to divine authority and that "th' Almighty Maker," as he pleases can "them ordain/ His dark materials to create more worlds" (2.913, 915–16). The personification of this state of matter is led to believe that Satan means to serve the constitutional interest of his realm and so cooperates with rather than resists him on his journey. Unlike Sin, however, Chaos declares no relationship or allegiance to Satan. He offers no resistance, either. Sin has in her origins agency adversarial to God; Chaos registers the absence of any volitional agency at all. He has no origin and is not *really* there, except as an infinite state of material possibility.

As in the encounter with Sin and Death, who as we have seen appear initially as threats to Satan's progress, Satan's encounter with Chaos as a threat precedes the allegorical elaboration of the character of Chaos. The sequencing is thus the same, but the nature of such threat as Chaos poses differs vastly from that personified by Sin and Death, and is not pinned down to a described shape or named shapelessness athwart Satan's path. We are again taken by surprise. Shortly after Satan launches himself from Hell, the physical realm of Chaos itself nearly writes an end to Satan's mission and does so merely by being what it is: infinite, random, and vacuous:

> Flutt'ring his pennons vain plumb down he drops
> Ten thousand fathoms deep, and to this hour
> Down had been falling, had not by ill chance
> The strong rebuff of some tumultuous cloud
> Instinct with fire and niter hurried him
> As many miles aloft. (2.933–38)

The material realm of Chaos – the indeterminate space that Satan crosses prior to his interview in the allegorical Court of Chaos and Night – presents a more spontaneous and unregulated challenge to the author of evil than anything else he confronts as he proceeds on his mission to destroy or pervert humanity. Only the "strong rebuff" of a random cloud saves Satan from being forever swallowed up by limitless depths. At this one moment during Satan's long journey from Hell's pit, God does not appear to be in control. It occurs in the wild. No volitional agent under divine management, such as Sin or Death or Gabriel, intervenes to enable the adversarial plotline to proceed. This singular moment instead occurs fortuitously, "by ill chance."

In the preceding episode, Sin, the representation of a moral state, deploys the key she has been provided but forbidden by God to use. The only connection we might draw between that moment and the one in which Satan is propelled from the depths of Chaos is in its explosive associations.

The doors of Hell open "with impetuous recoil and jarring sound/ ... and on their hinges grate/ Harsh thunder" as the mouth of Hell belches "smoke and ruddy flame" into the abyss (2.880–82, 889). The "tumultuous cloud" that blasts Satan out of endless material oblivion repeats the persistent association of Satan with fiery explosions and the sort of matter that is ripe with them. His original invention of gunpowder requires that materials "pregnant with infernal flame" be mined from beneath Heaven's surface and extracted "in their dark nativity [from] the deep" (6.482–83). But the cloud that propels Satan upward when he would otherwise have been forever lost in Chaos cannot be linked to him, his family, his new realm, or to divine providence. Unlike the birth of Sin, the construction of artillery in Heaven, or other related episodes, Satan's escape from an endless plummet through the abyss is merely humanity's bad luck rather than a product or punishment of Satanic invention. Such a moment may not absolve providence of its role or justify the ways of God to men, any more than the deep presence of the raw materials for gunpowder does, but in this instance during Satan's journey out of Hell, divine agency is at least not pushing the action along in the direction that God wants it to go.

Satanic forces of evil as represented by Sin and Death explicitly recognize themselves to be under God's thumb even though they appear horrifying and unstoppable. Chaos, although the narrator observes that his realm meekly complies with God's creative demands, makes no such admission. His face, like his realm, is "incomposed," but unlike Sin and Death he is not portrayed as hideous or frightening – only confused and ineffectual. He explains that his strife-ridden realm has been "encroached on still through our intestine broils" (2.1001). The constitutional confusion of his realm renders it inherently vulnerable to organization. He never mentions the agency behind such encroachments, only the ripeness of his realm for them. Milton's theological treatise provides no obviously pertinent explanation of a providential aspect to the part that Chaos plays in Satan's advancement toward Adam and Eve. The term "chaos" does not even appear in the treatise, although it is widely agreed that during the course of the Satanically inflected narrative the pagan mythological term "chaos," meaning "unfathomable gulf" is used to present the realm of the first matter. Elsewhere in the poem it is named the "deep," the "abyss," and various other, sometimes quite inventive, epithets (e.g., "wide interrupt"; "vast abrupt"; "palpable obscure"), and Milton's God insists that he "fills" it passively until he wishes to create out of it (7.168–69; for more detail on the matter of Chaos and Milton's God, see Rumrich).

The first matter does come under scrutiny at some length in chapter seven of the first book of *DDC*. Milton there insists that this state of matter is essential to God, being the material wherewithal of his creative power: "God is the first, absolute and sole cause of all things ... So the material cause must be either God or nothing" (*MLM* 1201). In the epic, Chaos is described as infinite and uncreated, adjectives that Milton reserves for God alone. In *Paradise Lost* the abyss of Chaos thus seems to represent what Milton in his theological treatise defines as the "heterogeneous, multiform and inexhaustible virtue" that "exist[s] in God, and exist[s] substantially" (*MLM* 1201). The most that might be said about the complicity of God in the material boost that Satan gets from the tumultuous cloud he encounters while plummeting through Chaos is that an affinity connects some aspect of the first matter to the Satanic initiative.

This dark connection is not a question of volition or design, and given the definition of Chaos it cannot be. But Milton's Chaos anticipates chaos theory of our day by allowing for strange attractors – a stable state or behavior, especially in turbulent systems, which can be represented as a non-repeating pattern. When Satan "springs upward like a pyramid of fire" from the Court of Chaos (2.1013), he assumes the elemental form that allowed him to persist in crossing through the infinite realm of Chaos (Kerrigan 138–9). There is coherence between the moment in which Satan blasts off from the Court of Chaos to approach our world and the earlier moment in which a fiery but random cloud propelled him toward that allegorical court. Satan could not exist as the adversary of God if the material potency of God did not substantiate him – as well as the realm of Hell, for that matter. Evidently, something there is in God that tends toward Satan even as he repudiates him. We later learn that material potency "adverse to life" is also part of Chaos (7.239), and although such matter is excluded from the original liveliness of creation, God ultimately substantiates the encroachment of Death on life. By the end of the epic, the allegorical conceits of Sin and Death, at first rendered as if they were hideous and threatening deterrents to Satan's progress, will abridge the realm of Chaos and, "following [Satan's] track," inhabit the newly created world in the persons of Adam and Eve (2.1025). Milton previews this postlapsarian episode directly after Satan departs from the Court of Chaos. In this last allegorical scene, one that unites Sin, Death, Chaos, and Satan in the same tableau, a literalized abridgement or "causey" dividing the indignant waves of Chaos is gathered out of and imposed on his dark realm by the divinely inspired Sin and Death, who have followed in Satan's wake through Chaos (10.293–305, 415). The epic action thus ultimately bonds the two similar but distinct narrative moments with which we began this chapter. Satan's interaction with Sin and Death prior to their incarnation in our world may be understood as a melancholy, proleptic allegory of the misery and the circumscribed scope of fallen human being – a fatal reduction of the divine potential represented in its rawest state by the realm of Chaos.

NOTES

1 From a display card account of the collage, "Bottle and Violin on a Table," *Museu Picasso*, Barcelona, Spain, on display July 2012. The argument of this chapter first occurred to me when I saw this collage and subsequently took shape with the help of commentary and suggestions from Katherine Cox, a graduate student at the University of Texas.
2 For the Latin text, see *CW* 15:68.

Further Reading

Defoe, Daniel, *Political History of the Devil*, 2nd ed. (London, 1727).
Johnson, Samuel, *Life of Milton*, ed. F. Ryland (London, 1894).
Kerrigan, William, *The Sacred Complex* (Cambridge, MA, 1983).
Rumrich, John, "Milton's God and the Matter of Chaos," *PMLA* 110 (1995), 1035–46.
Schwartz, Louis, *Milton and Maternal Mortality* (Cambridge, UK, 2009).
Schwartz, Regina, *Remembering and Repeating: Biblical Creation in "Paradise Lost"* (Cambridge, UK, 1988).
Treip, Mindele Anne, *Allegorical Poetics and the Epic: The Renaissance Tradition to "Paradise Lost"* (Lexington, KY, 1993).

4

VICTORIA SILVER

The Problem of God

> Now had th' Almighty Father from above,
> From the pure empyrean where he sits
> High throned above all highth, bent down his eye,
> His own works and their works at once to view:
> About him all the sanctities of Heaven
> Stood thick as stars, and from his sight received
> Beatitude past utterance; on his right
> The radiant image of his glory sat,
> His only Son… (3.56–64)

It is a truth universally acknowledged that Milton, unlike Homer, never nods. He may have conflicting and unconscious reasons for what he does in *Paradise Lost*, and truth in his great poem undoubtedly has more shapes than one; but he is not as a rule given to artistic inadvertency or poetic accidents. It has therefore been something of a puzzle to his modern readers that he begins the poem's great argument with the figure of Satan in all his ruined grandeur, giving him many of the poem's best lines and certainly most of its best speeches. Moreover, when in Book 3, the poet introduces God, Father and Son, whose eternal providence the speaker's argument professes to assert and whose ways it is supposed to justify, Milton assigns his version of the Christian deity a speech that no one ever wished longer. To make matters worse, the Father opens with a joke at the expense of a suffering Satan, mocking his tragic delusion that he has triumphed over countless obstacles, while yet remaining unseen by Heaven in his flight from Hell to Earth (3.80–81):

> And man there placed, with purpose to assay
> If him by force he can destroy, or worse,
> By some false guile pervert; and shall pervert;
> For man will hearken to his glozing lies,
> And easily transgress the sole command,
> Sole pledge of his obedience: so will fall

> He and his faithless progeny: whose fault?
> Whose but his own? Ingrate, he had of me
> All he could have; I made him just and right,
> Sufficient to have stood, though free to fall. (3.89–99)

It cannot but prejudice the reader against Milton's God to be greeted by the immediate and comprehensive condemnation of our species, with divine judgment on humanity's sin enunciated in sharp, strictly repetitive clauses. Although Milton's contemporary audience knew how the biblical story of Adam and Eve turned out, the Father's judgment on our first parents still comes miles ahead of the narrative event itself. We are, as it were, condemned before the poetic fact and from all eternity, which may lead us to resent Milton's God, whom the devilish propaganda of the poem's first two books portrays as a merely incumbent power "upheld by old repute,/ Consent or custom" (1.639–40).

Of course, the narrator tells us that the Father "foreseeing spake" (3.79): the oscillation of verb tenses in the speech from the present conditional to the future indicative in asserting Satan's strategy and dubious success signals the divine attributes of eternity and omniscience by which the Christian God is theologically characterized ("past, present, future he beholds" [3.78]). But unlike the conscientious archangel Raphael, who prefaces whatever he says to Adam and Eve with an account of the expressive problems involved in characterizing either the heavenly or the divine to his earthly auditors, the narrator has not prepared us for the peculiarities of divine revelation. Indeed, at this juncture in the poem, it is arguable that the narrator himself is not altogether clear, much less wise about what he reports. We are inclined to take for granted the iconological fact that, here as in most plastic representations of the divine Trinity since the early seventeenth century, the Father is seated, enthroned "above all highth" (3.58) with the Son placed honorably next to him, the Holy Spirit implied but anthropomorphically unseen, and the angels standing all about the heavenly throne in a state of utter, ecstatic bliss. The linguistic strangeness of the speech itself, however, goes unremarked. And outrageously, the bliss of the angels remains unabated at the end, when, contrary to the reader's probable indignation, "ambrosial fragrance" fills "All Heav'n, and .../ Sense of new joy ineffable" (3.135–37).

Presumably, they rejoice at God's final mention of grace and mercy toward a fallen humanity; but this comes only after the Father has devoted every other word to austere judgment on the frailty of his intelligent creatures, as well as dense, unrelenting justification of his own ordinances. One ordinance in particular preoccupies him, and that is the freedom he bestowed on Adam and Eve at their creation, thus enabling "our grand parents in that happy state,/ Favored of Heav'n so highly, to fall off/ From their Creator, and transgress his will/ For one restraint, lords of the world, besides" (1.29–32). These plaintive verses from Book 1 put the epic question of *Paradise Lost* as the speaker's importunate demand: what moved our first parents to disobey their God and plunge their posterity into suffering and death, like that he himself endures in his blindness and mortal peril? And although he immediately – and prematurely – blames it all on their seducer ("Th' infernal serpent, he it was" [1.34]), the Father in Book 3 replies to the unspoken thought raised in the minds of both speaker and reader – namely, that God Almighty could have prevented the fall of Adam and Eve, or as Satan more insidiously suggests, that it is God himself who tempted the revolt of human and angel kind, rendering their creator the ultimate, if not the sole, cause of all creatural evil. But Milton's God is having none of it:

> So without least impulse or shadow of fate,
> Or aught by me immutably foreseen,
> They trespass, authors to themselves in all
> Both what they judge and what they choose; for so
> I formed them free, and free they must remain,
> Till they enthrall themselves: I else must change
> Their nature, and revoke the high decree
> Unchangeable, eternal, which ordained
> Their freedom; they themselves ordained their fall. (3.120–28)

These peculiar poetic choices follow what many consider Milton's real blunder in *Paradise Lost* – his decision to make the one true God of Jewish and Christian tradition a mere character in his poem. The move offended more than a few of his devout readers, who regarded it not only as presumptuous, but blasphemous. And for all his vaunted artistry, what we seem to get is the doctrinal God baldly presented, lacking in the *mysterium tremendum* of biblical theophany – the ambient fire shrouded in dark cloud and heralded by thunder that Moses encounters on Horeb or Sinai, and that afterwards terrified his murmuring human flock into temporary submission. Moreover, God the Father does not so much speak as proclaim: there is none of the expressive modulation of the Lord's biblical appearances, created by circumstance and personal regard for the hearer – no "still small voice" in dream and vision, or in the heart (1 Kings 19:12). Instead, God the Father pronounces and ordains, while God the Son, the mediator between divine and human, interprets and extenuates in what Milton himself derisively called in his *De Doctrina Christiana* "all that play-acting of the persons of the godhead" (YP 6:213).

The almost algorithmic intricacy of the Father's exposition on creatural free will and divine foreknowledge does little to recommend him or his speech, which sounds mechanical, casuistical in the pejorative sense, and forced. Yet notwithstanding these impressions, the substance of the speech as such is hardly inhumane. For it is precisely because God is no tyrant that he repudiates the notion that his foreknowledge works like causal necessity upon his reasonable creatures, subjugating them to his will and a life of servile obedience that denies them the exercise of the very intelligence ("reason also is choice" [3.108]) that defines them. But then, Satan in his oratory professes not to believe in the existence of God, if by that name is understood the infinite and inconceivable creator of all things. Instead, he treats the person "styled almighty" as someone just like himself, only equipped with the concealed weapon of thunder, and so no more than supernatural and no less subject to the same supernatural physics as angelkind, whom Satan persists in calling "deities" and "gods." Moreover, with the speaker, we have seen Milton's devils speak, fly and march, build, congregate (with a little shapeshifting), and convene, moving with miraculous power in physical space and time, while God the Father and his Son, merely sit and talk (to each other and the heavenly hosts) on their high hill.

In *Paradise Lost* then, we seem to be in the familiar land of myth, where the supernatural is humanlike, only marvelously more sizeable, powerful, knowledgeable, and beautiful, which is as much as to say that Milton observes a degree of naturalism in his representation of Heaven and Hell. Yet such naturalism proves more superficial than fundamental to Milton's poetic art when, moments before the speaker is transported (no more physically than Milton's devil) to Heaven, he as well as Satan abruptly encounter in the cosmic netherworld four figures who are unquestionably personified abstractions – Sin, Death, Chaos, and Night. For they are the proper denizens of allegory, not myth, suggesting that, unlike Genesis, *Paradise Lost* is a species of allegory, and that Milton's God might be a personification along the same lines. In other words, Father and Son may not be what they seem.

The Bible offers a range of models for allegory, some intentional, some created by its theological interpreters. I would suggest that the version to which Milton has recourse is parable, and certain parables Jesus tells in particular. Parable often plays surreptitiously, ironically, upon the reader's beliefs and expectations, so that the shift from its naturalized to its figural meaning is frequently felt as startling, incongruous, and perverse, insofar as the narrative's implied significance directly challenges the way we habitually make sense of things. In the Gospels, Jesus tells the story of a father who kills a fatted calf not for his long-faithful son but for the prodigal who has defied him and wasted his own patrimony (Luke 15:11–32); of a vineyard owner who pays the same for one hour or twelve hours of work (Matthew 20:1–16); and of the master of a household who departs on a journey, entrusts his three servants with a descending scale of "talents," then casts the last of these into "outer darkness" for having buried his rather than risk its loss, rendering back upon his master's return exactly what he had been given (Matthew 25:14–30).

A reasonable person would condemn such behavior as unfair, but Jesus is speaking of religious things, where more is meant than meets the ear. Thus when these parabolic actions are shifted to the register of God, faith, and a sinful humanity their injustice astoundingly transforms into the opposite: the unfair father, the arbitrary employer, and the cruel master become the Lord in his long-suffering efforts to redeem humanity from its chronic apostasy, with faith the crux on which all human value depends. And the incongruity of these two meanings traces the distinction between ordinary and religious things, the naturalistic and the figural, the world and the one true God. When the disciples' question Jesus about his use of parables, he gives a pregnant answer, quoting the words of the Lord to the prophet Isaiah: "Therefore speak I to them in parables: because they seeing see not, and hearing they hear not, neither do they understand.... For this people's heart is waxed gross, and their ears are dull of hearing, and their eyes they have closed" (Matthew 13:9–17; cf. Isaiah 6:9–10). Unlike the disciples who grasp his meaning, Jesus' audience must learn to convert the ostensible sense of what he says to its religious meaning. At the same time, it is crucial to remember that any parable's religious significance cannot be divorced from its overt or naturalized sense, on which not only the allegory depends but the parable's characteristic impact. For we are meant to experience the ironic shift between the story's apparent and its allegorical significance as something of a shock: that is, we are meant to feel the chastening difference between how we are inclined to think about God and how he is rightly to be understood.

This textual revelation is one reason why Martin Luther calls religious knowledge *res non apparentes*, things that do not appear as such, after Hebrews 11:1: "Faith is the substance of things hoped for, the evidence of things not seen." It is not that religious things are simply invisible to the eye because physically obscured; rather, they are by their very nature antipathetic to sight and to the order of understanding and expectation it induces in us. Indeed, the prophet Isaiah observes of his God: "Verily, thou art a God that hidest thyself, O God of Israel, the Saviour" (45:15). Such hiddenness even in revelation expresses this God's perfect singularity and unique power of truth ("for I am God, and there is none else; I am God, and there is none like me" [Isaiah 46:9–10]). It also underscores deity's absolute distinction from the created world – the infinite and uncreated existence of the divine, as against that of its finite creatures whose ordained natures Adam could name just by looking at them. But we cannot draw such inferences from divine phenomena, because the expressions of what Luther calls the *Deus absconditus* do not describe the divine nature, but only what God wants us to know and understand about our relationship with him. And that is what the speaker and our first parents together learn in *Paradise Lost*, and what Milton would teach his reader.

We should not therefore presume to know the hidden God as we do his creatures. This is the sense of the Mosaic covenant's prohibitions against graven images, its acknowledgement of deity's freedom to manifest itself only as it wills. If the biblical God is said to think, feel, speak, hear, and touch, if he has a face, eyes, voice, hands, arms, and feet, these separate features do not coalesce into a body. They are the local, contingent elements of God's self-revelation – figures of speech, *façons de parler* or "ways of speaking," accommodations (see discussion later in this chapter) to human understanding.

Writing of the sacraments and their signs – the water of baptism, the bread and wine of the Eucharist – Milton observes in *DDC* that "a certain trope or figure of speech was frequently employed. By this I mean that a thing which in any way illustrates or signifies another thing is mentioned not so much for what it really is as for what it illustrates or signifies" (*YP* 6:555). And this is the peculiar character of divine revelation, Jesus' parables, and Milton's own allegory in *Paradise Lost*: they represent signs, not entities, and meanings, not actions or forces. In his self-alienation from God, Milton's Satan has forgotten this peculiarity of religious things, even as he has suppressed – at least for popular consumption – the distinction between himself as creature and God as his creator. That is why, as I said earlier, he regards the War in Heaven as being decided by creatural force – the matching of angelic strengths. But the unfallen angels know that the war, which reaches stalemate in its second day, was meant only to illustrate the infinite difference between creator and creature, made irrefutable on the third day when God the Son scours Heaven of the apostate forces in less poetic time than it takes him to arm and mount the Father's chariot.

Given the impossibility of perceiving a *Deus absconditus*, Milton recommends, again in *DDC*, that we approach the biblical God as a picture we entertain not of deity per se, but of deity as it chooses to represent itself. Instead of speculating where Scripture remains silent, or inventing a god out of whole cloth,

> [i]t is safest for us to form an image of God in our minds which corresponds to his representation and description of himself in the sacred writings. Admittedly, God is always described or outlined not as he really is but in such a way as will make him conceivable to us. Nevertheless, we ought to form just such a mental

image of him as he, in bringing himself within the limits of our understanding, wishes us to form. (*YP* 6:133–34)

The exegetical doctrine of "accommodation" (*accommodatio* or *condescencio*) that Milton invokes here was originally directed to the issue of biblical anthropomorphism, a usage that ascribes to God the characteristics of human personality and physical features, which insofar as deity is worshipped in this form could reasonably be regarded as violating the divine injunction against idolatry – the making and adoration of graven images *as* God. Accommodation is sometimes presented as a principle of simple analogy or resemblance between divine expressions and human experience, which can lead us to suppose that the divine is like enough to humanity that we can infer its invisible nature not only from the biblical picture, but also from the visible creation called God's other "book," and considered a revelation second only to the sacred Scriptures. But at other times, as here and in the Protestant reformers' theology, the doctrine is made to emphasize the theological grounds demanding such accommodated expression, which lie in deity's difference from the world. I refer to Luther's distinction between infinite and inconceivable deity, and the God who speaks to humanity in revelation: the one hidden for all time, the other the historical figure who walks in the garden in the cool of the evening. Similarly, if his hearers are uncomprehending or affronted by Jesus' parables, that is because they can no more move beyond the naturalistic sense of the text than Milton's Satan, or even if they do so, because they persist in structuring its inevident significance after the perceptible operations of ordinary things. But where the hidden God is concerned, drawing a correspondence between the seen and the unseen turns Jesus' *Abba* or "daddy" into the despot of the parables, and Milton's God into a tyrant and oppressor of his own kind.

Luther himself distinguishes between *invisibilia*, which the constraints of time and space render imperceptible to us, and what he terms *abscondita* – the "hidden things" of the *Deus absconditus*, which do not appear as such, and which he says observe "a new, and theological grammar" (*LW* 26:267). The difference is arguably between meaning again conceived as that discrete correspondence between word and thing, in which the meaning of a word is the object to which it refers, and meaning as usage, in which the sense of an expression depends on how we use it. It also captures how parable departs from simple allegory, inasmuch as parable enlists not one (the visual) but all the human dimensions of meaning and understanding to achieve its ironic, chastening impact, in which the failure to comprehend reflects our deficient or false ideas about God. In his 1535 lectures on Galatians, Luther personifies the difference in the opposition between God and a figure he calls "the white devil," who can appear in "the guise of an angel or even of God himself" (*LW* 26:41, 49), after Paul's remark in 2 Corinthians that "even Satan disguises himself as an angel of light" (2 Corinthians 11:14).

Conversely, he argues that God can look diabolical to us to the extent that his appearance or actions balk us of our vanity. For the picture of Jesus, Messiah and incarnate God, is an oblique, almost ironic picture of a deity whom Luther fittingly terms *Deus absconditus sub contrario*, "deity hidden beneath its contrary." Of course, as *theanthropos* or "God-man," Jesus' human nature conceals his divine one. However, Luther's sense of the incarnate God's contrary appearances is more pointed: he regards them as God's rebuke to human egotism and our consequent blindness to the meaning of divine revelation. For if the Jesus of the Gospels identifies himself as "the Son of Man," the Messiah of the prophets who will redeem God's chosen from their sufferings, he appears as a rustic, a vagrant, an agitator, and a blasphemer to those who condemned him to die as a criminal. But Luther would have it that Jesus' improbable appearances and ignoble death were fashioned by God himself to assuage human suffering, the utmost extremity of which he sent his only begotten Son to endure. On that account, what is most repugnant because abject in human eyes is glorious in those of the Christian God, who makes Jesus' suffering and death the heart of his new revelation.

Humanity is not inclined to associate such suffering with God, because it does not accord with our inflated image of ourselves, which in the figure of Luther's white devil we have made God to us; and this self-regarding decorum renders divine revelation more paradoxical still. For

> the world regards it as a sure sign that the Gospel is a heretical and seditious doctrine when it sees that the preaching of the Gospel is followed by great upheavals, disturbances, offenses, sects, etc. Thus God wears the mask of the devil, and the devil wears the mask of God; God wants to be recognized under the mask of the devil, and He wants the devil to be condemned under the mask of God. (*LW* 27:43)

Luther uses the word *larva* or "mask" to suggest how we are deceived by appearances in religious matters, precisely because deity is not like us and therefore discomfiting, repugnant, and disturbing to our ideas, whereas "the white devil" confirms them all in whatever ideological form he happens to take – as the "commonsensical," the "rational," the received, the fashionable – thus preventing humanity from recognizing its God.

Milton makes a comparable argument to Luther's in several of his prose tracts, where he contends that neither right order nor truth are self-evident, and so cannot be uniformly distinguished, much less imposed by any human authority. Order and truth (and the Church's reformation) together emerge over time and through conflict, contrariety, and contradiction – what he calls in *Areopagitica* "the wars of truth," which were fought in the arenas of public controversy and on the battlefields of sixteenth- and seventeenth-century Europe (*YP* 2:562). Whatever his subject in the tracts, he takes human controversy as a given, not only because he himself is engaged in polemic, but also because that is how he conceives truth and right to be found in the ambiguous flux of human experience:

> if we look but on the nature of elementall and mixt things, we know they cannot suffer any change of one kind, or quality into another, without the struggl of contrarieties. And in things artificiall, seldome any elegance is wrought without a superfluous wast and refuse in the transaction. No Marble statue can be politely carv'd, no fair edifice built, without almost as much rubbish and sweeping. Insomuch that even in the spiritual conflict of S. *Pauls* conversion there fell scales from his eyes, that were not perceav'd before. (*YP* 1:795–6)

These images from *The Reason of Church Government*, which Milton wrote in the early 1640s in the midst of public controversy over the structure of the Church of England, all depict the ideal arising from a human – indeed, an artistic – struggle to shape materials resistant yet essential to its expression and leaving detritus attending in its wake. Religious reform involves just such confusion and litter, expressed in the familiar image of snakelike scales falling from Paul's eyes – then Saul of Tarsus and the persecutor of Christians – who had been blinded by a vision of Jesus on the road to Damascus even as he gained the insight of faith (Acts 9:18). So Milton distinguishes between those who "choose to live by custome and catalogue, or, as S. *Paul* saith by sight and visibility, rather than by faith" (*YP* 1:778). That is, if we are to be reconciled to the one true God, we must learn to discriminate among our disparate and manifold impressions. In a world governed by a hidden God, truth and falsehood do not appear as such, or as Luther puts it, do not come with a label. Indeed, we are dealing here with the impalpable of meaning itself, which, like the unseen God, is more and other than its mere appearances in our eyes. For we remain hampered in our judgments by the congenital baggage of our own propensities, the assemblage of sins Milton sees expressed in the apostasy of Adam and Eve, and which leads him to aver, again in *Aereopagitica*: "Assuredly we bring not innocence into the world, we bring impurity much rather; that which purifies us is triall, and triall is by what is contrary" (*YP* 2:515):

> Good and evill we know in the field of this World grow up together almost inseparably; and the knowledge of good is so involv'd and interwoven with the knowledge of evill, and in so many cunning resemblances hardly to be discern'd, that those confused seeds which were impos'd on *Psyche* as an incessant labor to cull out, and sort asunder, were not more intermixt. (*YP* 2:514)

The "cunning resemblances" that obtain between the expressions of good and evil in this life enable Luther's white devil to appear as an angel of light, or God himself. Faith not only believes against the appearances our own vanity demands of God, it is a feat of the imagination, a response to an interpretive dilemma that reveals less about deity than it does about ourselves. Thus John Calvin opens the *Institutes* with the observation that to know God, we must first know ourselves, and that to know ourselves, we must first know God. Obviously, these twinned orders of knowledge are not the same, even as each implicates the other in the manner of that dialectic Luther orchestrates between the white devil and the hidden God, or the one Milton locates in the cunning resemblances of good and evil: for "while joined by many bonds, which one precedes and brings forth the other is not easy to discern" (Calvin 1:35). And a similar dialectic obtains between the ostensible and the figural sense of parable, and between what we see and what we think we see in *Paradise Lost*.

So what does the narrator show us in Milton's Heaven that he and we might not understand? Our authority comes from the angel choir that bursts into song at the decree of humanity's salvation and the Son's glad sacrifice. Like the speaker's initial picture of God enthroned on Heaven's high hill and in Jesus' comments about his parables, what their song describes owes everything to the sixth chapter of Isaiah, where the prophet is called to see an impossible sight – impossible, given the hiddenness of the biblical God:

> In the year that King Uzziah died I saw also the Lord sitting upon a throne, high and lifed up; and his train filled the temple. Above it stood the seraphims; each one had six wings: with twain he covered his face, and with twain he covered his feet, and with twain he did fly. (Isaiah 6:1–4)

Now Milton, in *DDC*, following Calvin, says that the figure Isaiah sees in his vision is not the hidden God: "I repeat, he did not see God himself, but perhaps some angel clothed in some measure of divine glory, or the Son of God himself, the image of his Father's glory" (*YP* 6:237); for "the name 'God' is, by the will and permission of God the Father, not infrequently bestowed even upon angels and men (how much more, then, upon the only begotten Son, the image of the Father!)" (*YP* 6:233). The angel choir, according to the narrator, concurs:

> Thee Father first they sung omnipotent,
> Immutable, immortal, infinite,
> Eternal King; thee Author of all being,
> Fountain of light, thyself invisible
> Amidst the glorious brightness where thou sitt'st
> Throned inaccessible, but when thou shad'st

> The full blaze of thy beams and through a cloud
> Drawn round about thee like a radiant shrine,
> Dark with excessive bright thy skirts appear,
> Yet dazzle Heav'n, that brightest Seraphim
> Approach not, but with both wings veil their eyes.
> Thee next they sang of all creation first,
> Begotten Son, divine similitude,
> In whose conspicuous count'nance, without cloud
> Made visible, th' Almighty Father shines,
> Whom else no creature can behold; on thee
> Impressed the effulgence of his glory abides,
> Transfused on thee his ample spirit rests. (3.373–87)

This is a theological interpretation of the spectacle the narrator himself described earlier on Heaven's high hill, and it entirely reorganizes the elements of that picture, which is why Isaiah's God tells the prophet, in that passage echoed by Matthew's Jesus, to say to his people: "Hear ye indeed, but understand not; and see ye indeed, but perceive not" (Isaiah 6:9–10). What the angels describe is not the hidden God, but the divine glory – the fierce luminescence that signals deity's presence in the sense of its attention or regard. The only figure they see is the Son's, who is indeed a *figure* – the personate image of God or "divine similitude" – in whose "conspicuous countenance" invisible deity is made manifest, as Father or Son. The word "conspicuous" says it all – eminently to see or perceive *together* – which is how Heaven views God, in the figure of the Son as preexistent Christ and Messiah. The only visible figure enthroned amidst the divine glory is the one who speaks now in the voice of the Father and now in the Son's, reflecting in his expressions the different aspects of scriptural deity – wrath and love, justice and mercy, the promulgation and interpretation of the divine decrees. Nor is it a coincidence that the early modern period saw an iconographic vogue in which Jesus' face adorns all three persons of the Trinity, or stranger still, in which his head possesses three faces, two in profile and all his own.

But in *DDC* Milton joins any number of Protestant scripturalists like himself in arguing against the orthodox doctrine of the Holy Trinity – Father, Son, and Holy Ghost, as three distinct persons sharing one and the same divine nature or essence. Having made the case that scriptural evidence for this doctrine is tenuous, he makes the positive argument that there is only one God and that, in "begetting" the Son by his decree, the Father "imparted to the Son as much as he wished of the divine nature, and indeed of the divine substance also[.] But do not take *substance* to mean total essence" (*YP* 6:211). Thus the Son is subordinate to the Father, and the Holy Spirit is the invisible expression of divine grace operating in the historical world, largely without a distinct personality of his own. It is because the Son possesses godhead only in a secondary sense, by divine ascription, that he is the *image* of God: he is a creature born within cosmic time; and he is both seen and heard, facts that distinguish his being from that of deity per se. As Milton sums up, following the first chapter of John's Gospel, "the Son existed in the beginning, under the title of the Word or Logos; ... he was the first of created things, and ... through him all other things, both in heaven and earth, were afterwards made" (*YP* 6:206).

The Son is made where God is unmade; he is divine but not eternal; he is seen and heard where deity is hidden; his status as God's Son is artificial, with the divine nature bestowed but not original to him. All of which describes his function as God's Word, the palpable sign of deity and the agent of its revelation: for it is his figure that has occupied God's heavenly throne from before the angels were born, and who has performed the acts of God, which Raphael, describing the creation of our universe in Book 7, says are "Immediate ... more swift/ Than time or motion" (7.176–79). As a consequence, a certain illogic attends the Son's actions (as it does the speech of the Father), who having, in Raphael's account, effortlessly calmed the roiling deep of Chaos and ordered it into intelligible form, returns to Heaven in the chariot of paternal deity. But lo! a miracle, as Raphael explains: "The Filial Power arrived, and sat him down/ With his great Father, for he also went/ Invisible, yet stayed (such privilege/ Hath omnipresence)" (7.587–90).

This illogic is a sign not only of deity's incomprehensible being but also of allegory's presence, which Satan in his self-idolatry refuses to recognize. Indeed, until the Son's exaltation, Satan believed that the divine image *was* ultimate deity and therefore comparable to himself. But Satan's delusion of likeness to God is exploded when its true identity is revealed with these peculiar paternal words: "This day I have begot whom I declare/ My only Son, and on this holy hill/ Him have anointed, whom ye now behold/ At my right hand" (5.603–06). At this moment of sublime illogic (because the acts of God defy "process of speech" [7.178] and the constraints of time and space that speech encodes), the foundations of Satan's own identity are shaken to the ground. For he can no longer liken himself to ultimate deity, and so he determines to revolt against the rule of the creature who resembles him, if only superficially, and whom he therefore assumes to be his equal. But as the outcome of the War in Heaven proves, Satan in his faithlessness reckons without Milton's God, whose "goodness infinite, goodness immense" (12.469) invariably brings good out of evil. The same is true on Earth, where the devil's seeming triumph in reducing our first parents to his own likeness has already been undone by the Son's self-sacrifice (the Pauline sense of predestination), while in Hell first he and then his legions all turn serpent, the contagious image of his evil.

Further Reading

Christopher, Georgia, *Milton and the Science of the Saints* (Princeton, NJ, 1982).

Danielson, Dennis, *Milton's Good God: A Study in Literary Theodicy* (Cambridge, UK, 1982).

Didron, Adolphe Napoleon, *Christian Iconography: The History of Christian Art in the Middle Ages*, tr. E. J. Millington, 2 vols. (1851; New York, 1965).

Dowey, Edward, *The Knowledge of God in Calvin's Theology* (New York, 1952).

Ebeling, Gerhard, *Luther: An Introduction to His Thought*, tr. R. A. Wilson (Philadelphia, 1970).

Empson, William, *Milton's God* (London, 1961).

Fish, Stanley, *Surprised by Sin*, 2nd ed. (Boston, 1998).

Fixler, Michael, *Milton and the Kingdoms of God* (Chicago, 1964).

Frye, Northrop, *The Return of Eden* (Toronto, 1965).

Grossman, Marshall, *Authors to Themselves: Milton and the Revelation of History* (Cambridge, UK, 1987).

MacCallum, Hugh, *Milton and the Sons of God: The Divine Image in Milton's Epic Poetry* (Toronto, 1986)

McNeill, John T., ed., *Calvin: The Institutes of the Christian Religion*, tr. Ford Lewis Battles, 2 vols. (Philadelphia, 1960) [Calvin].

Pelikan, Jaroslav and Walter A. Hansen, eds., *Luther's Works*, vols. 26–27: *Lectures on Galatians*, tr., Jaroslav Pelikan (Saint Louis, 1964) [LW].

Silver, Victoria, *Imperfect Sense: The Predicament of Milton's Irony* (Princeton, NJ, 2001).

Skulsky, Harold, *Milton and the Death of Man: Humanism on Trial in "Paradise Lost"* (Newark, DE, 2000).

Summers, Joseph, *The Muse's Method* (Boston, 1970).

PART II

5

MAGGIE KILGOUR

Classical Models

Modern readers sometimes feel intimidated by Milton's references to Greek and Roman literatures. It is of course quite possible to read, enjoy, and appreciate Milton's epic with no knowledge of his ancient sources. Yet attention to Milton's use of the classics greatly enriches our reading of the poem. It helps us understand his relation to tradition and can provide a handy introduction to that tradition. Moreover, in seeing how Milton responds to his models we learn something fundamental about how his imagination works. In a poem that imagines the beginnings of all things, Milton reminds us that his own poetry begins in encounters with the great minds and works of the past.

Since the Romantics, we have tended to think that poetry originates in the poet's unique genius. For Milton's generation, as well as earlier ones, such an idea would have made no sense, as authors learned to write by imitating the works of earlier writers. Beginning at grammar school, students were taught to read, write, and speak Latin. While Greek was taught at higher levels, Latin was the basis for all learning, and the language of writing and conversation. To learn to write, students copied the great authors, translating Latin poems first into English and often then back again into Latin. They made speeches, often in Latin as well, imagining what a classical author or character might have said in a particular situation. We can hardly imagine the effects of this training on students' minds. It not only made many of them bilingual, but also made them intimately familiar with the ways in which ancient writers thought. We can see one effect in the explosion of literary creativity in England from the mid-sixteenth century on. Imitating others clearly did not stifle originality in this period, it stimulated it. Seeing the world through the eyes of others broadened and challenged Renaissance writers' imaginations; the classics helped them find their own unique and original voices, while the past gave them a perspective from which to understand and critique their own present. Moreover, as well as reading the classical texts, Renaissance writers studied and copied each other's adaptations; for them tradition was not a static body of remote knowledge but an ongoing process of transformation in which they themselves played a dynamic role.

It is in this context that we need to see the young Milton, who was an omnivorous reader and a superb linguist, fluent in Latin and Greek (as well as Italian) and able to read many other languages. The classics helped him become a poet, as he experimented with different classical meters and genres. The very conventionality of these forms inspired him, as for Milton freedom comes through submitting to rather than rebelling against restraints. Roughly half of his first volume of poetry, the 1645 *Poems*, is written in Latin. Both his Latin and English poems are full of echoes and allusions to classical epics, odes, pastoral, elegy, drama, satire, and invective, and show his knowledge also of earlier European and English translations and adaptations of the ancients. This early study of classical genres, techniques, and themes prepared him to be a writer, and ultimately to write *Paradise Lost*. In "Lycidas," Milton drew upon the tradition of pastoral poetry, especially the *Eclogues* of the Roman poet Virgil, to which he would return to represent life in the Garden of Eden. As part of his apprenticeship, Milton especially enjoyed imitating Latin love elegies, and in particular those of Ovid whose representation of desire and courtship would later help shape the relationship between Adam and Eve. The young Milton also wrote a striking number of funeral elegies, from his earliest English poem, "On the Death of a Fair Infant dying of a Cough," to "Lycidas" and his poignant Latin lament on the death of his best friend, "*Epitaphium Damonis*." Critics have sometimes hinted that this suggests a rather ghoulish side to his character, but Milton knew that writers learned the tricks of their trade by writing such elegies. The end of *Paradise Lost* is itself a kind of elegy on the loss of Eden and the entrance of death and evil into the world.

While Milton tried out different classical forms, he knew that the epic was considered to be, as John Dryden claimed, "undoubtedly the greatest work which the soul of man is capable to perform" (5:267). In his early "*Elegia Sexta*," Milton calls the epic writer the "priest to the gods" (77), in Latin, a *vates*, a seer or prophet, who is inspired by the celestial muses. Early Renaissance writers were eager to write epics to claim authority for themselves while also showing that their own nations were as culturally mature and worthy of celebration as Greece and Rome. Milton was influenced by the examples of writers on the continent, like Ariosto and Tasso, and in England, like Spenser, who had written modern epics. He knew that to write an epic took hard work and time, as the poet needed not only to master poetic technique, particularly the ability to sustain a long narrative, but also to acquire knowledge in a wide range of subjects: science, geography, religion, philosophy, and history. The invocation to *Paradise Lost*,

Book 9 reminds us that Milton was "long choosing" (26) both the subject and form of his most ambitious work. Moreover, his poetic ambitions were put on hold by political and personal upheaval, which prevented him from publishing any poetry between 1645 and 1667. By the time *Paradise Lost* appeared, scientific advances and the experience of the Civil War had made the epic genre seem anachronistic, a throwback to a primitive and violent time. So in *Paradise Lost* Milton feared that he might be writing in "an age too late" (9.44), in which his epic appeared old-fashioned to the modern tastes of the Restoration. But this self-consciousness of belatedness makes *Paradise Lost* a very modern work, which does not merely summarize the traditions of the ancients but also subjects them to scrutiny. Milton considers what it means to write an epic in the late seventeenth century and to use pagan forms for a Christian subject.

While writers before Milton had used the epic for Christian narratives – especially stories of the crusades – in *Paradise Lost* the relation between classical and Christian is itself an important theme. Like all genres, the epic has its own conventions and set of properties, which readers would expect: invocations to the muses, a great hero, catalogs, epic similes, battles, games, inset narratives, the intervention of the gods, a descent to the underworld, a prophecy of the future, and so on. However, from the very first lines of the poem, Milton shows how these conventions take on new meanings in a Christian context. The opening invocation follows closely the epic openings of Homer and Virgil and their followers, which introduce the poems' subjects and heroes, and then ask for the help of muses. But Milton's "heav'nly Muse" (1.6) inspired not Homer and Virgil but the "shepherd" Moses (1.8), traditionally seen as the author of the first five books of the Bible, and is accompanied by the Christian Holy Spirit (1.17). With such support, the narrator claims he can "soar/ Above th'Aonian mount" (1.14–15), the conventional home of the muses. While he compares himself with famous classical bards, such as "Blind Thamyris and blind Maeonides [Homer],/ And Tiresias and Phineus Prophets old" (3.35–36), he also distances himself from them. In the invocation to Book 7 (17–20), he hopes not to suffer the fate of the hero Bellerophon, the rider of the winged horse Pegasus, a symbol of poetry, who flew too high and plummeted to the earth. The narrator recalls too the archetypal poet Orpheus, who failed to bring back to life his beloved wife Eurydice and himself finally suffered a painful death (7.32–38). Christians had frequently compared Orpheus with Christ, who also suffered and died, but who successfully went down to hell to free mankind. For Milton the Christian poet can go where the classical ones could not, as his muse, unlike Orpheus's, is real; as he cries to her: "thou art Heav'nly, she an empty dream" (7.39).

The unreality of classical myths is foregrounded in Book 1, during the building of Pandemonium, the devils' new home in hell. Milton tells how this grand palace was designed by Mulciber (commonly known as Vulcan or, in Greek, Hephaestus). He pauses first to remember the stories that the ancients told about Mulciber and then to correct them:

> Men called him Mulciber; and how he fell
> From Heav'n, they fabled, thrown by angry Jove
> Sheer o'er the crystal battlements; from morn
> To noon he fell, from noon to dewy eve,
> A summer's day; and with the setting sun
> Dropped from the zenith like a falling star,
> On Lemnos th' Aegean isle: thus they relate,
> Erring; for he with his rebellious rout
> Fell long before. (1.740–48)

The story told here is based primarily on the account of Homer in *Iliad* 1.589–94. The general tension in the poem between classical and Christian is epitomized in the contrast here between the gorgeous lyrical passage, which suspends Mulciber's fall in mid-flight for seven lines (740–46), and the abrupt ending (746–48). The verse lets us feel the enchantment of the pagan myths, but then brings us back to the blunt and simple truth: they are false. Milton here draws also on the once common belief that the biblical books of Moses had been written before the writings of the Greeks and then copied badly: as the Son in *Paradise Regained* claims, "Greece from us these arts derived;/ Ill imitated" (4.338–39). Classical myths are distorted shadows of the Christian truth that Milton tells.

It is too simple, however, to see the relation between classical and Christian in the poem as merely one of stark opposition. The sheer beauty of the description of Mulciber's fall gives the pagan myth remarkable power and shows how deeply Milton responded to classical poetry. In many ways his relation to classical models should be seen as one of elaboration rather than strict correction. His ability to expand and tease out the significance of conventions is apparent in his use of the epic simile. In classical epics, extended comparisons of what is happening in the poem to something outside of it stop the action for a moment and ask the reader to view it from a new perspective. For a moment the poet's imagination offers a different way of seeing what is happening. So, for example, a famous simile in Virgil's *Aeneid* describes the dying soldier, Euryalus:

> And blood streamed on his handsome length, his neck
> Collapsing let his head fall on his shoulder –
> As a bright flower cut by a passing plow

> Will droop and wither slowly, or a poppy
> Bow its head upon its tired stalk
> When overborne by a passing rain. (9.615–20)

The simile hurls us out of the brutal battlefield into a different world, one that really belongs to pastoral poetry or to Virgil's long poem the *Georgics*, which celebrates the rural life of farming. It can be – and should be – disorienting, juxtaposing the world of killing and war with that of farming and peace. But the effect is not just one of contrast, as the simile asks us to consider the relations between the two antithetical worlds. While war is the opposite of peace, war is also fought to bring peace. And in the *Georgics*, Virgil suggests that farming itself is a form of warfare, a struggle against hostile forces. Amidst relentless scenes of savage violence, the comparison of the dying soldier to a flower also reminds us of the beauty and fragility of human life.

Epic similes thus pause the main action to make us reflect on it and life in general; they open up into an alternative reality that shadows the epic world of fighting. Milton's similes go even further by focusing on the perspective from which the action is viewed. So for example in Book 1, Satan's shield is described:

> his ponderous shield
> Ethereal temper, massy, large and round,
> Behind him cast; the broad circumference
> Hung on his shoulders like the moon, whose orb
> Through optic glass the Tuscan artist views
> At evening from the top of Fesole,
> Or in Valdarno, to descry new lands,
> Rivers or mountains in her spotty globe. (1.284–91)

At the start, the purpose of this simile is to convey size: Satan's shield is really big, as big as the moon. But this is not just any moon: this is the moon seen by a specific viewer, "the Tuscan artist," Galileo, and from a specific place in Tuscany. Milton is drawing attention to how we see things. Galileo, whom Milton met when he traveled in Italy in 1638, is the only contemporary person directly alluded to in the poem; Milton clearly was struck by this visionary who was, as Milton himself would later be, blind. Moreover, with his "optic glass," the telescope, Galileo had proven that, contrary to appearances, the Earth revolves around the Sun. Like this scientific revolutionary, Milton offers a revolution in perspective, revealing a reality contrary to the way we usually see things. *Paradise Lost* itself becomes our telescope, a means through which the writer and reader are able to perceive things that are very far away from us, including the epic world itself.

In juxtaposing unlike things, similes create patterns of likeness and difference: they draw together the dying warrior and the flower, killing and farming. Milton also asks us to think about his likeness and difference to his classical models, and to notice the tension between the Christian plot and the classical subtexts. His account of the fall of man is haunted by stories of the fall of Troy, the great and ancient civilization whose tragic end preoccupied the Renaissance imagination. In particular, Homer's and Virgil's epics offered him alternative myths of fall and redemption, exile and return, and contrasting models for the epic hero.

The *Iliad* and the *Odyssey* represent events that lead up to and follow upon the fall of Troy. The *Iliad* recounts the penultimate days of the war, focusing on the Greek warrior, Achilles, and his wrath first against Agamemnon, the leader of Greeks whom he feels dishonored him, and then against the Trojan hero Hector, who kills his beloved friend Patroclus. Although readers know that Troy will soon fall and Achilles himself die, neither event is told in the poem, which ends with Achilles's slaying of Hector. But knowledge of the coming future hangs over the poem, and the death of Hector makes the fall of Troy and indeed Achilles's own death inevitable. Achilles's awareness of his coming end drives him to achieve immortality through fame. In character and concerns, Achilles is very different from Odysseus, the hero of the *Odyssey*, who is primarily interested in getting home. Odysseus's adventures take place after the fall of Troy, making him an appropriate hero for a later, fallen, world. The main action of the *Iliad* is confined to the battlefields of Troy; that of the *Odyssey* includes the entire Mediterranean, and a wide range of peoples, monsters, and enchantresses, like Calypso and Circe, who try to keep Odysseus from reaching his goal. Where Achilles is defined by his anger and his strength, Odysseus is known for his intelligence and cunning, which enable him to survive not only ten years of fighting, but also ten years of traveling, and finally to return home to his family in Ithaca.

Homer's two poems seem very different, and critics still debate whether they were indeed written by the same person. But Milton would have assumed that they were, and they complement each other well, offering two types of heroes: the fighter and the thinker. A third model for heroism which combines elements from both of these appears in Virgil's response to Homer in the *Aeneid*. Virgil's poem celebrating the power of Rome is also a sequel to the story of Troy's fall, as Romans claimed that the Trojan Aeneas had survived and come to Italy where he founded the new nation. In Virgil's epic, Aeneas is like Odysseus in that he is trying to get home. But unlike Odysseus, he is going to a new home, and whereas Odysseus was desperate to leave Troy and get back to his own country, Aeneas resists leaving Troy, which is his homeland. He is a reluctant hero, who wants to stay and die in his country, and has to be pushed and prodded by various gods to get and keep on going. Where Achilles and Odysseus are both in their different ways very selfish, Aeneas is driven by duty. Such self-sacrifice can make him a rather unappealing hero to modern readers, but it made him extremely attractive for Christian readers of the Middle Ages and Renaissance who saw in his story a prototype of that of Christ. For this reason, and given the continued dominance of Latin over Greek in the curriculum, the *Aeneid* was the central model for epic in the Renaissance.

As these quick summaries suggest, the ancient epic is not homogeneous, and contains debates over the nature of the hero and the meaning of heroic action. By writing an epic, Milton entered into a long-standing discussion that had been active in the ancient world and that had become more complicated in a Christian context with the introduction of a new mode of heroism in Christ. Satan looks very much like a classical hero: like Achilles he is angry and feels dishonored; like Odysseus he is a cunning traveler; like Aeneas, he leads his people to a new homeland. A composite of many earlier heroes, he is accompanied by other conventional generic markers: for example, catalogs, especially that of the devils in Book 1.376–521, and epic similes, such as the one I noted earlier. The fact that he has a shield allies him specifically with Achilles and Aeneas, whose shields are described at length in *Iliad* 18 and *Aeneid* 8. For these reasons and others, the Romantics thought that he was the true hero of the poem, with whom the revolutionary Milton was subconsciously in sympathy. But such parallels may in fact undermine Satan's heroism when viewed from a Christian perspective from which such forms of military valor seem destructive. In showing Adam the future of the world, Michael criticizes traditional models of heroism, denouncing

> giants, men of high renown;
> For in those days might only shall be admired,
> And valor and heroic virtue called;
> To overcome in battle, and subdue
> Nations, and bring home spoils with infinite
> Manslaughter shall be held the highest pitch
> Of human glory, and for glory done,
> Of triumph, to be styled great conquerors,
> Patrons of mankind, gods, and sons of gods,
> Destroyers rightlier called and plagues of men. (11.688–97)

In the War in Heaven, the Son appears as an impressive classical hero in his war chariot, but the true conquest of evil will be achieved through his self-sacrifice (*Paradise Lost* 12.386–465). While the invocations to Homer's and Virgil's poems introduce as heroes Achilles, Odysseus, and Aeneas, that of *Paradise Lost* presents Christ as "one greater man" (1.4), who is greater because he will lead all mankind back to their heavenly home. In *Paradise Lost* 9.14, Milton insists therefore that his subject is "Not less but more heroic" than those of the classical epics.

In challenging epic ideas of the heroic, therefore, Milton develops a central concern of epic itself. But in so doing he draws on other classical forms. As I have already suggested, the classical tradition included many kinds of literary works, which the young Milton studied and imitated. The epic had been partly admired for its ability to subsume other genres. *Paradise Lost* embraces this capaciousness, enlisting all kinds of poetry into its encyclopedic vision. Its inclusion of debate and dialogue shows Milton's study of classical tragedies, drawn on also for *Samson Agonistes*, which themselves had reimagined the Homeric hero from other points of view in order to question the nature of epic heroism. As I noted earlier, the scenes in the Garden of Eden look back to the pastoral tradition, while Milton's insistence that Adam and Eve work recalls Virgil's *Georgics*, which praise the farmer's labor (although the work in Eden is much more pleasant and fun). In the classical world, moreover, literary genres were associated with contrasting values and ways of life. While the epic celebrated military glory, the pastoral and georgic praised the peaceful, simple life in nature. The love elegy in particular offered an alternative to the epic by focusing on love and individual happiness as the most important things in life. The epic, especially the influential *Aeneid*, emphasized conquest and national destiny, and so made personal desire a temptation that interferes with the hero's quest: Virgil's Aeneas must give up his wife, and later his lover Dido, in order to become the founder of Rome. From the perspective of love poetry, however, the epic glorifies violence, which elegiac writers renounced for more peaceful pleasures. While Virgil celebrated *arma*, arms, the elegiac poets asserted *amor*, encouraging readers to make love, not war.

As I noted earlier, the young Milton recognized the status and power of the epic but was also drawn to the elegy. He especially loved Ovid, whose elegies had been the model for an earlier generation of great English writers – Spenser, Marlowe, Shakespeare, and Donne – as well as for many of Milton's contemporaries, such as Thomas Randolph and Abraham Cowley. Moreover, in the Renaissance, Ovid's epic *Metamorphoses* was frequently read as an alternative to that of Virgil. Lacking a single hero, and indeed a single narrative, filled with fascinating stories of change and desire, the *Metamorphoses* inspired Renaissance artists of all kinds; according to Milton's daughter, it was one of his favorite works. In *Paradise Lost*, references to Ovid's poetry contribute to Milton's representation of an ideal and innocent world of pleasure and desire in which heroism is not confined to military battles and where the lonely epic hero waging war has been replaced by the Son, as well as by a loving couple who face complex spiritual tests as they learn and grow (the epic War in Heaven in Books 5–6 may seem rather crude and remote from Adam and Eve's experience of trial). If Milton's Eden includes Virgilian pastoral and georgic, it is also a place where the Ovidian love elegy comes to life. Ovid, the poet of change, helps Milton capture the dynamism of a freshly made and growing garden world. Milton alludes to Ovidian figures like Proserpina, Pomona, and Ceres, goddesses associated with fertility (4.269; 9.393–96). While the description of the creation of the world in Book 7 follows carefully the very brief account told in Genesis 1, the biblical narrative has been exuberantly elaborated with Ovidian details to capture a world in motion that is bursting with the energy of innumerable changing forms.

Ovid has another role, however, in the poem. Most famously, or infamously, the account of Eve's creation, which she tells in Book 4, is based on the tale in *Metamorphoses* 3 of Narcissus, the boy who fell in love with his own image reflected in water. Freud made this story famous in our time; by Milton's time, however, it had already been used often as an allegory showing the destructiveness of pride and self-love. It is therefore a disturbing model for Eve. Milton's scene follows Ovid's account closely. Like Narcissus, Eve is drawn to a beautiful reflection that she mistakes for a real person. However, Milton breaks from Ovid to take the story in a new direction to a happy ending. When Narcissus realizes his double error – that he is in love not only with himself but also with a mere image – he dies of frustrated desire. Eve knows that she also might have met such an end: "there I had fixt/ Mine eyes till now, and pined with vain desire" (4.465–67). Unlike the self-absorbed Narcissus, however, when Eve finds out that she is in love with an empty reflection of herself she turns from her own image to Adam, with whom she can enjoy the pleasure of sexual and social intercourse that Milton puts at the center of paradisal life.

The scene reminds us how Milton uses classical characters to imagine his own: Satan is defined through Achilles, Odysseus, and Aeneas. But the decision to present the character of Eve through this particular Ovidian story is provocative. What does it tell us about her? For some critics, it indicates Eve's inherent and fatal narcissism, which makes the fall inevitable from the start. Others have argued that it shows her development from a stage of innocent self-love into mature love of another. Unlike Narcissus, who chose to remain trapped in illusion and self-love, Eve chooses reality and union with Adam. But the story is not just all about Eve. In explicitly copying Ovid, Milton asks us to think not only about the relation between Eve and Narcissus, but also about his own relation to Ovid: to figure out the play of likeness and difference between text and model. The scene is a meditation on the act of imitation itself, showing how the poet follows but must break from the past. It is telling therefore that Satan clings to outmoded forms of epic heroism. For all of Satan's shape-shifting, he resists real change, and ironically, copies Ovid too closely: his final metamorphosis into a snake in Book 10 is based on a scene in *Metamorphoses* 4.563–603. His offspring Sin is herself a copy of Ovid's monster Scylla from *Metamorphoses* 13–14, a famous figure who had already been imitated by Spenser and other writers.

For Milton, the need to create change is a political as well as poetical concern. The failure of the English Revolution to bring about change gave Ovidian stories and themes even greater meaning for him. Other classical epics would have spoken directly to his own situation in the 1660s: the plot of the unfinished *Civil War*, written in the first century AD by the brilliant young Roman Lucan, which told of the civil wars in Rome that ultimately gave Caesar dictatorial power, has many parallels with Milton's own experience of revolution, war, and the restoration of monarchy. As well, throughout his life Milton drew on classical works when thinking about political liberty. But Ovidian figures especially offer Milton the possibility of imagining future change. The most immediate and perhaps devastating consequence of the fall for Adam and Eve is their alienation from each other, as their joyous lovemaking turns into bickering and recrimination. The epic War in Heaven becomes the domestic war of the sexes. However, the couple slowly begin to repair their relationship, and unite to seek forgiveness from God. Their humble appearance reminds Milton of a scene in Ovid:

> their port
> Not of mean suiters, nor important less
> Seemed their petition, than when th'ancient pair
> In fables old, less ancient yet then these,
> Deucalion and chaste Pyrrha to restore
> The race of mankind drowned, before the shrine
> Of Themis stood devout. (11.8–14)

In *Metamorphoses* 1, Ovid tells how the world was created by an unknown god. When the newly made human race became corrupt, Jove sent a flood to destroy it, rescuing only one pious couple, Deucalion and Pyrrha. When the flood ended, they threw to the ground stones that turned into a new race of people, and so recreated the world that had been destroyed. Ovid's story is appropriate for Milton, as it is reminiscent of the account of the biblical flood, which Michael will tell later in Book 11 (the aside in line 11, "less ancient yet than these," reminds us again that Ovid's version was supposedly a copy of the earlier biblical narrative). It suggests also that, like Deucalion and Pyrrha, Adam and Eve are about to start remaking the world; they begin an ongoing process of creative revision that the poet himself also continues.

Dr. Johnson claimed that Milton "saw Nature ... *through the spectacles of books*" (287), complaining further that he "had read much, and knew what books could teach; but had mingled little in the world, and was deficient in the knowledge which experience must confer" (293). This hardly seems a fair description of a man who traveled in Europe where he was enthusiastically received by some of the most interesting men of the time, who was deeply involved in politics, and who had a wide circle of friends, not to mention three wives and three daughters. Milton was very much engaged in the world, and *Paradise Lost* is as much a record of his personal experience and the failure of the Revolution as it is a digest of his reading and parade of the fruits of an expensive education. Johnson creates a false opposition between knowledge based on learning and that based on experience. It is true that Milton saw the world through books. But so do many lovers of literature, who believe that what we read shapes us and changes the way we see the world. For a writer like Milton the classical motif of the invocation of the muse is doubly significant as the classics were his muse. The past gave him a revolutionary perspective on his own experience, offering the forms through which he could create a modern myth that is both highly personal and also speaks to a universal experience of loss, alienation, and the longing for love and home.

Further Reading

Burrow, Colin, *Epic Romance: Homer to Milton* (Oxford, 1993).

Clark, Donald Lemen, *John Milton at St Paul's School: A Study of Ancient Rhetoric in English Renaissance Education* (New York, 1948).

Dryden, John, *The Works of John Dryden*, gen. ed. H. T. Swedenberg, Jr., 20 vols. (Berkeley, CA, 1956–89).

Green, Mandy, *Milton's Ovidian Eve* (Farnham, UK, 2009).

Johnson, Samuel, *Lives of the English Poets*, ed. Roger H. Lonsdale, 4 vols. (Oxford, 2006).

Kilgour, Maggie, *Milton and the Metamorphosis of Ovid* (Oxford, 2012).

Lewalski, Barbara, *"Paradise Lost" and the Rhetoric of Literary Forms* (Princeton, NJ, 1985).

Martindale, Charles, *John Milton and the Transformation of Ancient Epic* (Totowa, NJ, 1986).

Revard, Stella P., "Classical Literature and Learning," in *Milton in Context*, ed. Stephen B. Dobranski (Cambridge, UK, 2010), 270–80.

Virgil, *The Aeneid*, tr. Robert Fitzgerald (New York, 1990).

6

JEFFREY SHOULSON

Milton's Bible

Paradise Lost is inconceivable without the Bible. Although the poem takes its epic form and many of its literary conventions from classical precedents, nearly all of its central stories, themes, and characters are drawn from biblical materials. Yet to acknowledge the epic's primary debt to the Bible is also to require of its readers a sensitivity not only to the ways in which Milton draws on the Bible, but, even more importantly, to how his versions of biblical materials diverge – often radically – from those scriptural precedents. Readers must resist the temptation to explain the poem's idiosyncrasies and difficulties simply by attributing them to biblical pretexts. For although Milton is on record as having asserted the sufficiency of scriptural authority, that is, Scripture's capacity to convey its meanings in an unmediated fashion, without the aid of an interpreter, his approach to depicting those meanings, in both his prose and his poetry, is notorious for its tendentious selections, juxtapositions, and reorderings. Milton describes his method of argumentation in the prefatory remarks to his theological treatise, *De Doctrina Christiana*, as follows: "I ... have striven to cram my pages even to overflowing, with quotations drawn from all parts of the Bible" (*YP* 6:122). While *Paradise Lost* is a different kind of text than *De Doctrina*, the approach depicted in this account is not unrelated to the manner of the poet's appropriation of biblical materials in the epic. The poem is, indeed, crammed to overflowing with biblical references, but when we remember that the Bible is itself comprised of extraordinarily diverse kinds of writings, often in direct or implicit conflict with one another, we can begin to see that Milton's collocation of scriptural passages and stories is anything but innocent or unmediated.

So before we undertake an overview of the role the Bible plays in Milton's poem, it is important to review some key features of the Bible itself. First, as the etymology of the word suggests, the Bible, from the Greek plural form, *ta biblia* (the books), is an anthology, not a single, univocal text. It is comprised of a range of different kinds of writings – narratives, legal codes, ritual practices, songs and poems, philosophical meditations, prophecies, letters of instruction or rebuke, and more – and these texts were composed over a period of more than one thousand years. Modern scholarship has helped to recover the extensive redaction histories of many books in the Bible, that is, the synthetic process of editing together multiple oral and/ or written traditions into a single book like Genesis or Daniel or Matthew. But even for a reader in Milton's time, who would probably not have entertained the idea of multiple sources for a single book, the differences in tone, in focus, in general interest among various books would have been readily apparent. For example, the book of Leviticus, with its intensive focus on ritual sacrifices, presents a very different view of the value attributed to these practices than does, say, the book of Isaiah, with its attacks on Israel's hypocritical and empty observances of these same rituals. Deuteronomy's elaboration of the fraught covenantal relationship between God and Israel stands in stark contrast to the non-parochial, very nearly Stoic depiction of life's relentless cycles, unguided by any apparent providence, in the book of Ecclesiastes. And these differences within what is known to Christian readers as the Old Testament do not even begin to acknowledge the far more stark shifts between those texts that are part of the Hebrew canon and the texts known as the New Testament. The writers of the New Testament were certainly attentive readers of the Hebrew Scriptures (although probably mostly in the Greek translation, the Septuagint, that came to dominate the Jewish Hellenistic world); but these writers were, just as importantly, interpreters of those texts, seeking to redefine them in ways that spoke to their own first century CE concerns. The book of Psalms, for example, is an essential text for the gospel narratives. Yet Mark's use of the Psalms in shaping the passion story is a far cry from how these Psalms would have been read by earlier generations or even by other Jewish sects in the first century. Indeed, it may be useful to think of the way New Testament writers reframed, rewrote, or redefined the Hebrew Bible as, itself, a kind of precedent for Milton's own reframing, rewriting, and redefining of the Bible in *Paradise Lost*. We shall return to this point in greater detail later in the chapter.

Second, Milton's seventeenth-century encounter with the Bible would have been through a variety of different versions. A talented linguist, he certainly could and did read portions of the Bible in their original languages – mostly Hebrew, for the Old Testament, and Greek for the New Testament. Milton's linguistic skills were not unlimited, however, and he also came to rely on some of the newly available work of classical philologists and Christian Hebraists, citing scholars like Paul Fagius, Hugo Grotius, John Selden, and others throughout his prose tracts. Still, that Milton could consult a Hebrew

Bible or Greek New Testament in the original language meant that he would have had occasion to make use of his own understanding of nuance and connotation, even as he read the texts in the English translations circulating at the time. As for these translations, it is likely that Milton would have known and read from several of them. He probably knew the 1539 Great Bible, the 1568 Bishop's Bible, and even the 1610 Catholic Douay-Rheims version. We can be even more confident that he was familiar with the 1560 Geneva Bible, the single most important Protestant translation of the sixteenth century, noteworthy for its extensive headnotes and glosses, many of them having the explicit purpose of arguing for the Reformed theology its translators were developing during their years of exile in Geneva while the Catholic Mary sat on the throne of England. It has been largely accepted, however, that Milton's English Bible translation of choice was the King James, or Authorized, Version, first published in 1611, when he was just two or three years old. Distinctive for the absence of all but a few marginal glosses and annotations (and thus very different from the Geneva translation), this version came to dominate English culture, just as its translators and sponsor had hoped, within a half-century of its first appearance. In using the King James Version, Milton would have read a translation based on much of the best textual and philological scholarship of the time, produced through an extraordinarily thorough and systematic process of committee review. Not without its flaws, informed by certain High Church religious and cultural sensibilities, and certainly not cut from whole cloth – scholars have shown just how much of the translation is indebted to earlier English versions from Tyndale's and on – the King James Version nevertheless marked an important step forward in the history of biblical scholarship, allowing readers to encounter the text largely free from the heavy hand of polemical annotations and partisan translations.

Given the availability of new translations and the flourishing textual and philological scholarship of the period, the seventeenth century was a particularly rich time for reading and rereading the Bible, an activity English Protestants of nearly all varieties undertook regularly and seriously. Private Bible reading was, after all, one of the linchpins of the Reformation. Milton would have expected his "fit audience ... though few" to have a comprehensive familiarity with biblical texts, and his decision to use the biblical story "of Man's first disobedience" as the basis for an epic poem must be understood within this context. Far more than a biblical paraphrase, *Paradise Lost* marks a spectacularly audacious rewriting and rearranging of the Bible in which new – sometimes revolutionary – scholarship combines with reshapings of classical and medieval literary history in the crucible of Milton's own sprawling, imaginative intellect.

The Bible appears in different ways throughout the epic and it will be helpful to consider this variety along an (admittedly contrived) spectrum, ranging from nearly direct quotation to the recycling of a phrase or story from one part of the Bible in the service of an entirely different moment in Milton's poem.

Raphael's hexameral account of the creation in Book 7 is the site of many (though by no means all) of the poem's most explicit and direct quotations from the Bible. On the second day, for example, the archangel tells Adam, "Again, God said, 'Let there be firmament/ Amid the waters, and let it divide/ The waters from the waters'; and God made/ The firmament" (7.261–64). These lines closely match the King James Version's words in Genesis 1:6–7, "And God said, Let there be a firmament in the midst of the waters, and let it divide the waters from the waters. And God made the firmament.... " But Milton never allows the Bible only to speak for itself, quickly following this approximate quotation with his own poetic elaboration:

> expanse of liquid, pure,
> Transparent, elemental air, diffused
> In circuit to the uttermost convex
> Of this great round: partition firm and sure,
> The waters underneath from those above
> Dividing: for as earth, so he the world
> Built on circumfluous waters calm, in wide
> Crystalline ocean, and the loud misrule
> Of Chaos far removed, lest fierce extremes
> Contiguous might distemper the whole frame: (7.265–73)

An embellishment like this reveals a good deal about how Milton invests his biblical references with an array of further meanings, some of them linked to other moments in the poem, others reaching well beyond the margins of the page to engage with the poem's historical context. In their efforts at greater precision and detail, these lines resonate, for example, with the emergent language of scientific inquiry and description, characteristic of the newly formed Royal Society. The word "expanse" offers a further linguistic refinement to the meaning of the Hebrew *raqi'a*, which the King James Version has rendered as "firmament." These lines also recollect the poem's earlier depiction of Chaos in Book 2, as Satan traveled through the unformed space between Hell and the created universe. Perhaps most significantly, the portrayal of the firmament as a peacekeeping device, holding warring elements at bay lest they threaten to "distemper the whole frame," reminds the reader, on the one hand, of the War in Heaven in Book 6, for which this creation story serves as a direct counterpoint, and, on the other hand, of traumatized and strife-torn England in the wake of the more than ten years of civil wars that had drawn to a close with the Restoration. By embedding direct quotations from the Bible within an elaborated framework that includes both tacit and explicit connections to the most troubling matters of Milton's time, matters that may be said to have contributed to the theodical pressures of the whole poem, Milton projects onto these biblical allusions a sense of urgency and contemporaneity that they might not otherwise have for the reader. That is, if Milton's stated project, "to justify the ways of God to men," is understood as informing all aspects of the epic poem, we can begin to see how such a theodicy works its way even into a seemingly unrelated detail about the nature of the firmament dividing heavenly and earthly waters and how a biblical reference might be exploited in such a context.

It may not be surprising to find Milton relying most directly on the exact words in the Bible for his own rendition of divine creation, given the poetic hubris entailed in creating something new to describe *the* paradigmatic instance of creation. It *is* surprising, however, to find Milton diverging from his biblical pretexts when he undertakes an equally daunting feature of the poem, its representation of God. In his *DDC* Milton went to great lengths to argue for the exclusive reliance on God's self-representation in the Bible for any human apprehensions of divinity: "It is safest for us to form an image of God in our minds which corresponds to his representation and description of himself in the sacred writings" (*YP* 6:133). In *Paradise Lost*, most notably in Book 3, Milton seems directly to violate his own rule, imagining an exchange between the Father and the Son with virtually no biblical precedent. Critics like to link the dialogue between an irate Father demanding justice and a tranquil Son pleading for mercy to the Bible by means of a diffuse (and misleading) characterization of the difference between the vengeful God of the Old Testament and the compassionate God of the New Testament. The Celestial Dialogue itself has no scriptural paradigm, but the details of the exchange are fraught with fragmentary biblical allusions, and such allusions do not always conform to the simple dichotomy of Old Testament Father and New Testament Son. It is true that generations of readers have accepted such oversimplifications, but Milton's dialectical combination of Old and New Testament representation of divinity is far more subtle and complex.

Beyond explicit citation, the poem also abounds with examples of narrative elements that directly point to biblical precedents for their authority but move well beyond quotation or even paraphrase. Book 9's narration of the Fall, for example, depends on the characteristically elliptical account of this first disobedience in Genesis 3:1–7. The outline of the story is there for Milton to develop and the poet nowhere directly contradicts the Bible's story.

Of course, he does not leave it as such, either, expanding and dilating the story over a stretch of more than one thousand lines. Setting aside the differences and additions in language and dialogue, we may briefly note some of the details of this part of the story that *are not* to be found in the biblical version: the exchange between Adam and Eve that leads to their working apart; Satan's intrusion into, and use of, the unknowing serpent for the purposes of his temptation; the extensive interchange between Satan and Eve leading to her decision to eat from the fruit; Eve's praise of the tree followed by her long deliberation about whether to share the fruit with Adam; Eve's return to Adam, his shock at her news, his interior meditation on whether to follow Eve's lead, and his explanation to Eve for why he chooses to eat with her; the sexual encounter between Adam and Eve immediately following their Fall; Adam's recriminatory accusations. Each of these facets of the poem's version of the Fall expands on, interrogates, and proposes a variety of interpretive responses to the Bible's terse account. These poetic expansions open up matters of theology, of government, of gender and sexuality, of ontology, of epistemology, and more. What makes this extraordinary enlargement of the Bible's seven verses possible is one of the most distinctive features of biblical writing, its elliptical quality. In his seminal essay on the differences between biblical and classical narrative, "Odysseus' Scar," Erich Auerbach describes the characteristic reticence of biblical writing as being "fraught with background" (1953, 12). That is, the Bible's withholding of details, its absence of interiority, its laconic, paratactic sequencing of events, invites its readers to infer and invent many of the features of storytelling – subjective impressions, personal motivations, causal relations between events, and so forth – one finds more directly provided in other kinds of narratives. If we pursue Auerbach's distinction in his essay between Homer and the Bible, Milton's reinvention of the narrative of the Fall may be understood as the product of his imposition of a classical form that demands excursus and dilation – the epic poem – onto a biblical story originally rendered in such evocative and opaque fashion. The generic hybridity of a biblical epic demands, as it were, the kinds of interpretive and imaginative expansions found in Book 9. The nature of these expansions is not determined or delimited by this convergence of two different kinds of "representation of reality," to use Auerbach's phrase, but there certainly are instances of the poem's supplementation of the biblical account that draw on classical precedent for both their form and content, Book 6's War in Heaven being one of the most obvious (and notoriously problematic) examples.

The conjunction of the biblical and the classical offers one kind of explanation for Milton's supplementation of the Bible's story. It may also be productive to regard Milton's interpretive expansion of the biblical narrative as an early modern Christian version of rabbinic midrash, a Jewish mode of biblical exegesis that emerged at almost the same time as the writings in the New Testament and Church Fathers and continued to be developed in a variety of contexts for a number of centuries. Midrash takes many forms and serves many functions, but one of its primary methods is to locate narrative gaps, ambiguities, and openings in biblical texts that then become occasions for imaginative expansions and rewritings. The rabbis used these expansions to develop arguments about normative behavior ("*halakhic midrash*"); but they also used them to formulate (sometimes tacit, sometimes explicit) polemics against their religious or political rivals (competing Jewish sects, the Roman or Sassanid empires), to meditate on God's role in history or lodge complaints against God's apparent indifference or abandonment, to consider the complicated interactions between Jewish and non-Jewish culture, and to find guidance in matters of ethics and morality not directly addressed in Scripture. Such a range of interpretive applications matches, to a striking degree, the different ways in which Milton's expansions of biblical materials function in *Paradise Lost*. Indeed, the conspicuous resemblances between midrash and Milton's poem have given rise to numerous scholarly efforts to discover direct or indirect influences of rabbinic writing on the epic.

There are plenty of supplementary details in Milton's poem not found in the Bible that have counterparts in *midrash aggadah*, the narrative portions of these rabbinic writings. In Book 4, for example, Satan's malignant response to the sight of the first couple's embrace includes the (extra-biblical) suggestion of sexual jealousy:

> Sight hateful, sight tormenting! Thus these two
> Imparadised in on another's arms
> The happier Eden, shall enjoy their fill
> Of bliss on bliss, while I to Hell am thrust,
> Where neither joy nor love, but fierce desire,
> Among our other torments not the least,
> Still unfulfilled with pain of longing pines; (4.505–11)

As has been noted by several critics, the idea of Satanic envy of Adam and Eve expressed specifically in terms of unfulfilled erotic desire appears to have originated in Jewish sources, including *Genesis Rabbah*, *Avot de-Rabbi Nathan*, and others. The influence of texts like these remains an intriguing possibility. Certainly with the proliferation of works by Christian Hebraists in the sixteenth and seventeenth centuries, Milton would have been able to gain access to quite a lot of rabbinic materials even without any particular expertise in the original texts. The parallels between midrashic approaches and Milton's methods in *Paradise Lost*, however, are just as important for what they have to say about the kinds of readings the Bible, in all its ambiguity, obliqueness, and not-infrequent contradictions, elicits – especially from readers who turn to the Scriptures for answers to questions about their own historical moments and crises.

Comparisons between Milton and rabbinic writers are quite illuminating, but there can be little doubt that far more influential to Milton's way of reading and retelling the Bible are the range of interpretive approaches developed as a function of the New Testament's reimagining of the Hebrew Bible. Perhaps the most important of these exegetical strategies is the mode known as typology, a comprehensive interpretive scheme concerning the relationship between the Hebrew Bible and the New Testament. In general terms, the Christian transformation of the Hebrew Scriptures into the Old Testament via typology is built upon the presumption that events in the Old Testament prefigure aspects of the New Testament, especially those pertaining directly to Christ's life, death, and resurrection. Each detail in the Old Testament comes to be understood as a type, anticipating its completion or fulfillment in the antitype of Christ. This hermeneutical strategy presumes a full theory of history in which events are no longer understood to have meanings in and of themselves, but rather only take on their full significance in relation to subsequent events – and most radically, in light of the one and only *real* event, the Crucifixion and Resurrection of Christ. So, for example, the stories in Genesis of Noah or Abraham, presented as lone, righteous men during times of corruption, all come to be understood as adumbrations, "shadowy types," of the one truth, the one truly just man, Jesus Christ.

Milton expands on these typological suppositions throughout his poem. Most obviously, he calls upon this historical framework for the condensed (future) history lesson Michael gives to Adam in Books 11 and 12, depicting successive types of the "one just Man" (11.818). The reiterative, cumulative force of the examples Michael provides to Adam is modeled on the Letter to the Hebrews (the most overtly typological book in the entire New Testament), particularly chapter 11's roster of biblical figures who are said to have exhibited the power of faith, famously defined at the beginning of that chapter as "the substance of things hoped for, the evidence of things not seen" (Hebrews 11:1). A tension emerges, however, in the role biblical precedent plays in the narrative dilation of these final two books of the epic. On the one hand, although Milton has invented the entire episode of Michael's visitation to Adam and their ascent up the "hill/ Of Paradise the highest, from whose top/ The hemisphere of earth in clearest ken/ Stretched out to the amplest reach of prospect lay" (11.377–80), this supplementary episode is not cut entirely from whole cloth. Milton draws on the final chapter in the book of Deuteronomy for his scriptural precedent (though it is temporally subsequent), in which Moses climbs to the top of Pisgah, from which God shows the Israelite leader "all the land of Gilead, unto Dan, and all Naphtali, and the land of Ephraim, and Manasseh, and all the land of Judah, unto the utmost sea, and the south, and the plain of the valley of Jericho, the city of palm trees, unto Zoar" (Deuteronomy 34:1–3). And each of the vignettes Michael reveals to Adam in Book 11 or narrates to him in Book 12 derives from biblical episodes in Genesis, Exodus, Numbers, Joshua, Judges, 1 and 2 Samuel, and the Gospels. So in these respects, Milton uses the Bible to supplement and expand a biblical narrative that is ostensibly occasioned by the first three chapters of Genesis. On the other hand, insofar as Milton follows the example of Hebrews, he also flattens out and condenses so much that makes each of these biblical stories different, interesting, and far from straightforward. C. S. Lewis famously described the last two books of *Paradise Lost* as an "untransmuted lump of futurity" (Lewis 125). It might be more accurate, however, to say that by deploying the typological mode so overtly in these books, Milton has offered his reader a "lump of futurity" defined precisely by how it has been transmuted through a very particular kind of reading practice that emerges with the rise of Christianity.

There is more to be seen, however, in the ways typology informs the biblical features of Milton's poem. Within the typological view of history, time is no longer understood exclusively in a linear fashion, with events organized by sequence and succession. The typological reader discovers connections between events at disparate moments in history and these convergences displace temporal sequence as the most useful means for understanding historical relations. Biblical and historical episodes are layered over each other, collapsing the time that seems to separate them, sometimes even reversing that temporality. And God's role comes to be understood as that of an author, inscribing his providential authority on history by means of the events whose significances reveal themselves in relation to one another. This authorial role attributed to God functions as a model for Milton, too, as he deploys the typological reorganization of temporality to great effect in the recycling of biblical precedents for many of his expansions on the story of the Fall. So in the example I have already cited of Moses' Pisgah vision serving as a precedent for Adam's mountain history lesson we have an instance of inversion: the Bible's account of Moses was written long before Milton's poem and yet the episode in his poem for which it serves as precedent itself precedes the life of Moses.

Other examples of this kind of inverted historical continuity or relation abound. Book 3's dialogue between the Father and the Son over the future of humanity in the aftermath of the yet-to-occur Fall may not have an explicit biblical precedent, but the Son's defense of humanity echoes at least three episodes in the Hebrew Bible: Genesis 18 describes Abraham's efforts to dissuade God from destroying Sodom and Gomorrah; Exodus 32 depicts Moses' pleas with God not to destroy the children of Israel after their sin of worshipping the golden calf; and Numbers 14:13–17 describes Moses pleading with God, yet once more, after God has expressed his intention to destroy completely the Israelites and to begin again with a nation descended from Moses. Standard Christian typology would read these three biblical exempla from the Old Testament as types, foreshadowing the intercessionary and soteriological role Christ plays in the Gospel narratives. The Son's words in the Celestial Dialogue recollect all of these Old Testament passages, directly echoing the first version in Genesis 18:25, "That be far from thee to do after this manner, to slay the righteous with the wicked, that be far from thee," when Milton has the Son observe to the Father, "That be from thee far,/ That far be from thee" (3.153–54). The poem's Celestial Dialogue posits an original for these biblical moments, not in the New Testament accounts of Jesus, but rather in a prebiblical encounter between the unincarnated Son and the Father. It seems especially fitting, too, that this temporal disorientation helps to shape an exchange that has introduced the reader to the epistemological disjunction between the human experience of time as some form of sequence and divine perception, which stands outside of time and allows God to behold "past, present, future" in a singular "prospect high" (3.77–78). Human understanding may be incapable of fully grasping divine trans-temporality, but the poem's recursive overlays and typological convergences of discreet biblical exempla challenge the reader to interrogate any presuppositions she or he might have about the inevitability of linear, chronological sequence.

Another significant set of additions to the sparse narrative of creation and disobedience in Genesis 1–3 includes the poem's extended account of the begetting of the Son, Satan's rejection of and rebellion against that elevation, the ensuing War in Heaven, the defeat of the rebel angels, and their subsequent decision to seek revenge through the corruption of humanity. In listing these key features of Milton's epic in this sequence, I have, of course, defied the order in which they appear in *Paradise Lost* for the purposes of imposing on them some sense of chronology, a sense that, as we have just seen, ought to be examined carefully and critically for what kinds of meanings it does and does not permit the reader to perceive. The War in Heaven is a noteworthy instance of biblical supplementation that arises from the convergence of the generic demands of a classical epic and the temporal realignments made possible by Christian teleology, that is, the sense or meaning imparted to the whole from its ending. In providing the poem with the fireworks of military engagement and battlefield heroism, Milton appears to be conforming to the classical precedents of epic poems like the *Iliad* or the *Aeneid*. Yet the poet also insists that such feats of martial prowess ought not be regarded as evidence of true heroism. The invocation to Book 9 explains that the ensuing account of the humanity's disobedience and punishment is "Not less but more heroic than the wrath/ Of stern Achilles on his foe pursued/ Thrice fugitive about Troy wall; or rage/ Of Turnus for Lavinia disespoused" (9.14–17). Taken in this light, then, the incorporation of the epic battles into a biblical story would appear to elevate the Bible at the expense of classical literature. Yet the pagan classics are not the only precedent for the War in Heaven: in addition to drawing heavily on Ezekiel's vision of the divine chariot for his depiction of the "chariot of paternal deity" (Ezekiel 1–3:14; *PL* 6.750), Milton also depends on many of the images of cosmic conflict found in the book of Revelation, which speaks directly of its own war in heaven between Michael and his angels and the great dragon, "that old serpent, called the Devil, and Satan" (Revelation 12:7–9). The culminating position of Revelation within the biblical canon, teleologically imposing its vision backwards on all that has preceded it, serves also to authorize Milton's insertion of the War in Heaven into what is both a primordial moment in prehistory (precisely at the opposite end of time from the eschatological visions of Revelation) and a central position in the poem (it comes midway through the text). So what the diminishment of classical models takes away with one hand, the elevation of biblical authority bestows with the other.

Paradise Lost presents itself as something new, something "unattempted yet in prose or rhyme" (1.16). In its very echoes of a similar claim in Ariosto's *Orlando Furioso* (1.2), however, the line signals to its readers that such an audacious claim is not identical with Satan's bold denial of creatureliness, of having been created by a greater power, in his confrontation with Abdiel: "who saw/ When this creation was? Remember'st thou/ Thy making, while the Maker gave thee being?/ We know no time when we were not as now;/ Know none before us, self-begot, self-raised/ By our own quick'ning power" (5.856–61). Satan refuses his origins and his Original in order to deny his indebtedness and obedience to God. Milton always and everywhere acknowledges his poem's origins in biblical authority. His rebellion, then, is potentially far more subversive than that of the infernal serpent. Satan denies divine authority. Milton appropriates the divine authority of the biblical texts in the service of his own imagination, and his own poetical, political, and theological agenda. A fit reader will be sensitive to the difference between the Bible speaking for itself and a poem that invites careful, thoughtful engagement with its interrogation of scriptural authority.

Further Reading

Auerbach, Erich, "Odysseus' Scar," in *Mimesis: The Representation of Reality in Western Literature*, tr. William R. Trask (Princeton, NJ, 1953), 3–23.

Auerbach, Erich, "Figura," in *Scenes from the Drama of European History*, tr. Ralph Manheim (Minneapolis, MN, 1994), 11–78.

Broadbent, John, "The Poet's Bible," in *John Milton: Introductions*, ed. John Broadbent (Cambridge, UK, 1973), 145–61.

Conklin, George Newton, *Biblical Criticism and Heresy in Milton* (New York, 1972).

Corcoran, Mary Irma, *Milton's Paradise with Reference to the Hexameral Background* (Washington, DC, 1945).

Dobbins, Austin, *Milton and the Book of Revelation: The Heavenly Cycle* (University, AL, 1975).

Evans, J. Martin, *"Paradise Lost" and the Genesis Tradition* (Oxford, 1968).

Fisch, Harold, *Jerusalem and Albion: The Hebraic Factor in Seventeenth-Century Literature* (New York, 1964).

The Biblical Presence in Shakespeare, Milton, and Blake (Oxford, 1999).

Fletcher, Harris F., *The Use of the Bible in Milton's Prose* (New York, 1929).

Fresch, Cheryl H. "'As the Rabbines Expound': Milton, Genesis, and the Rabbis," *MS* 15 (1981), 59–80.

Frye, Northrop, *The Great Code: The Bible and Literature* (New York, 1982).

Gallagher, Philip J., *Milton, the Bible, and Misogyny* (Columbia, MO, 1990).

Haskin, Dayton, *Milton's Burden of Interpretation* (Philadelphia, 1994).

Haublein, Ernst, "Milton's Paraphrase of Genesis: A Stylistic Reading of *Paradise Lost*, Book VII," *MS* 7 (1975), 101–25

Kelly, Maurice, *This Great Argument: A Study of Milton's "De Doctrina Christiana" as a Gloss upon "Paradise Lost"* (Gloucester, MA, 1962).

Kurth, Burton O, *Milton and Christian Heroism: Biblical Epic Themes and Forms in Seventeenth Century England* (Berkeley, CA, 1959).

Lewis, C. S., *A Preface to "Paradise Lost"* (London, 1943).

Lim, Walter S. H., "Adam, Eve, and Biblical Analogy in *Paradise Lost*," *SEL* 30 (1990), 115–31.

MacCallum, H. R., "Milton and Figurative Interpretation of the Bible," *University of Toronto Quarterly* 31 (1962), 397–415.

"Milton and Sacred History: Books XI and XII of *Paradise Lost*," *Essays in English Literature Presented to A. S. P. Woodhouse* (Toronto, 1964), 149–68.

Mattern, Frank, *Milton and Christian Hebraism: Rabbinic Exegesis in "Paradise Lost"* (Heidelberg, 2009).

Nicholson, Marjorie Hope, "Milton and the Bible," in *The Bible and its Literary Associations*, ed. Margaret B. Crook (New York, 1937), 35–72.

O'Keefe, Timothy J., *Milton and the Pauline Tradition: A Study of Theme and Symbolism* (Washington, DC, 1982).

Park, Youngwon, *Milton and Isaiah: A Journey through the Drama of Salvation in "Paradise Lost"* (New York, 2000).

Patrides, C. A, *Milton and the Christian Tradition* (Oxford, 1966).

Radzinowicz, Mary Ann, *Milton's Epics and the Book of Psalms* (Princeton, NJ, 1989).

Reichart, John, *Milton's Wisdom: Nature and Scripture in "Paradise Lost"* (Ann Arbor, MI, 1992).

Rosenblatt, Jason P., *Torah and Law in "Paradise Lost"* (Princeton, NJ, 1994).

Ryken, Leland and James H. Sims, eds., *Milton and the Scriptural Tradition: The Bible into Poetry* (Columbia, MO, 1984).

Schwartz, Regina, *Remembering and Repeating: Biblical Creation in "Paradise Lost"* (Cambridge, UK, 1988).

Shawcross, John T., "*Paradise Lost* and the Theme of Exodus," *MS* 2 (1970), 3–26.

Shoulson, Jeffrey S., *Milton and the Rabbis: Hebraism, Hellenism, and Christianity* (New York, 2001).

Sims, James H., *The Bible in Milton's Epics* (Gainesville, FL, 1962).

Stallard, Matthew, ed., *"Paradise Lost": A Biblically Annotated Edition* (Macon, GA, 2011).

Steadman, John M., *Milton's Biblical and Classical Imagery* (Pittsburgh, 1984).

Werman, Golda, *Milton and Midrash* (Washington, DC, 1995).

7

JOHN CREASER

The Line in *Paradise Lost*

Here, in modernized spelling, is what might appear to be a striking seventeenth-century account of Satan, prince of devils, newly exiled to Hell:

> … aspiring to set himself in glory above his peers, he trusted to have equaled the Most High, if he opposed; and with ambitious aim against the throne and monarchy of God raised impious war in Heav'n and battle proud with vain attempt. Him the Almighty Power hurled headlong flaming from th' ethereal sky with hideous ruin and combustion down to bottomless perdition, there to dwell in adamantine chains and penal fire, who durst defy th' Omnipotent to arms.

And here, with further lines added, is the passage as it actually appears early in *Paradise Lost*:

           … aspiring
To set himself in glory above his peers,
He trusted to have equaled the Most High,   40
If he opposed; and with ambitious aim
Against the throne and monarchy of God
Raised impious war in Heav'n and battle proud
With vain attempt. Him the Almighty Power
Hurled headlong flaming from th' ethereal sky   45
With hideous ruin and combustion down
To bottomless perdition, there to dwell
In adamantine chains and penal fire,
Who durst defy th' Omnipotent to arms.
Nine times the space that measures day and night   50
To mortal men, he with his horrid crew
Lay vanquished, rolling in the fiery gulf
Confounded though immortal: but his doom
Reserved him to more wrath; for now the thought
Both of lost happiness and lasting pain   55
Torments him; round he throws his baleful eyes

That witnessed huge affliction and dismay
Mixed with obdurate pride and steadfast hate:
At once as far as angels ken he views
The dismal situation waste and wild,   60
A dungeon horrible, on all sides round
As one great furnace flamed, yet from those flames
No light, but rather darkness visible
Served only to discover sights of woe,
Regions of sorrow, doleful shades, where peace   65
And rest can never dwell, hope never comes
That comes to all; but torture without end
Still urges, and a fiery deluge, fed
With ever-burning sulphur unconsumed: (1.38–69)

Lineation apart, the passages are identical, yet the experience of reading is transformed. Why does this formal and non-semantic distinction matter so much, even where there is no rhyme to mark the turning of the lines? Why is lineation the fundamental distinction between verse and prose, and how central is this to *Paradise Lost*?

Lineation has major repercussions, both general and specific, and the first general consequence is that, before a poem is read, its look on the page establishes a heightened sense of artifice and invites a special attention – or, from a reciter, mode of utterance, something unhurried, pointed, and alive to rhythm. With a capital letter beginning each line and white space at the line-end, it draws attention to the verbal medium and declares: this is not everyday discourse but a particular kind of symbolic representation.

Secondly, there is the paradoxical heightening and distancing of emotion characteristic of art. The expressive forms of verse made possible by lineation (and to be examined later in this chapter) intensify emotion. Yet in the 1802 Preface to *Lyrical Ballads* Wordsworth argues that, even though meter imparts passion to words, more painful subjects can be endured in verse than in prose. Powerful language, he says, threatens "an undue proportion of pain," but the tendency of meter is "to divest language in a certain degree of its reality, and thus to throw a sort of half consciousness of unsubstantial existence over the whole composition" (Wordsworth 264–5). The form of verse distances while the expressiveness of verse involves. So, in the artifice of the theater, the fall of greatness concentrated in a tragedy elevates emotion even while it brings an awareness of fiction, distancing us into contemplation.

Thirdly, lineation's isolation of brief utterances into distinct lines – which may or may not be grammatical units – heightens consciousness of the rhythms of language. In the language of poetry, even of free verse, there is a higher regularity, order, and patterning than in almost all prose. Everyday prosaic reading is usually too hurried to pay much attention to rhythm, but lineation organizes the pulsations of language into patterns, and invites steady reading aloud – or as if aloud, with the mind alert to sound and articulation. This is not simply listening out for attractive sounds; indeed, the melody of consonants and vowels is slight beside the melody and harmony of music. Still, reading verse aloud, conscious of lineation, opens up the prevailing rhythm and its variations, resonating with something deep in human nature. A newborn baby makes rhythmic movements of the hands in time to the rhythms of meaningful speech addressed to it. Later, a baby's babblings fall into rhythmical sequences. If we hear a stream of undifferentiated sound – from the ticking of a clock to a burst of machine-gun fire, for example – we impose a rhythm on it, some alternation of strong and weak pulses: TICK-tock, RAT-a-TAT. Artistic creation is the pinnacle of this automatic turning of monotony into rhythm, of mere sequence into pattern. Out of the randomness and arbitrary sequences of living, we create significance and order, establishing some permanence and meaning amid irresistible mutability. In the arts, what Wallace Stevens terms the "blessed rage for order" is unequivocally benign, without the personal constraints and frustrations of social norms. The artistic forms that most acknowledge order, such as Milton's strictly disciplined verse, also enjoy the readiest freedom, for the tighter the form, the more telling is any variation, the more resilient the departure and return. In highlighting the rhythms of language, poetry such as Milton's calls upon deep responses: our joy in pattern, order, and yet freedom.

The first of the more specific consequences of lineation is that, as T. S. Eliot wrote, "a different metre is a different mode of thought" (1965, 129). Particular meters are suited to particular kinds of experience: the limerick to one kind, the Italian sonnet to another, the English sonnet to a third. A mode of versification is not a neutral implement or medium, but a range of potentials, with given aptitudes and correspondent limitations. As I shall show, the almost unprecedented choice of narrative blank verse for the epic *Paradise Lost* is profoundly apt for the poem's vision.

Secondly, a line of verse brings not only a sense of purposeful utterance but also certain rhythmical expectations, self-evidently so in metrical verse. From these expectations comes a norm that makes possible an incessant and expressive play of fulfillment and deviation, a continual interchange of repetition and surprise. Deviation heightens tension; return to the regular brings relaxation and familiarity. Few poets match Milton for such expressive energy within the line.

Thirdly, there is the line-turn itself. In rhymed verse, the rhymes fall at the end of the line because this is its strongest point. A sensitive reader always registers the line-turn, and normally dwells on it by a slight emphasis or delay. This does not have to be marked enough to be perceptible on a recording – although it usually is – but it certainly has to be felt by the reader or listener. The line-break is a real presence in English verse, even when the syntax runs over the line, as so often in *Paradise Lost*, and as I shall demonstrate, it can even stand in as a virtual syllable. It creates a special mode of punctuation, a point of emphasis, which may or may not coincide with a pause in grammar and meaning. A good poet may sometimes seem to treat the line-turn casually, but will never treat it carelessly.

To appreciate how Milton makes the most of these three specific consequences, a theory of prosody – a way of registering and analyzing verse rhythm – is needed, and the most resourceful and responsive available is that of Derek Attridge, which is based not on classical precedent but on the nature of English speech. As he shows, the major prosodies in English verse descend from two norms of the living language, the first of which is isochrony or the equal timing of stress. Utter the sequences "salt/mustard/vinegar" or "Huck Finn/Huckle Fickle/Huckleberry Finnegan" and the stressed syllables – the first syllable in every word – naturally fall at equal intervals. This leads to the *accentual verse* of many popular forms, such as ballads, nursery rhymes, and playground chants, where the structural principle is simply the number of beats or heavily emphasized syllables in the line, invariably four, irrespective of the shifting total of unstressed or lightly stressed syllables. Sophisticated poets have often exploited this: an extreme instance is T. S. Eliot in *Sweeney Agonistes*, moving immediately from the four beats and up to fifteen syllables per line of "In a NICE little, WHITE little, SOFT little, TEN-der little | JUIC-y little, RIGHT little, MISS-ionary STEW" to the four beats in four emphatic syllables of "YOU SEE THIS EGG" (here and throughout this chapter, stressed syllables are marked by roman capitals) (1963, 130).

Secondly, there is the duple movement of English, the tendency to alternate stressed and unstressed syllables, as is evident in any polysyllable and audible in careful utterance. The dominant prosody in Milton and throughout literary rather than popular verse since the sixteenth century – *accentual-syllabic verse* – combines isochrony with this duple tendency. Now not only the beats but the less than fully stressed syllables, the offbeats, have a prosodic function, and in regular verse such as *Paradise Lost* the unstressed syllable is as structural as the stressed. The prevailing movement is duple, and the prevailing line, eluding the elementary symmetries of four-beat accentual verse, is the iambic pentameter, a fivefold alternation of syllables rising from the less to the more stressed, as in "at ONCE as FAR as ANG-els KEN he VIEWS" (1.59). In verse as resourceful as Milton's, however, relatively few lines are straightforward realizations of this pattern; individual lines show an incalculable variety of movement. Even so, Attridge is able to demonstrate that all this requires only three deviations from duple alternation, all still in keeping with English speech. When three stressed syllables occur together, we tend in careful speech to give the second the time of a stress but slightly less emphasis than the others, hence "POPE *JOHN* PAUL" or "THREE *BLIND* MICE" (with italics indicating syllables that, while stressed, would only be given full emphasis to distinguish Pope John Paul from, say, "Pope Mark Paul" or the three blind mice from, say, three white mice). In verse, this becomes the *demotion* of the second of three consecutive stresses, as in: "as ONE *GREAT* FURN-ace flamed, yet from those flames" (1.63). Here "one" and the first syllable of "furnace" are the first two structural beats of the line (followed by "flamed," "from," and "flames"), while "great," necessarily stressed not only because of its meaning but as a monosyllabic adjective (Attridge 1995, 26–7), is given the time but not the full weight of the adjacent beats. A demoted syllable like this is a stressed offbeat and makes a line slower and more weighty.

The obverse of this, in careful speech, is that when three nonstressed syllables occur together, we tend to give slightly more weight or time to the second. Compare "NOW is the HOUR" and "NOW is ON the HOUR" (with the secondary emphasis indicated by small capitals). In accentual-syllabic verse, this becomes the *promotion* of the second of three adjacent nonstresses by a lengthening or pause, as here in the last syllable of "monarchy:" "a-GAINST the THRONE and MON-arch-Y of GOD" (1.42). A promotion is a syllable, often a pronoun or preposition, naturally given only a subsidiary emphasis that, through its placing, is allotted the time – or at least is felt as having been allotted the time – of a metrical beat. Without due presence being allowed a promoted syllable, many iambic pentameters would deviate into the alien prosody of four-beat accentual verse: "a-GAINST the THRONE and MON-archy of GOD" or the patter of some other invasive rhythm: "served ON-ly to dis-COV-er sights of WOE" (64); "to BOT-tomless per-DI-tion, there to DWELL" (47). Sensitive readers will often mark a promotion less by emphatic utterance and more by a slight pause to create the time of a beat, reproducing Milton's subtle effects in lines such as Eve's yielding to love-play with pride "And SWEET re-LUC-tant AM-or-OUS de-LAY" (4.311). Milton usually allocates "amorous" two metrical syllables (as in effect "AM'rous"), but the full three syllables required by the meter here draw out the bliss of loving foreplay, with adjectives expanding from one beat and one syllable ("sweet") to one beat in three syllables ("reluctant") to two beats in three syllables. Compare the four-beat accentual rush of omitting that promotion: "and SWEET re-LUC-tant AM-rous de-LAY."

The third deviation is *pairing*, where there are only two adjacent stresses, both of them beats, and therefore no demotion. Given that two stresses disrupt the duple flow and throw the line off-kilter, the imbalance is kept as brief as possible by immediately preceding or following the pair by a matching pair of offbeats, as in "reserved him to MORE WRATH; for now the thought" (1.54) or "with vain at-TEMPT. HIM the al-mighty power" (44) (the four syllables of a pairing, whether stress-final or stress-initial, are indicated by underlining). These four-syllable groupings are incompatible with more traditional prosody and have sometimes been denied or obscured under meaningless terms such as "double iamb," but Milton often uses them to avoid an iambic jog-trot and to create sudden and potent emphasis, as on "more" and "him" in the preceding lines.

A crucial refinement is that in precise circumstances the line-turn itself may stand in for a single syllable, whether stressed or unstressed, so that two rather than three syllables create a demotion or promotion, and a single stress is in effect a pairing. In iambic verse, promotion occurs at the end of the line, as in: "no LIGHT, but RATH-er DARK-ness VIS-i-BLE [x]" (63) with the "[x]" of the line-turn representing the third unstressed syllable. Conversely, demotion may occur at the start of a line, as in: "Him the almighty power | [/] *HURLED* HEAD-long FLAM-ing FROM th' e-THER-eal SKIE" (44–45), with [/] indicating the virtual stress at the line-turn and italic capitals the demotion. The paradoxical pairing of a single syllable occurs as the common reversal of stress at the beginning of a line: "[/] REG-ions of sor-row, doleful shades, where peace" (65). It might initially be thought that the line-turn [/] or [x] is merely the stressed syllable ending the preceding line or the nonstress opening the following line. But the effect is just the same when the preceding line ends with a feminine or unstressed syllable, or the following line begins with a reversed stress; "hurled" is demoted in the example just given even if the preceding word "power" is pronounced as a disyllable. Compare Adam in despair: "the BOD-y PROP-er-LY hath NEITH-er. | ALL of me THEN shall DIE" (10.791–92) where "all" is heavily emphatic although preceded by the feminine ending of "neither." The felt pause of the line-turn creates an absolute metrical barrier between adjacent lines, however interwoven they are in meaning, and however much someone reading aloud chooses to run them together. The real presence of the pause is the fundamental reason why the words cited at the head of this chapter read so differently as prose and as verse. Blank verse is not, as Samuel Johnson complained in his *Life* of Milton, "verse only to the eye."

Prosodic analysis of *Paradise Lost* reveals how Milton is disciplined to the point of austerity. In the later Shakespeare and the dramatists he influenced, blank verse had become extremely free, even licentious. Licenses such as lines of four or six beats, of around eight to thirteen or fourteen syllables, headless lines with the first syllable missing, the so-called epic caesura of an extra offbeat at the midline pause, and the feminine ending of an unstressed syllable were common. In *Paradise Lost*, even the feminine ending is rare, and virtually every line has precisely ten metrical syllables, allowing for some colloquial elision or running together of adjacent vowels (as in "to set himself in glor-*y a*-bove his peers" [39], with elision indicated by italics). There are no headless lines and hardly any epic caesuras. Similarly, paragraphs always begin and end at a line-turn; even speeches are never broken off jaggedly in midline. Shakespeare and his followers had tended to subordinate the individual line to the speech; often, the sense of a line's ending is deliberately weakened by closing on a lightly stressed word and a feminine ending. Milton, however, retains a strong sense of the integrity of the individual line. It is typical that in the passage of thirty-two lines cited above, thirty end on a weighty syllable, twenty-eight of them monosyllables; there is only one feminine ending ("aspiring") and only one promoted final syllable ("visi-BLE"). A line never ends with a mere function-word such as "and" or "that."

Yet this disciplined verse feels anything but constricted and austere. The perceived integrity of the line brings out all the more clearly Milton's incessant modulations within it. Normative iambic pentameters are very much in the minority. Almost all adopt deviations not merely for variety but to intensify meaning through expressive effect: in "with VAIN at-<u>TEMPT. HIM the</u> <u>al</u>-MIGHT-y POWER" (44) and "to MORT-al <u>MEN, HE with his</u> HORR-id CREW" (51), the stress-initial pairings invite the reader to throw contemptuous but awestruck power on the Satanic pronouns. At "*HURLED* HEAD-long FLAM-ing FROM th' e-THER-eal SKY" (45), the extra stress on "hurled" alliterating with the main stress on "headlong" – and those h's require deliberate utterance – plus the concentration of four long syllables at the start of the line, evoke the massive energies of the divine expulsion. The line "he TRUST-ed TO have E-<u>qualed the MOST HIGH</u>" (40), with only two full stresses in the first eight syllables, may seem like Satan himself almost out of control, but, again like Satan, it is firmly brought into shape by the final pairing.

So Milton is no slave to the strict version of prosody he has devised. Elsewhere in the poem he shows himself ready to push his rhythms to the limit. For example, in a line such as "Hypocrisy, the <u>ON-*LY*' *EV*-il that</u> walks" (3.683) the pairing requires three syllables to be elided into two. In a line such as "<u>when the FIERCE FOE HUNG on our</u> BROKen REAR" (2.78), where the three adjacent stresses are all metrical beats and there can be no demotion, there are two concentered pairings, the stress-final ending "fierce foe" and the stress-initial beginning "foe hung." Moreover, there can be principled exceptions to Milton's norms. For example, at the sole promoted and therefore unemphatic line-ending of the excerpt, "DARK-ness VIS-i-BLE" (1.63), the lack of a clear-cut ending is appropriate for the paradoxical mystery being evoked. Similarly, Milton's avoidance of the feminine ending is breached at the start of the excerpt with Satan's "aspiring" above his peers; with hindsight one perceives that Milton tends to use such endings for acts of disobedience and illegitimate aspiration. For example, two more follow shortly after in the "vaunting aloud" (1.126) of Satan's first speech: "And high disdain, from sense of injured merit" (98) and "That durst dislike his reign, and me preferring" (102). At the fall in Book 9 and especially at Adam's savage bitterness in Book 10, the clustering of feminine endings makes the principle unmistakeable.

Very occasionally, Milton is also prepared to disrupt his prosodic norms and write aberrant rhythms. There are, for example, a few dislocated pairings, where the paired beats and offbeats are separated and the line is out of balance for a few words; this produces an awkward line unless there is some expressive purpose. At "On th' other SIDE, AD-am, SOON as he heard" (9.888), the advancing of the unpaired stress on "soon" to an odd syllable, before the anticipated paired offbeat, brings out how quick Adam is to feel horror at Eve's sin (compare the rhythmically more straightforward: "On th' other SIDE, AD-am, as SOON was heard"). A related license is what may be termed the 1–3–6 sequence, where the line begins not, as commonly, with one reversed stress but with two, so that the verse is out of balance until the sixth syllable. The alienation of Adam and Eve from one another and from God when, soon after the fall, they are summoned to the divine presence is marked by the aberrant rhythm: "[/] LOVE was NOT in their LOOKS, either to God" (10.111). Compare: "[/] LOVE from their LOOKS was absent, both to God." Another telling example is when Eve recommends working apart: "[/] AD-am, WELL may we LAB-our still to dress" (9.205) (compare "AD-am we WELL may LAB-our still to dress"). The presumption lurking within this apparently practical suggestion is evident not only in her blunt opening of the discussion, without any of the unfallen world's loving modes of address, but also by the abnormal rhythm, bringing a sardonic tinge to their life of joint labor through the premature and out of balance stress on "well."

The constant modulations of rhythm within the line sketched out so far contribute much to the dynamic energy that pervades the poem, but equally potent is the modulation of the verse from line to line, engendered by Milton's notorious dismissal of rhyme as "troublesome and modern bondage." Rhyme inevitably brings a sense of closure and of shaped destiny to the line and the passage, quite contrary to Milton's vision. Hence the testy note on the verse elicited from him by the publisher for the poem's reissue in 1668, where rhyme is "the invention of a barbarous age ... a thing of itself, to all judicious ears, trivial and of no true musical delight; which consists only in apt numbers, fit quantity of syllables, and the sense variously drawn out from one verse into another, not in the jingling sound of like endings."

The references to "numbers" and syllables are too brief and conventional to mean more than an appropriate prosody well-handled (Koehler 1958). What is striking is the unorthodox emphasis on enjambment, an overflow of semantic energy alien to the steady line-by-line and couplet-by-couplet procession of Restoration verse. For example, as many as twenty-four of the thirty-two lines of the cited passage flow without a syntactic pause into the following line; only three lines end with a heavy stop, only one of these a full stop. This is not uncharacteristic: in the poem as a whole, three lines in every five run on. Such freedom is matched by freedom of division within the line; whereas conventionally the caesura or internal pause fell after the fourth or sixth syllable, in *Paradise Lost* it is disposed freely across the line. In the poem as a whole, less than half fall at the orthodox syllables, and fully a third are "lyric caesuras," falling at an odd rather than even syllable, encouraging onward movement rather than a pause, or disquiet rather than rest, as in the cited passage with the third syllable pause of: "Torments him; round he throws his baleful eyes" (1.56).

The sentences of *Paradise Lost* are as unprecedented in their length as in their disposition from line to line and within the line. They average some ten lines or eighty words even though short sentences for rhetorical emphasis are not rare – such as the short quasi-sentence between colons in the cited passage: "But his doom | Reserved him to more wrath" (53–54) – the "b" of "But" is capitalized in the early editions, even though it follows a colon. The outcome is the dynamic unpredictability of the verse: the huge spans of syntax with incessant variations of local movement demand a lot of the reader's concentration, but the reward is verse of unparalleled energy, weight, and flexibility.

How is one to read verse such as this, when reading aloud or as if aloud? On the one hand, it is vital not to lose the prosody in the syntax and read it as prose like the paragraph of rewriting at the head of this chapter. On the other hand, it is equally vital not to impose a regular singsong or predictable inflection of the voice when the line runs on. The best solution was recommended long ago by the actor Thomas Sheridan (father of the playwright Richard) in his *Lectures on the Art of Reading* (1775), who proposes what he terms "the stop of suspension" – or "pause of suspension" – at the enjambment. There should be no change at all in the voice, he urges, at the final pause. "This will sufficiently distinguish it from the other [grammatical] pauses; because some change of note precedes the others, either by raising, or depressing the voice…. [T]he pause [of suspension] itself perfectly marks the bound of the metre, and being made only by a suspension, not change of note in the voice, can never affect the sense" (Sheridan 264–5). In practice, the pause may sometimes be of negligible length; individual readers may well feel the need to run over some line-turns for expressive reasons; what is important is that the line-turn is *felt*, by reader and listener alike. Uninflected by the intonations of grammar, this pause puts its own shape on the flow of meaning, for the pause of suspension is also a pause of suspense, a moment of conjecture. However well one knows *The Winter's Tale* or *Oedipus Rex*, the survival of Hermione or the downfall of the king are profoundly surprising and shaking when experienced afresh. However well one knows the 10,565 lines of *Paradise Lost*, there is a fleeting moment of diverse possibilities and conjecture at the line-turn: "Of man's first disobedience, and the fruit …" (1.1) – what fruit, and is it literal or symbolic? The poem ends in uncertainty – "the world was all before them" (12.646) – and the reader shares in uncertainties and opening possibilities generated throughout.

The effects of enjambment are as diverse as Milton's art is inexhaustible. Evoking the depths of the universe, God announces:

> Boundless the deep, because I am who fill
> Infinitude, nor vacuous the space. (7.168–69)

The pause between "fill" and "infinitude" draws out how the divine – epitomized by the divine name "I AM" (Exodus 3:14) – is awe-inspiringly present throughout the infinities of space. When the birds of the air are created at 7.431–32, "the prudent crane" steers

> Her annual voyage, born on winds; the air
> Floats, as they pass, fanned with unnumbered plumes …

There is a joyous ease and exultation in the floating of the rhythm around that pause of suspension and the comma early in the next line. In the passage cited at the beginning of this chapter, however, horror and tragedy lurk at the turn of the lines. Satan has trusted in his power and "Raised impious war in Heav'n and battle proud," but only to meet his comeuppance in the next line: "With vain attempt" (1.43–44). The line "At once as far as angels ken he views" (59) recalls the archangelic traces of Lucifer still there in Satan, only for the "dismal situation" to crowd in on him at the next line. As the passage continues, the hellish dungeon flames like a great furnace, yet the line-turn at "from those flames" reveals uncannily that they give off "No light," and then more horrors are discovered from the still more uncanny "darkness visible." "Hope never comes," and the tragic loss is yet more intensified by the illogical addition at the line-turn: "That comes to all," underlining the devils' alienation from universal grace. This line's unstopped ending at "torture without end" evokes the endlessness of their pain. The turning of the line to "still urges" fuses the immediate energies of the verb with the unchanging eternity of "still" (meaning "always"), while the late caesura's isolation of "fed" at the end of the line clashes a term of sustenance and consumption against what never can be "consumed," the "ever-burning" sulphur. The elliptical syntax of these lines piles grief on grief yet more emphatically.

In such verse, the experience and indeed the meaning of the lines are quite distinct from the same words uttered as prose, as also in this tremendous sentence:

> Him the Almighty Power
> Hurled headlong flaming from th' ethereal sky
> With hideous ruin and combustion down
> To bottomless perdition, there to dwell
> In adamantine chains and penal fire,
> Who durst defy th' Omnipotent to arms. (44–49)

Although the relative clause of the last line eventually loops the whole sentence together, this is anything but a period with one overarching syntactic shape. Read in the prose transcription offered at the beginning of the chapter, it all flows on smoothly enough, but the lineation brings out that it might easily have been completed at the line-endings "sky," "down," "dwell," or "fire," as well as at the sole marked caesura, "perdition" (compare Hollander 98). Line is added to line without syntactic necessity, although with a dynamic effect rather than the inertia of comparable syntax in the opening soliloquy of *Samson Agonistes* (lines 53–57):

> But what is strength without a double share
> Of wisdom? Vast, unwieldy, burdensome,
> Proudly secure, yet liable to fall
> By weakest subtleties, not made to rule,
> But to subserve where wisdom bears command.

Unwieldy and burdensome indeed – all the more in the 1671 edition, where it is rightly all one sentence – the invertebrate syntax lumbers on as Samson, sunk in despair and self-pity, merely heaps excuse on excuse. But each line-turn in the passage on Satan adds new force to divine power and new horror to his destiny. This anticipates the dread and despair he comes to realize in his most searching soliloquy:

> Which way I fly is Hell; myself am Hell;
> And in the lowest deep a lower deep

> Still threat'ning to devour me opens wide,
> To which the Hell I suffer seems a Heav'n. (4.75–78)

Milton's skill at the line-turn means that readers share in such terrifying plunges. Introducing this soliloquy, for example, the narrator tells how here on Earth Satan's "conscience wakes despair" and "wakes the bitter memory | Of what he was, what is, and what must be | Worse;" (4.24–26). The resonant and liturgical phrase apparently completed in line 25 is exploded by the shocking turn to "Worse" isolated at the head of the next line, with the verb "be" wrenched from meaning "happen" to "become" – an epitome of how Milton's turns can undermine the stability of reader and character alike (see also Hollander 95). For Satan the only way is down. Whereas Samson's sequence is a self-indulgence, Satan foresees an irresistible, ever-worsening doom.

Even so, Satan chooses this destiny – it is foreknown by God but not predestined by him. Right up to the moment of the human fall, Satan feels repeated promptings of remorse but chooses to suppress them. Although the poem sets out to assert "eternal providence" (1.25) and eventually leaves the human pair with "providence their guide" (12.647), Adam and Eve – like the devils, the angels, and in part even the Son himself – repeatedly face real choices between "the ways of God" and their creaturely impulses, between allegiance and disobedience. Earlier epics had been stories of predestined triumph and of the restoration of a culture, and the heroes are the instruments of the gods. As decreed by the divine, the Greeks are on the verge of overwhelming Troy and regaining Helen; Attica is purified; Troy is about to be reestablished in Italy; Jerusalem is liberated. On the other hand, *Paradise Lost* is, as the title proclaims, a tragedy and a poem of loss. The last two books prophesy generations of human misery. Yet this is also the guarantee of human freedom; *Paradise Lost* is the epic of free will in a genre dominated by fate. The "[p]revenient grace" (11.3) that has descended to Adam and Eve when they pray together in love and contrition after the fall enables but does not cause their reconciliation and penitence. That has been brought about by their mutual love and trust. Indeed, "The world [is] all before them" to make of it what they can. This ultimately is why the poem lacks the shaped destiny of rhyme with rhyme's preordained sense of closure. In *Areopagitica*, Milton had written that truth is as a streaming fountain: "if her waters flow not in a perpetual progression, they sicken into a muddy pool of conformity and tradition;" truth is not fixed and handed down, but ever to be striven toward, though never fully achieved (*YP* 2:543). The unrhymed verse of *Paradise Lost*, with its continually modulating rhythms and divisions within the line and constant opening into new perspectives at the line-turn, makes reading "a perpetual progression" and requires of the responsive reader continual acts of choice and discrimination.

Further Reading

Attridge, Derek, *The Rhythms of English Poetry* (New York, 1982).
  Poetic Rhythm: An Introduction (Cambridge, UK, 1995).
Beum, Robert, "So Much Gravity and Ease," in *Language and Style in Milton*, ed.
  Ronald David Emma and John T. Shawcross (New York, 1967), 333–68.
Bradford, Richard, "'Verse Only to the Eye?' Line Endings in *Paradise Lost*," *EIC* 33
  (1983), 187–204.
  Silence and Sound: Theories of Poetics from the Eighteenth Century (Rutherford,
  NJ, 1992).
Bridges, Robert, *Milton's Prosody*, rev. ed. (Oxford, 1921).
Burnett, Archie, "'Sense Variously Drawn Out': The Line in *Paradise Lost*," *Literary
  Imagination* 5 (2003), 69–92.
Creaser, John, "'Through Mazes Running': Rhythmic Verve in Milton's *L'Allegro
  and Il Penseroso*," *RES* 52 (2001), 376–410.
  "Prosody and Liberty in Milton and Marvell," in *Milton and the Terms of Liberty*,
  ed. Graham Parry and Joad Raymond (Cambridge, UK, 2002), 37–55.
  "'Service Is Perfect Freedom': Paradox and Prosodic Style in *Paradise Lost*," *RES*
  58 (2007), 268–315.
Eliot, T. S., *To Criticise the Critic and Other Writings* (London, 1965).
  Collected Poems 1909–1962 (London, 1963).
Hollander, John, *Vision and Resonance: Two Senses of Poetic Form* (New York,
  1975).
Koehler, G. Stanley, "Milton on 'Numbers,' 'Quantity,' and Rime," *SP* 55 (1958),
  201–17
Mueller, Janel, "Just Measures? Versification in *Samson Agonistes*," *MS* 33 (1996),
  47–82.
Prince, F. T., *The Italian Element in Milton's Verse* (Oxford, 1954).
Ricks, Christopher, "John Milton: Sound and Sense in *Paradise Lost*," in *The Force
  of Poetry* (Oxford, 1987), 60–79.
Sheridan, Thomas, *Lectures on the Art of Reading ... Part II, The Art of Reading
  Verse*, 4th ed. (London, 1794).
Snell, Ada L. F., "An Objective Study of Syllabic Quantity in English Verse," *PMLA*
  33 (1918), 396–408.
Sprott, S. Ernes, *Milton's Art of Prosody* (Oxford, 1953).
Weismiller, Edward R., "The 'Dry' and 'Rugged' Verse," in *The Lyric and Dramatic
  Milton*, ed. Joseph H. Summers (New York, 1965), 115–52.
  "Studies of Verse Form in the Minor English Poems," *Variorum Commentary on
  the Poems of John Milton: The Minor English Poems*, ed. A. S. P. Woodhouse
  and Douglas Bush (1972), 2.3.1007–87.
  "Studies of Style and Verse Form in *Paradise Regained*," in *Variorum Commentary*,
  ed. Walter MacKellar (1975), 4.263–363.
  Entries on "Blank Verse" and "Versification," in *A Milton Encyclopedia*, gen. ed.
  W. B. Hunter, Jr., 9 vols. (Lewisburg, PA, 1978–83), 1.179–92 and 8.113–35.
Wordsworth, William and Samuel Taylor Coleridge, *Lyrical Ballads*, ed. R. L. Brett
  and A. R. Jones (London, 1963, rpt. 1971).

8

PAUL STEVENS

The Pre-Secular Politics of *Paradise Lost*

When *Paradise Lost* was first published in 1667, while few doubted its extraordinary quality, many still felt the poem to be tainted by the republican politics of its author. On first reading the poem, the royalist parson John Beale, for instance, wrote to his friend, John Evelyn, "You will join with me to whisper in a smile, that [Milton] writes so good verse, that tis pity he ever wrote in prose" (Poole 80). But as he reread the poem, Beale became increasingly alarmed at its political register. Besides the "long blasphemies" of the devils, he bristled at Milton's Charles I-like representation of Nimrod, the tyrant who, not content with "fair equality," falsely claims "sovereignty" from heaven and arrogates dominion over others even while he accuses them of rebellion (*PL* 12.24–82). In passages like this, Beale heard the old defender of regicide at his unreconstructed worst (Poole 80). As memory of the Civil Wars faded and readers became increasingly focused on the literary achievement of the poem, this sensitivity to its immediate political context disappeared. Although *Paradise Lost* was re-politicized in the late eighteenth century with the Romantic idealization of Satan, only with the advent of modern academic criticism has there been any sustained analysis of the poem's contemporary political orientation. For all its flaws, Christopher Hill's remarkable 1977 *Milton and the English Revolution* opened the way for a plethora of compelling new political interpretations. What is perhaps most striking, however, is not the quality of these various approaches but their failure to arrive at consensus on the precise political argument of the poem. This is the case, as Alastair Fowler suspects, because the poem's political concerns are so tightly woven into the fabric of its religious and aesthetic aims that the poem's fiction defies any kind of easy political allegorization (Fowler 41–5). Indeed it is probably for this reason that so many early readers were not as disturbed as Beale: Milton may be a "criminal and obsolete person," says the Presbyterian Sir John Hobart in January 1668, but as for *Paradise Lost*, "[I] never read anything more august, and withal more grateful to my (too much limited) understanding" (von Maltzahn 490–1).

Even so, the poem is clearly, intensely political, passionately concerned with the nature of liberty and its concomitant, sovereignty. Given Milton's way of being in the world, especially the peculiar way his Protestant sense of justification by faith was refracted through his humanist education, it could hardly be otherwise. In order to develop this point and fully explain what the poem reveals about political liberty and sovereignty, I want to focus on three moments in Milton's narrative: first, Michael's education of Adam (Books 11–12), then God the Son's challenge to the Father (Book 3), and finally Satan's challenge to God (Book 5). But before turning to these, I want begin with the work's genesis in order to explain exactly why the poem's politics are so integral to its overall aims. In re-writing Scripture as an epic poem, Milton sets out to fulfill his peculiar talent for poetry not for its own sake, but in order to *justify* himself before God and *educate* his fellow countrymen and women, to present them with a vision that, however political, will rise above mere polemic. In so doing, I want to suggest, he offers what modern religious thinkers like John Milbank and Charles Taylor would call a "pre-secular" understanding of politics.

Justification and Education

Although biblical epics were by 1667 anything but unprecedented, the sheer scope of Milton's effort clearly surprised many readers, not least Andrew Marvell who feared he might be ruining Scripture's "sacred truths" (*MLM* 287). Milton's authority for rewriting the Bible was, however, both perfectly scriptural and carefully set out in the poem as such. His rationale for re-writing Scripture lies in the Protestant emphasis on *sola fide* or "justification by faith by alone," a religious doctrine whose implications in the case of Milton are every bit as political as they are confessional.

When the poet confesses that the immediate purpose of *Paradise Lost* is to "justify the ways of God to men" (1.26), he is not doing God "a favor" by explaining what the deity had somewhat absentmindedly left obscure (Frye 8). The darkness is not out there, Milton says, but "in me" (1.22). At its most personal level, the poem is an act of faith, specifically a speech act that announces the poet's belief in God's justice in order to demonstrate his own election; that is, to realize his God-given talent and to make manifest the prevenient grace that actually makes belief possible. It is for this reason that the poem's opening is not so much a thesis statement or declaration of intent as an invocation or prayer. And the faith Milton expresses in this prayer is real, for ultimately Christian revelation even for Milton is irrational, mere "foolishness" to the wise (1 Corinthians 1:23): as he says in *DDC*, "when discussing sacred matters, let us disregard reason ... and follow exclusively what the Bible teaches" (*YP* 6:213). At such moments the humanist scholar gives way to the Protestant believer. Like the disciples at Pentecost, he hopes to breathe out the life-giving Word through the divine agency of *spiritus* or the "rushing mighty wind" (Acts 2:2) and so repeat and recreate "the wonders of God's works" (Acts 2:11). The poem is, however, not only an expression of faith, but as a speech act, it is also a good work produced by faith – that is, it has a pragmatic dimension.

While never seeking to undermine the Pauline simplicity of *sola fide*, Milton is consistent throughout his writings in insisting on faith's need to manifest itself in action. We are certainly "justified by faith," he says in *DDC*, but by "a living faith, not a dead one, and the only living faith is a faith that acts" (*YP* 6:490). In other words, "faith has its own works" (490) and for Milton chief among those works is politics. In this it is difficult not to see the enduring influence of his humanist education. In *De Officiis*, for instance, one of the core texts of that education, Cicero insists that we "are not born for ourselves, but our country claims for itself one part of our birth, and our friends another" (9–10). He is as emphatic about faith as Paul is, but what Cicero means by faith is not belief in the impossible, Christ crucified, or the wonders of God, but in the perfectly possible – that is, community, the polis and *amicitia*, the nation and fellowship. Most relevant here, he is adamant that faith needs to substantiate itself in action: "the keeping of faith is fundamental to justice ... and let us trust that the keeping of faith is so called because what has been said is actually done" (10). In Milton, then, to a surprisingly consistent degree, Protestant and humanist demands coalesce to emphasize *praxis* and render virtuous action political. This is imperative: if *Paradise Lost* as an act of faith is to live, it must, even after 1660, do "good work" in the life of the polis. But since *Paradise Lost* is merely a poem, how is this to be?

The answer is, of course, education: that is, the degree to which the poem's aesthetic power may persuade its readers to understand and practice or, as Milton puts it in *Areopagitica*, re-member the truth. Poets are after all better teachers than scholars, "our sage and serious Poet *Spencer*" than "*Scotus* or *Aquinas*" (*YP* 2:549, 516), precisely because poetry, unlike more direct forms of discourse, exercises its readers; it works by indirection, enabling them to enact or perform its moral lessons. And it is through the moral and religious education of the individual rather than any specific constitutional arrangements that the health of the polis is to be established. This is how he puts it in his desperate 1660 pamphlet, *The Ready and Easy Way to Establish a Free Commonwealth*, a work he wrote while composing

Paradise Lost: "To make the people fittest to chuse, and the chosen fittest to govern, will be to mend our corrupt and faulty education, to teach the people faith not without virtue" (7:443). If the people are to be free and sovereign, then, not simply education but education in "faith not without virtue," education sensitive to the pressure of God's grace, is essential. As direct political action was denied him after the Restoration, nothing could do this as well as the great poem he was already embarked upon. But not surprisingly, as he continues to work on the poem in the early 1660s, much of *The Ready and Easy Way* never leaves him.

The "Pre-Secular" Education of Adam

The poem, as Beale recognized, is at its most overtly political in Michael's account of human history. Michael teaching Adam is a mirror image of Milton teaching his "old principle" (Poole 80). As a historian, Michael's method appears to be that of philosophy or doctrine teaching by example, but as his narrative proceeds his examples are assimilated into a typological order that transcends history (on typology, see Shoulson in this volume). This is critically important because it suggests the degree to which Adam's moral and political education, like that projected for the people in *The Ready and Easy Way*, is "pre-secular." That is, even though Adam's education takes place during the *saeculum*, the interval between the fall and the end of days, it is not simply a matter of reasoning well or following the law of nature but of being inspired to do so by the hope of transcendence so powerfully articulated in revelation. Rational liberty, conscience, or right reason, ultimately depend on the animating force of God's grace, personified here in Michael. As the Son reminds the Father, grace is the "speediest of thy winged messengers" and like Michael comes "unprevented, unimplored, unsought" (*PL* 3.229–31). Without sensitivity to the revelations of grace, the poem increasingly suggests, secular political theory will lead nowhere.

Adam's political education resolves itself into three lessons: first, that spiritual regeneration includes the possibility of political renewal; second, that the Bible's saints might thus be understood as citizens; and third, that the mediating role of these citizen-saints between the divine and the human is most powerfully modeled in the actions of God the Son. The narrative through which Michael conveys these points falls into two discrete sequences, the climax of the first being a type of the second; that is, the triumph of Noah is a prefiguration of the resurrection of the Son. In the first sequence (11.424–901), Michael offers Adam six scenes for analysis from pre-Israelite history, from the curse of Cain to the new covenant with Noah. The fallen Adam routinely misreads these scenes, but under instruction gradually gets the idea. What the sequence describes, and what Adam at least in part perceives, is the universal and paradoxically timeless event of regeneration: how what seems like a relentless torrent of defeat and degeneration may be reversed in an instant. The moment of joy Adam feels when he sees the de-creative tide of Noah's flood reversed (11.871–72) prefigures the culmination of his moral and political education at the end of the second sequence of Michael's narrative (12.13–465). Here when he finally comes to understand that God's curse on the serpent's head is in fact a promise of humankind's final regeneration in the Son, his renewed joy is unrestrained: "O goodness infinite, goodness immense!" (469). The story of Christ's death and impossible resurrection precipitates an epiphany, specifically a perception of the transcendent, endlessly creative energy of God's grace: it is a reversal of de-creation "more wonderful" than the creation itself (471–73). Most importantly, as the metaphoric patterns in both Michael's history and *The Ready and Easy Way* suggest, it includes the possibility of a renewal that is specifically political even in the most vitiated of worlds. Communal life in the *saeculum* is not, as the Catholic theologian John Milbank imagines it, a time that is irredeemably "secular," an interval "where coercive justice, private property, and impaired natural reason must make shift to cope with the unredeemed effects of sinful humanity" (9). For Milton, God's grace is always there capable of repairing the ruin of our first parents, both saving souls and rebuilding the polis.

While de-creation is figured in the flood, its reversal is recurrently imagined as the effect of *spiritus*, the divine wind that both inspires the poet and moves on the face of the waters in Genesis. In the story of Noah, *spiritus* appears in the form of the "keen north wind, that blowing dry/ Wrinkled the face of deluge" (*PL* 11.842–43). In the earlier story of Adam and Eve's regeneration (11.1–20), it appears in the faith with which the survivors of Ovid's flood, Deucalion and Pyrrha, throw stones behind them to repopulate the world and "restore/ The race of mankind drowned" (13–14). Similarly and most importantly for the present argument it appears in the faith with which the author of *The Ready and Easy Way* defiantly asserts providence and assigns himself the same role of Deucalion and Pyrrha. In the torrent driving the nation toward the Restoration, "the deluge of this epidemic madness," Milton imagines his words as the stones that God will surely raise "to become the children of reviving libertie" (*YP* 7:463). In Milton's imagination, then, the re-creation of humankind after Noah's flood is inseparable from the re-creation of the polis. Here, as Beale suspects, when Milton is talking about "saints" (*PL* 11.705), he is also talking about citizens. Noah, the "one just man" (818) whose faith has brought about the new covenant, is a type of the ideal citizen. That is, in Michael's teaching, the religious concept of the saint assimilates and remodels the secular concept of the citizen – not the other way around. For what distinguishes this citizen-saint are not simply classically-derived republican principles but those principles as they are illuminated, driven, and qualified by what Alain Badiou would call the revolutionary truth or "pure event" of Christian revelation (Badiou 45; Mohamed; and Stevens 2013). Consider the relation between the tyrant Nimrod and the citizen-saint Moses.

The critical difference between the two leaders is not simply Nimrod's arrogation of dominion over his fellow human beings, but his arrogation of God's freedom or sovereignty: assuming what amounts to an early version of the divine right of kings, he claims a "second sovereignty" (*PL* 12.35). He will rule on Earth as God does in Heaven. While the tyrant falsely identifies himself with God, Moses, the citizen-saint, is insistently identified with the Son of God. This, so I want to suggest, is the pre-secular radical at the center of the poem's politics. Michael's representation of Moses is a carefully religious recalibration of the argument of *The Ready and Easy Way*. Having parted the Red Sea, reversing the threat of another flood, Moses does not take the easy or "readiest way" (12.216) to establish his free commonwealth, but eschewing "rashness" leads his people into the desert (222). There they establish their government, choose the kind of perpetual senate Milton had imagined in his 1660 pamphlet (*YP* 7:436), and ordain their laws. The laws it turns out are both theirs and God's, mediated through Moses. Since God, as he really is, is incomprehensible, a source of terror – his voice "dreadful" to mortal ear (12.235–36) – there is no access to his will other than through a mediator. In undertaking that role, the citizen-saint becomes a type of the Son: "Moses in figure bears" the high office of mediator "to introduce/ One greater, of whose day he shall foretell" (238–42). And it is in the relation between the citizen-saint and the Son that we come to the heart of Milton's political vision. If he is to educate the English in "faith not without virtue," they will need to focus on the Son.

As the Word, the Son is Scripture personified and it is for this reason that Milton insistently imagines himself as a scripturalist among the theologians (*DDC*, *YP* 6:204–05). The centrality of Scripture as opposed to theology, whether traditional or otherwise, is evident everywhere in *Paradise Lost*. Most importantly, it subsumes the poem's epic structure. *Paradise Lost* is in fact not one epic, but three – the Satanic and Angelic stories are enclosed within God's overarching narrative. The poem opens with a "parody-demonic" epic (Frye 52) in which Satan presents himself as the hero whose mission is to defy God, conquer the new world, and colonize it with Sin and Death. After the first two books, however, Satan's disorder is shown to be simply a part of God's order and is rapidly assimilated into God's epic, a story in which humankind will become the hero. In order to facilitate this, Milton interpolates a third epic, told by the Archangel Raphael, in which the Son appears as the hero, showing exactly what it means to create order out of disorder, life out of death. Each one of these stories, like the great classical epics, begins with a heavenly or in the case of the Satan's narrative an infernal council. Both the specifically heavenly councils, one in Book 3 and the other in Book 5, struggle to articulate the relation between God and the citizen-saint through the mediating image of the Son. This is as important as it is because the Son is the sole "image of God" (2 Corinthians 4:4), the only way humankind can come to an understanding of God. The two divine epic councils, therefore, resolve themselves into a series of hermeneutical exercises or deeply thoughtful contemplations of Scripture, specifically of Genesis 18 and Exodus 32 (Book 3) and Psalm 2 (Book 5). Taken together they crystallize Milton's post-Restoration understanding of political sovereignty or how power is to be distributed in the polis. And as we will see, while the one offers the promise of a new politics, the other constitutes a critique of politics without grace.

The Son's Scriptural Challenge to the Father

Given the poem's overall epic structure, the divine council of Book 3 is clearly meant to command special attention (Stevens 1985, 145–77). In each one of the classical councils on which it is modeled, a subordinate deity intercedes with the supreme deity on behalf of the hero of the poem. The particular issue is some injustice or broken promise and the intercession precipitates the main action of the poem. In the *Aeneid*, Venus intercedes with Jupiter on behalf of Aeneas, the issue being Jupiter's apparent failure to facilitate Aeneas's political destiny, the renewal of Troy in Rome: "Is this our reward for piety and obedience?" she passionately challenges the supreme deity (1.253). Jupiter reassures her, insisting that what he has predestined will happen, and that Rome's future will be an "empire without end" (1.279). In Milton's version of the divine council, because of his distinctively scriptural understanding of the Trinity – specifically his conviction, articulated in *DDC*, that God the Son is not coessential but subordinate to the Father because he is "begotten" (Psalm 2:7) by him (*YP* 6:203–80) – he is able to assign the role of Venus to the Son. Unlike the intercession of Venus, however, not only does the intercession of the Son precipitate the main action of *Paradise Lost*, there is a sense in which it *is* the main action.

Milton is a child of the Reformation. While he insists over and again that his understanding of God is exclusively scriptural, he is also, like any other Reformation thinker, intoxicated "with the majesty of God" (Rice 163), that is, with his sovereignty, transcendent otherness, and "absolute freedom" (*DDC*, *YP* 6:209). At the same time, Milton is equally a child of his humanist education, and his distinctive conception of the Son is ultimately a response to both these influences. In the same way that his understanding of *sola fide* emphasizes the degree to which a faith that does not lead to action is dead, so his understanding of God's majesty is qualified by a conception of the Son that allows enormous scope for human agency. This is not the case with John Calvin, for instance, who confronts the terrible majesty of God's freedom without any qualification: "Again I ask, whence does it happen that Adam's fall irremediably involved so many peoples, together with their infant offspring, in eternal death unless it so pleased God?"(955). That he could take pleasure in such human suffering is "dreadful indeed," Calvin confesses, but such a conclusion is logically unavoidable – for if God foreknew what would happen, then not only did he permit it but he willed it for the sake of his "glory" (957). Milton the humanist vehemently rejects this view of God. God the Father's opening speech in Book 3 is indeed full of dread: he appears as an "incensed deity" (3.187), angry and resentful. But even here, where he is meant to be so remote, the Father categorically rejects Calvin's terrifying understanding of "predestination" (114): "if I foreknew,/ Foreknowledge had no influence on their fault" (117–18). He insists that human freedom is necessary to his own divine freedom, "necessary" specifically in the sense that his pleasure would be inhibited without it: "What pleasure I from such [blind] obedience paid,/ When will and reason (reason also is choice)/ Useless and vain, of freedom both despoiled,/ Made passive both, had served necessity,/ Not me" (107–11). The Son capitalizes on this and is even more forceful in his rejection of human passivity, for his intercession is not simply an interpretation but a tough Venus-like challenge: "For should man finally be lost," he admonishes the Father in one of the poem's most astonishing moments, "So should thy goodness and thy greatness both/ Be questioned and blasphemed without defence" (150–66).

The challenge is of critical importance. On the one hand, the Son's response merely interprets, amplifies, or re-sounds the grace note with which the Father closed his opening speech: "man therefore shall find grace" is echoed in the Son's refrain, "gracious was that word which closed/ Thy sovereign sentence, that man should find grace" (131, 144–45). As he does this, the Son confirms God's freedom, the sovereignty of his sentence. Despite Adam and Eve's understandable folly, by the terms of their "pledge" or contract with God, the Father's act of mercy is absolutely unnecessary: it is gracious, gratuitous, entirely without constraint whether logical or juridical. On the other hand, the Son's response effectively refutes its own affirmation of God's freedom. The challenge embedded in his response somewhat bewilderingly insists that God's mercy is necessary, for were humankind finally to be lost then both God's goodness and greatness would be indefensible. The key to this impasse is scriptural: the Son's allusions to the agency of his own imperfect biblical types – Abraham before Sodom and Gomorrah and Moses after Israel's apostasy at Mount Sinai – reveal the principle to which Milton seems most concerned to bear witness, the devolution of sovereignty. And Scripture, not political theory or even "political theology," will explain how exactly this works.

Both Abraham and Moses refuse to believe that God will renege on his commitment to the people. Unlike Calvin, Abraham cannot believe that God would countenance or take pleasure in any kind of injustice: "That be far from thee to do after this manner, to slay the righteous with the wicked: and that the righteous should be as the wicked, that be far from thee: Shall not the Judge of all earth do right?" (Genesis 18:25). Similarly, Moses cannot believe that God, although he has the right, would abandon his plan for the Israelites. If he were to do so, his adversaries, the Egyptians, would obtain their end, exulting "For mischief did he bring [the Israelites out of Egypt] to slay them in the mountains, and to consume them from the face of the earth" (Exodus 32:11–12). Far from being overawed, in the security of their faith both these figures become free to speak out and so share in God's sovereignty. So much so that Moses can command God to change his mind: "Turn from thy fierce wrath, and repent of this evil against thy people," he demands. And God does (Exodus 32:12–14).

These biblical passages clearly had an enormous impact on Milton (see, for instance, DDC, YP 6:134–35). As the Son appeals to both the Father's righteousness and sovereignty, he both assumes and fulfills the agency of his own human prefigurations. Speaking of man's loss, he becomes Abraham: "that be from thee far,/ That far be from thee, Father, who art judge/ Of all things made, and judgest only right" (PL 3.153–55). Then he becomes Moses: "shall the adversary thus obtain/ His end," he asks, would you, Father, "Abolish thy creation, and unmake .../ ... what for thy glory thou hast made?" (156–54). As he does this, the Son pointedly transforms humankind into a version of himself: the impersonal "man" becomes God's "creature late so loved, thy youngest son" (151) – he speaks of humankind in a way that the Father finds himself completely unable to do in his opening speech. This move, which anticipates the Son's climactic offer to "Account me man" (238), has two immediate implications. First, it reinforces a growing awareness that while God's mercy may be unnecessary in terms of the law, it is absolutely necessary in terms of the grace or love that is imagined as the source of all being and the substance of God's glory. If it fails to answer fully Calvin's dreadful logic, it confounds it in a magisterial act of faith.

Second and more importantly, it foregrounds the relation between the "faith that worketh by love" (Galatians 5:6) and the devolution of God's sovereignty. Far from being overawed by the Father, in the security of his faith, the Son is free to speak out and share in the sovereignty of the Father. He becomes his "word," "wisdom," and "effectual might" (3.168–70). David Norbrook may be right to argue that there is no room in Milton's heaven for "deliberative rhetoric, the arguments of the forum" (Norbrook 480), but there is plenty of room for dialogue within the "analogy of faith" – that is, within the trust that always interprets the particular and contingent within the light of God's whole design, and vice versa. If the Father's angry, theological assertion of his freedom serves as a provocation to the Son in Book 3, even more so does his brutal, scriptural exaltation of the Messiah serve to incense Satan in Book 5.

Satan's Republican Challenge to God

One of the curiosities of the Father's opening speech in Book 3, unlike those that follow the Son's intercession, is how unscriptural it is. Although it is clearly meant to capture God's remoteness and anger, it contains no specific allusions to the text of the Bible. In fact, the Father is made to reason in a way disturbingly similar to the devils in Book 2 – of "providence, foreknowledge, will and fate,/ Fixed fate, free will, foreknowledge absolute" (2.558–60): he argues in such a similar way that it is difficult not to feel that such "philosophical" rhetoric is being deliberately parodied. If this rationalizing, "theological" speech provokes a pointedly scriptural response from the Son, the pattern is reversed in Book 5. The Father's opening declaration here (5.600–15) is intensely scriptural, pregnant with the Word, while the response it elicits from Satan is irredeemably secular, republican, or "neo-Roman" (Skinner 10–16). While the Father's speech is a redaction of Psalm 2, Satan's response seems more like a Ciceronian appeal to patriotism and liberty. In reversing the pattern, not only does Milton emphasize the degree to which God and Satan are talking past each other, but he foregrounds the scriptural orientation of the poem's politics. Forms of human reasoning as prestigious as theology and classical republicanism fall away before the sheer creative force of the Word. This is not a rejection of politics but their transumption.

Paradise Lost begins like all its epic models *in medias res*. The formal purpose of Raphael's story, like the one Aeneas tells Dido's rapt court, is to provide a flashback and so pinpoint what first set the action of the epic in motion. For Aeneas, the ultimate cause of the fall of Troy is to be found in the intemperate decision to recover the wooden horse. Milton dramatically ups the ante. For Raphael, the ultimate cause of the Fall itself is to be found in Satan's decision to challenge God. In Milton's "story of all things" the action begins not with the creation but with the begetting of the agent of creation, the exaltation of the Son (Frye 3–31), that is, his "Word" (John 1:1). In order to emphasize the scriptural origin of this idea, Milton focuses on Psalm 2 (see YP 6:206–07). The result is strangely provocative – suggesting the degree to which, for Milton, God's "offered grace" only invites by means of a textual problem, a provocation to intense hermeneutic endeavor (3.187–88).

The begetting of the Son is the supremely good act – the original act of grace from which everything else flows. Read at face value, however, this act as it is represented in Psalm 2 seems curiously less than gracious or charitable. As Yahweh anoints David king of Israel, delegating his sovereignty and raising up the lowliest of shepherds, he expresses his rage at the enemies of Israel: he will "vex them in his sore displeasure," declaring that in spite of their opposition, "Yet have I set my king upon my holy hill of Zion." Then addressing David directly, he says, "Thou art my Son; this day have I begotten thee. Ask of me and I will give thee the heathen for thine inheritance.... Thou shall break them with a rod of iron; thou shalt dash them in pieces like a potter's vessel" (Psalm 2:5–9). When this becomes the Father's opening declaration in Raphael's story, a declaration addressed not to the enemies of Israel but to his beloved and utterly loyal angelic host, it becomes a provocation: "This day I have begot whom I declare/ My only son." Whoever disobeys him disobeys me, and will be cast out from God "without redemption, without end" (5.603–15). It is not immediately clear why this supreme act of charity should be articulated as a threat – as Satan wonders, why issue laws to those "who without law/ Err not" (5.798–99)?

From a secular perspective, Satan's response to this intemperate declaration is not difficult to understand. He is made to feel humiliated, "impaired" (5.665). He cannot see that the Father's words might be some kind of test. From a classical republican perspective, he is made to feel "obnoxious," a term he himself uses to describe his abject state when he later enters the body of the serpent (9.170). "Obnoxious" means vulnerable, mastered, and open to harm; in Roman law, it describes the dependent status of women, children, and slaves. For neo-Roman writers like Marchamont Nedham, James Harrington, and on occasion Milton himself, it captures a sense of "unfreedom" determined not by coercion or constraint but *dependency*. As Quentin Skinner puts it, for neo-Roman writers, "to live in a condition of dependence is in itself a source or form of constraint" (84), the full pain of which can only be expressed by likening it to a state of slavery. For these writers individual liberty is violated by what might seem to us relatively innocuous or necessary forms of legal or political dependency, suggesting an extraordinarily aggressive or heightened sense of individual agency or personal virtue. Dependency saps virtue, the specific quality of *virtus* that makes a man a man and truly free, or in Latin, a *vir*. Satan's pride may ultimately derive from Augustine, exemplifying the solipsistic desire of a creature to live unto itself alone (*City of God* 14:13), but here because it is cast in classical republican terms, it constitutes a critique of secular political theory at its most persuasive. The implication is that just as faith without good works is dead, so any system of politics without grace – not least all the republicanism, "all the oratory" of Greece and Rome (*PR* 4.360), so loved by the humanist Milton – is ultimately doomed to failure.

Satan finds that grace abhorrent. Milton's devil often appears false, self-serving, a caricature of vaulting ambition, but in certain moments of tragic authenticity he remains a figure of compelling force. On Mount Niphates, for instance, he reveals the degree to which he finds God's grace an unbearable burden. Although he feels God's endless love, it suffocates him, curtails his freedom, and renders him dependent or obnoxious, a mastered "man." He speaks out of the sensibility of a classical republican or Roman aristocrat. He fully understands the principle of Christian grace, but like Tacitus or Pliny who considered Christianity the religion of slaves, he despises it. He remembers the pain with which he felt the "debt immense of endless gratitude/So burdensome still paying, still to owe" (*PL* 4.52–53), and although he now realizes that this debt might be quit in a moment of reciprocal love, he continues to challenge God. Driven by his desire for the individuation or "unbounded hope" (4.60) implicit in the promise of classical liberty, he disdains subjection.

On Niphates, his challenge is immediately confounded by the Word: when he insists "Evil be thou my good" (110), Scripture echoes his words and interprets his defiance as the solipsism of unaided reason: "Woe unto them that call evil good, and good evil.... Woe unto them that are wise in their own eyes, and prudent in their own sight!" (Isaiah 5:20). But in Raphael's narrative he is allowed more latitude and speaks as though he were Cicero or, to some extent but not quite, Milton himself in *The Tenure of Kings and Magistrates*. Although what he has to say is only "counterfeited truth" (*PL* 5.771), he appeals movingly to reason and the law of nature independent of revelation. As one would expect from a deeply committed secular thinker, he argues from the evidence of things seen: "We know no time when we were not as now" (5.859). Addressing the rebel host, he appeals to what appear to be longstanding republican traditions. If you know yourselves to be who you truly are, he says, "Natives and sons of heaven possessed before/ By none," then you will not submit to this new decree. For who "can in reason … or right assume/ Monarchy over such as live by right/ His equals, if in power and splendour less,/ In freedom equal?" (789–97). Abdiel, imitating the scriptural intercession of the Son in Book 3, provides the answer. But the critical question then becomes how does Abdiel know what Satan and his followers fail to grasp?

The two divine councils offer Milton's English readers two models of political sovereignty and its devolution – one secular and one pre-secular. From Satan's secular perspective, the exaltation of the Son is a tyrannical arrogation of power. He takes the Father's declaration at face value, bristles at his threats, and appeals to rational liberty. We are citizens of this "our native heaven," he argues. We are indigenous, autochthonous, we know "none before us, self-begot, self-raised/ By our own quickening power" (5.863, 860–64). Sovereignty is natural, a birthright. Something of this extreme form of humanist reasoning is evident in *The Tenure*: "No man who knows ought, can be so stupid to deny that all men naturally were borne free, … born to command and not to obey" (YP 3:198–9). But in failing to add Milton's saving clause, that this is so because we are made in "the image and resemblance of God himself" (198), Satan's challenge points to the progressive secularization of contemporary political theory, where as confidence grows in human reason so God gradually disappears. From Abdiel's pre-secular perspective, this autonomous humanism is demonic. The loyal angel speaks out of the sensibility not of a classical republican but of a citizen-saint from Scripture. His startling challenge to Satan, "Shalt thou give law to God, shalt thou dispute/ With him the points of liberty" (*PL* 5.822–23), echoes the words not only of Job's friend Eliphaz, "Shall mortal man be more just than God?" (Job 4:17), but of Yahweh himself, "wilt thou condemn me, that thou mayst be righteous?" (Job 40:8). For some reason, Abdiel knows that in exalting the Son, God is not arrogating power but freely devolving it, revealing the source of all being in the Word – quite literally in Scripture's Psalm 2 – and raising the angels up to partake in that power as they interpret the Word. They are not "obscured" by the Son's reign, Abdiel says, but "more illustrious made, since he the head/ One of our number thus reduced becomes" (*PL* 5.842–43); that is, as God shares his sovereignty in the begetting of the Son, his creatures are raised up; they join the Son as he becomes one of their number, now "reduced" or reordered. Psalm 2 is so foregrounded in Milton's poem, not because the analogy between divine and human kingship is being reinforced (as Royalists might argue), but *because it is being deconstructed*. In exalting the Son, God is allowing the distinction between divine and human to be transumed. Ultimately, as the Father makes clear in Book 3, the metaphor of kingship itself will be cast aside and God's sovereignty will be enjoyed by all – "God shall be all in all" (*PL* 3.341).

How does Abdiel know this? Because he reads the Father's opening declaration in Book 5, the redaction of Psalm 2's harsh triumphalism, within the "analogy of faith." Just as the Son knows in Book 3, so Abdiel knows "how far [it is] from [God's] thought/ To make us less:" we know "by experience taught ... how good" he is, and "of our good, and of our dignity/ How provident" (5.826–31). From a secular perspective, these are merely religious pieties, and the sacred has little to do with either the new science of political theory or the hardheaded world of everyday politics. But such a perspective misses the revolutionary nature of Milton's poem. From the poem's pre-secular perspective, the very distinction between secular and sacred is being collapsed, the sovereignty of the secular as an independent domain and politics as a field of study or activity independent of the Word is being called into question.

According to Catholic thinkers like John Milbank and Charles Taylor, what distinguishes modernity is the transformation of the *saeculum* from a time into a place. God is made to withdraw from the world, which becomes increasingly disenchanted – cut off from his presence. It is God who is expelled from the garden, which increasingly grows to seed. Protestantism is frequently represented as a Trojan horse, one of the key instruments in effecting this transformation, a "secularizing religion" (Sommerville 8). A great Protestant text like *Paradise Lost* gives the lie to this argument because, for all its faults, it so forcefully presents a vision of human life, including its politics, suffused with the presence of God, the immediate and insistent pressure of Scripture, and the grace it offers. This is what the English, according to Milton, needed to learn if the nation were to flourish and escape tyranny.

Further Reading

Augustine, *City of God*, trans. Henry Bettenson (1972; rpt. London, 2003).

Badiou, Alain, *Saint Paul: The Foundation of Universalism*, trans. Ray Brassier (Stanford, CA, 2003).

Calvin, John, *Institutes of the Christian Religion*, ed. John T. McNeill, 2 vols. (Philadelphia, PA, 1960).

Cicero, *On Duties [De Officiis]*, ed. M. T. Griffin and E. M. Atkins (1991; rpt. Cambridge, UK, 2008).

Fowler, Alastair, ed., *Paradise Lost* (1968; rev. and rpt. London, 1998).

Frye, Northrop, *The Return of Eden: Five Essays on Milton's Epics* (Toronto, 1965).

Hill, Christopher, *Milton and the English Revolution* (1977; rpt. London, 1979).

Loewenstein, David and Paul Stevens, eds., *Early Modern Nationalism and Milton's England* (Toronto, 2008).

Maltzahn, Nicholas von, "The First Reception of *Paradise Lost* (1667)," *RES* 47:188 (1996), 479–99.

Milbank, John, *Theology and Social Theory* (1990; rpt. London, 2006).

Mohamed, Feisal G., *Milton and the Post-Secular Present* (Stanford, CA, 2011).

Norbrook, David, *Writing the English Republic* (Cambridge, UK, 1999).

Poole, William, "Two Early Readers of Milton," *MQ* 38:2 (2004), 76–99.

Rice, Eugene Jr., with Anthony Grafton, *The Foundations of Early Modern Europe, 1460–1559* (1970; rpt. and rev. New York, 1994).

Skinner, Quentin, *Liberty before Liberalism* (1998; rpt. Cambridge, UK, 2008).

Sommerville, John C., *The Secularization of Early Modern England: From Religious Culture to Religious Faith* (Oxford, 1992).

Stevens, Paul, "Literary History and the Turn to Religion: Milton Reading Badiou," *Religion and Literature* 45:1 (2013), 6–17.

Imagination and the Presence of Shakespeare in "Paradise Lost" (Madison, WI, 1985).

Taylor, Charles, *A Secular Age* (Cambridge, MA, 2007).

Virgil, *The Aeneid*, trans. David West (1990; rpt. London, 2003).

9

KAREN L. EDWARDS

Cosmology

To understand Adam's question about the structure of the universe and Raphael's response to it at the beginning of *Paradise Lost*, Book 8, has seemed to many readers to require a great deal of specialized knowledge about Renaissance cosmology, and the thicket of footnotes found in most scholarly editions of the poem reinforces the assumption.[1] This essay argues that the poem's representation of the universe explicitly *rejects* the need for specialized knowledge about cosmology. Nonetheless, the fact that such knowledge existed by the early sixteenth century is significant. It indicates that, in the history of science, cosmology is a special case. It does not fit into standard accounts of the scientific revolution, usually assigned to the mid-seventeenth century. Not only had cosmologists refined their methods of observation decades before other natural philosophers began to do so, but their theories (especially those of Copernican cosmologists) disturbed the era's primary metaphoric conception of the natural world, that it is God's other book, second to the Bible, and is immediately legible. Contradicting what seems plainly obvious to the untrained eye, that the sun moves around the Earth, Copernicans raised doubts about the value of ordinary observers' experience of the heavens. Is the chapter on the heavens in God's great book of nature, then, too difficult for ordinary readers? Can the heavens be read only by those with advanced and specialized training? Is the psalmist's claim that "the heavens declare the glory of God" (Psalm 19:1) relevant to only a select few? With Adam's question to Raphael about how to read the heavens, Milton directly faces this exegetical crisis. In philosophical terms, we might say, prelapsarian Adam's is not an innocent question.

Paradise Lost, I will argue, allows us to see that the value of human experience can be appreciated only by those who understand the enabling limitations of that experience. This position implies, with much else, a practice of textual interpretation informed by the concept of accommodation. Milton invokes accommodation (although not by name) in *De Doctrina Christiana*. There he states that we have permission to imagine God with some human attributes, as, for instance, a right hand, a voice, or a throne, for in the Bible he "has disclosed just such an idea of himself to our understanding as he wishes us to possess." Accommodation means a dialogue between God and humankind, Milton implies:

> Let there be no question about it: they understand best what God is like who adjust their understanding to the word of God, for he has adjusted his word to our understanding, and has shown what kind of an idea of him he wishes us to have. (*YP* 6:136)

The Bible *also* accommodates to human understanding, so biblical exegetes explain, its references to sun and moon, stars and planets. Raphael's answer to Adam in Book 8 self-consciously invokes accommodation and in so doing sheds important light on the archangel's apparent refusal to choose between a geocentric and a heliocentric universe. This refusal, which has troubled many readers, will be the initial concern of the essay. I will then turn briefly to Raphael's narrative of Creation in Book 7 to look at the relationship between the structure of the universe and the Creator's command at Genesis 1:22, "Be fruitful and multiply." The essay will end with some speculations about the unspatialized totality that envelops and contains the spatialized universe discussed by Raphael and Adam. But let us begin by considering accommodation.

In employing and reflecting on accommodated language for the cosmology of *Paradise Lost,* Milton draws on (even as he bends to his own uses) a long exegetical tradition that attempted to reconcile biblical and "scientific" accounts of astronomy. The tradition had its main source in Augustine, who insisted that the Bible shapes the profound mysteries of God's creation to fit weak human understanding. His insistence freed readers from having to adhere to a literal reading of verses that concern heavenly bodies. Thus, Augustine explained, Genesis 1:16 ("And God made two great lights; the greater light to rule the day, and the lesser light to rule the night") describes how the sun and moon *appear* to human eyes (Augustine 1:70–71). Of course, at the time Augustine was writing, the Ptolemaic system was universally accepted, and his accommodated readings assume and demonstrate that the Bible supports geocentrism. Centuries later, accommodated readings were called upon to support the new heliocentric system proposed by Copernicus in *De revolutionibus* (1543). Thus redirected and reemployed, accommodation turned out to be one of the Copernicans' most effective polemical weapons.

Copernicans justified invoking accommodation on the principle that God's "two books" cannot be in opposition, as divine truth is one and does not contradict itself. Moreover, they declared, the Bible is not a manual of physics: the book of Scripture teaches spiritual truths; the book of nature teaches truths about Creation. As the Lutheran Georg Joachim Rheticus asked, "who would maintain that knowledge of physics is necessary to salvation?" (qtd. in Snobelen 701). The truths of nature, insisted Copernican astronomers, are best available to those trained specially in observing the heavens. Determined to show that the Bible does not challenge their findings, they devoted particular attention to explicating two biblical verses frequently called upon to support geocentrism: Joshua 10:13 ("And the sun stood still, and the moon stayed, until the people had avenged themselves upon their enemies") and Psalm 19:6 ("[The sun's] going forth *is* from the end of the heaven, and his circuit unto the ends of it"). Neither of these verses, Copernicans admitted, can sustain the theory that the Earth moves around the sun. But they are not intended to, nor to demonstrate *any* astronomical truths, for they use the language and viewpoint of ordinary observers. Deliberately echoing Augustine, Rheticus stated that in such passages the Scriptures "speak of the apparent motion of the Sun, not its absolute state of being" (qtd. in Snobelen 702; see Howell 65). Nor does this reading of the verses imply that the Bible has spoken falsely. As Johannes Kepler put it, "the perception of the eyes also has its truth" (Kepler 60).

In keeping with their conviction that it is not a manual of physics, Copernicans did not claim that the Bible irrefutably demonstrates heliocentrism. Rather, they showed themselves aware of the "inherent flexibility" of accommodation as an interpretive practice (Snobelen 729). The Carmelite priest Paolo Antonio Foscarini pointed in 1615 to the problem of linking the authority of the Bible to a particular cosmological theory, given the tendency of such theories to become outdated over time. Foscarini argued that if Copernicanism were eventually established as true (which he regarded as likely), the Church would save face if in the meantime it were tolerant of accommodated readings of the Bible that supported heliocentrism (Blackwell 261). Tommaso Campanella, a Dominican priest more radical than Foscarini and, like Foscarini, largely, although not entirely, convinced of the truth of Copernicanism, also implied that knowledge about the cosmos is a work in progress to those with the requisite training. He stated in his *Apologia pro Galileo*, published in 1622: "it is clear that Moses set no limits on human knowledge, and that through him God did not teach either physics or astronomy." Nor did Christ: "it would have been superfluous for him, who came to redeem us from sin, to teach us what we are able and obliged to learn on our own" (Campanella 65–66). In his *Astronomia nova* of 1609, Kepler concluded that *both* the book of nature and the book of Scripture are accommodated to human understanding. In terms of the former, he cited the fact that God has deliberately adjusted the speed of planets to musical ratios intelligible to the human intellect (Ravetz 212). In terms of the latter, he pointed to the everyday language in which the Bible speaks of the heavens, which, he insisted, should be retained in preference to obscure technical terminology. For Kepler, in Kenneth Howell's words, "*all* God's dealings with the universe are coloured by accommodation because the cosmos was to be an instrument (sacrament) of celebration and adoration" (Howell 131, emphasis added).

Kepler does not appear in *Paradise Lost*, but there are three allusions in the poem to Kepler's Copernican contemporary, Galileo Galilei. This insistent presence – famously, he is the only contemporary of Milton's mentioned in the poem – has intrigued readers. Without question, Galileo is the most outspoken of all those Copernicans who attempted to reconcile the Bible and heliocentrism by way of accommodation, most notably in his "Letter to the Grand Duchess Christina" (see Drake 145–216 for a translation of "Letter"). In *Paradise Lost*, however, the astronomer's appearances are marked by a concern not with exegesis but with instrumentality. The first allusion to Galileo occurs in Book 1, when Satan's shield is said to hang

> on his shoulders like the moon, whose orb
> Through optic glass the Tuscan artist views
> At evening from the top of Fesole,
> Or in Valdarno, to descry new lands,
> Rivers or mountains in her spotty globe. (1.287–91)

The fact that Galileo is called an "artist" (the only use of the word in *Paradise Lost*) has occasioned some discussion. Since the nineteenth century, it has generally been assumed that Galileo was a heroic figure and would have been recognized as such by Milton. Yet the word "artist" in the early modern period implies a restricted achievement, and Milton never uses the word of himself or any other poet. The earliest sense of the word, still extant in Milton's day, is of one skilled in a practical craft, an artisan. Galileo's craft is the invention, or at least the refining and expert wielding, of the telescope, mentioned in each of his three appearances in *Paradise Lost*. This reiteration hints at dependence, as if Galileo were enclosed in a world of his own manufacture, a sense figuratively expressed in his finding in the moon what he already knows – that is, terrestrial landscapes. Moreover, Galileo, unlike Raphael, can bring only part of the universe into partial focus; he does not have access to the whole picture. The deficiencies of Galileo's vision, in both physical and figurative senses, accordingly become important in the poem's allusions to him. In Book 3, we see, although the astronomer does not, Satan's arrival on the sun:

> There lands the fiend, a spot like which perhaps
> Astronomer in the sun's lucent orb
> Through his glazed optic tube yet never saw. (3.588–90)

Even the most acclaimed "artist" cannot see what a poet can. In Book 5, Galileo's vision is compared directly to Raphael's. Whereas the archangel, descending to Earth, looks down and sees everything at once and without obstruction, the astronomer, looking up, confirms his own preconceptions:

> As when by night the glass
> Of Galileo, less assured, observes
> Imagined lands and regions in the moon: (5.261–63)

The irony of "[a]s when" is considerable, for Raphael's unobstructed angelic vision has little in common with Galileo's "less assured" human observations. The allusions to Galileo thus prepare the way for the dialogue about astronomy in Book 8, when Raphael will show Adam that the truth for which it is his privilege, or fate, to strive is relative to the conditions of human existence.

In *Paradise Lost*, Adam and Eve have only the book of nature in which to read the glory of the Creator. Adam's question to Raphael at 8.15–38 ("When I behold this goodly frame ...") shows him to be a literal reader of the heavens, though one of uncommon ability. Raphael's answer is designed to free him from his literalism. Adam's question begins with an echo of Psalm 8:3 ("When I consider thy heavens, the work of thy fingers, the moon and the stars, which thou hast ordained"). It ends, however, not in wonder, as the psalm does, but in calculation (8.16), and this leads Adam to ask why nature allows the huge sun to revolve around the tiny Earth. By not *simply* explaining heliocentrism to him, Raphael guides Adam, and arguably himself, toward a more subtle, open, and imaginative reading of what the archangel shows is an accommodated text. It is significant that the form of their conversation is a dialogue, the traditional form in which cosmological treatises were written. Meaning emerges dialectically in a dialogue, which implies that Raphael and Adam – and, vicariously, the reader – learn from their interaction with each other. Eve's much-remarked departure at 8.44 insures the continuation of the tradition: Adam's answering her questions and relating to her what he has learned will necessarily give rise to another cosmological dialogue. We might even say that Raphael and Adam's dialogue itself has stemmed from an earlier dialogue between Adam and Eve in Book 4, when Eve, looking up at the stars, asks Adam, "But wherefore all night long shine these, for whom/ This glorious sight, when sleep hath shut all eyes?" (4.657–58). Adam attempts to provide an answer at 4.660–88 but without complete success. It seems likely that his question to Raphael, informed by his newly acquired knowledge of Creation, represents a refined and elaborated version of Eve's question. As for her decision to leave the table, may it not be influenced by her memory that cosmology was the theme of an intimate bedtime conversation with her husband, a conversation that made her "forget all time" (4.639), and by the hope that she and he will enjoy another such conversation before long?

Learning through dialogue is crucial both to the one who asks and to the one who answers questions about cosmology in *Paradise Lost*. To assume an anthropomorphized Raphael who delivers a preexisting body of knowledge to Adam is to fail to recognize the imaginative power of Milton's poem. This power is manifest in the creation of an angelic other whose thinking is intuitive and who understands immediately the implications of Adam's circumstances (the source of his questions) and spells them out, instantly, as he goes. Raphael is not prepared, instructed, or trained: he is not a product of culture. Does he *know* "whether heav'n move or Earth" (8.70)? The answer must be that he figures out the structure of the universe as he talks with Adam – just as, in dialogue with the Father in Book 3, the Son figures out that he will "not long/ Lie vanquished" under Death's power (3.242–43). It is appropriate that Raphael should come to know the human universe through Adam. At the same time, the archangel accepts without demur the fact that God has withheld certain knowledge from angels as well as men, knowledge called simply "the rest" at 8.71. Raphael is thus in a position to say that attaining knowledge of the movement of the Earth or sun "[i]mports not, if thou reckon right" (8.71). This true reckoning (which has nothing to do with measuring and everything to do with judgment) is exemplified in his response to Adam.

What the archangel does not tell Adam, or does not know, can be seen as secondary compared to what he *does* tell and know:

> heav'n
> Is as the book of God before thee set,
> Wherein to read his wondrous works, and learn
> His seasons, hours, or days, or months, or years ... (8.66–69)

Milton's practice throughout *Paradise Lost* embodies the archangel's words, which echo Genesis 1:14: "And God said, Let there be lights in the firmament of the heaven to divide the day from the night; and let them be for signs, and for seasons, and for days, and years." Raphael's words also imply that reading and rereading God's works is what matters, because the book of the world is inexhaustible. To arrive at a fixed interpretation is not the aim of reading a divinely accommodated text. Rather, it is to realize that the text requires and repays continual interpretive activity, the consequence of which is to magnify the Creator. Thus with subtle wordplay Raphael redirects Adam's interest in creatures' "magnitudes" (8.17) to their source in the Creator's "high magnificence" (8.101). Those who will in future "gird the sphere/ With centric and eccentric scribbled o'er,/ Cycle and epicycle, orb in orb," Raphael explains, will make the book of the heavens illegible (8.82–84). Scribblers rather than scribes, they render themselves unable to read and reread God's "wondrous works" (8.68). The tone of ironic amusement in which Raphael dismisses their efforts frees readers of *Paradise Lost* from an obligation to attend to the precise definition of "epicycles" and "eccentrics." For a reader of the poem, as for a reader of the book of the heavens, the danger lies in substituting the annotations for the text itself.

Let us look closely at Raphael's explicit statement about the necessity for an accommodated interpretation of the book of the heavens:

> But this I urge,
> Admitting motion in the heav'ns, to show
> Invalid that which thee to doubt it moved;
> Not that I so affirm, though so it seem
> To thee who hast thy dwelling here on Earth.
> God to remove his ways from human sense,
> Placed heav'n from Earth so far, that earthly sight,
> If it presume, might err in things too high,
> And no advantage gain. (8.114–22)

What Raphael achieves is to help Adam understand and appreciate the text's complexity. The fact that God has removed his ways from human sense (*not* from human intellection) is a reminder that the author of the book of the heavens is spirit, infinite, eternal, immutable, omniscient. From such an author, one cannot expect a text that yields up its richness to those who read literally, or who simply calculate – especially as *seeming* is an integral part of the text (8.117). This is initially surprising. Seeming, after all, is strongly associated with Satanic and postlapsarian erring in *Paradise Lost*. Yet Raphael's words clearly suggest that reading the book of the heavens includes the possibility (if not the inevitability) of misreading it, and that this is beneficial. At this perhaps unexpected point, we would do well to turn for help to what Milton thought about reading the *other* book of God, the book of Scripture.

Over the course of his life, as Dayton Haskins has persuasively demonstrated, Milton moved from the position of affirming "the simple truth plainly revealed in the Scriptures" to a "mature understanding of the Bible as a book marked by many tangles and obscurities" (Haskin 53, 237). The latter conception implies that meaning in Scripture does not reveal itself at once, or even finally, and that therefore a reader's interpretive engagement with the Bible never ends. Each return to the text requires readers to reassess what they had understood before. The Bible provides for such a progressive model of spiritual understanding in Paul's admonition to the

Corinthians: "When I was a child, I spake as a child, I understood as a child, I thought as a child: but when I became a man, I put away childish things" (1 Corinthians 13:11). A "childish" reading is a "misreading" in the sense that it is provisional or intermediate, in accord with an earlier stage of the reader's spiritual maturity. This is not to say, however, that a reader will eventually attain something we might call adult interpretive certainty, for the Bible's obscurities remain. What, we need to ask, is to be gained from giving humanity a text of such interpretive complexity that readers are required continually to engage in rereading it? The answer must surely be that such a text is a never-failing source of creative discovery, discovery that encompasses reader, text, and author. Readers engage in dialogue with their earlier and less mature interpretive selves and thus grow in understanding of themselves; the text, unfolding itself in ever richer and more subtle ways, yields new perceptions about the ways of God to men; and worship of the author of the text is continually renewed in wonder.

It is possible, Dayton Haskin suggests, that Milton found in the interpretive complexities of the book of the world (being revealed ever more clearly by the developments in natural philosophy occurring in his lifetime) a model for the interpretive complexities of the Bible. That is, Milton's realization that the Bible is obscure and tangled may have led him to search "both inside and outside the exegetical tradition to find models for imagining that interpretive complexity was an aspect of the original creation" (Haskin 237). Not only does the book of the world, specifically the book of the heavens, provide such a model, but it also demonstrates the intrinsic worth of the human perspective. The interpretive difficulties that human beings encounter when reading the heavens are the *sine qua non* for deepening their understanding. These are difficulties that stem precisely from the human vantage point, from humans' standing on Earth, in both senses of "standing." Raphael's point at 8.119–22 is that "advantage" is not to be gained by presumption in "things too high," but from the "lowly" human perspective, which encourages the re-creative readings that are one fulfillment of the Creator's command to "be fruitful and multiply." To "err in things too high" is to regard as a disadvantage the indeterminacy that the human vantage point gives. It is to choose to scribble over the heavens, equivalent to blotting out the text, rather than to call upon growing experience and wisdom for successive rereadings.

We might pause here to note that although Raphael declines to recommend one cosmological system over another, it is possible to argue that *Paradise Lost* itself embraces heliocentrism. It does so in ways that exercise readers' interpretive subtlety, in accordance with Raphael's freeing Adam to be a better reader. First, geocentrism is implicitly denigrated in Book 3. There, the seven planetary spheres of the Ptolemaic system, along with the eighth sphere of fixed stars and the ninth or crystalline sphere, appear in the satiric context of the Paradise of Fools, that windy depository of delusion and superstition (3.481–83; see Leonard 2:705–08). One hundred lines later, as the narrator tracks Satan's flight to Earth, heliocentrism appears in the guise of the wondrous cosmic dance. Derived ultimately from Plato's *Timaeus* and elaborated over the centuries, the notion of the cosmic dance envisages the stars and planets moving harmonically around the sun. In Book 3 the narrator describes what Satan would have seen (had he looked) as he flies toward the sun:

> the great luminary
> Aloof the vulgar constellations thick,
> That from his lordly eye keep distance due,
> Dispenses light from far; they as they move
> Their starry dance in numbers that compute
> Days, months, and years, towards his all-cheering lamp
> Turn swift their various motions, or are turned
> By his magnetic beam, that gently warms
> The universe, and to each inward part
> With gentle penetration, though unseen,
> Shoots invisible virtue even to the deep ... (3.576–86)

The heliocentric leaning of this passage is enhanced by the inclusion of the word "magnetic" (3.583), a term associated with Kepler, who famously posited magnetism as the force that holds the planets in their orbits around the sun. Another version of the cosmic dance appears in Book 5, when Raphael describes the angels' "Mystical dance" "about the sacred hill" and likens it to "yonder starry sphere/ Of planets and of fixed in all her wheels .../ mazes intricate,/ Eccentric, intervolved, yet regular/ Then most, when most irregular they seem" (5.619–24). At the center of *this* starry dance is not the sun, but the Son, newly begotten. In contrast, the Satanic version of the cosmic dance is geocentric. It emerges in the lengthy address to the Earth that precedes Satan's temptation of Eve:

> Terrestrial Heav'n, danced round by other heav'ns
> That shine, yet bear their bright officious lamps,
> Light above light, for thee alone, as seems,
> In thee concent'ring all their precious beams
> Of sacred influence: As God in Heav'n
> Is center, yet extends to all, so thou
> Cent'ring receiv'st from all those orbs ... (9.103–09)

A preoccupation with hierarchy is the most striking feature of this Satanic geocentrism. In Satan's imagination, other heavenly bodies dance attendance on Earth, which sits in their midst like an emperor receiving tribute.

The archfiend's term "officious" reminds us that Adam, too, assumes that the stars serve "merely to officiate light/ Round this opacous Earth, this punctual spot,/ One day and night" (8.22–24). But what Satan regards, with perhaps some envy, as the subservience due to rank, Adam regards as disproportionate and superfluous, for, as he claims, Earth is dark and tiny, "opacous" and "punctual" (8.23). Raphael at once challenges Adam's implicit criticism. "[C]onsider first," says the archangel, "that great/ Or bright infers not excellence" (8.90–91). In any case, Raphael declares, "not to Earth are those bright luminaries/ Officious, but to thee Earth's habitant" (8.98–99). The central position of "to thee" in line 99 emphasizes the point. Humanity is the center of the universe. It is essential to keep this centrality in mind when reading Raphael's final cosmological exhortation to Adam: "be lowly wise:/ Think only what concerns thee and thy being" (8.173–74). The archangel's statement is as far as possible from condescension. On the contrary, it asserts the unique place of human beings in the universe: they are the culmination of its creative fruitfulness, and Adam must not let himself be intimidated by the wide expanses of space. Nor should Raphael be taken as meaning that the heavens do *not* concern Adam and his being. *How* they concern Adam and his being is what is at stake, for by reading and rereading the book of the heavens, human beings may realize anew the Creator's glory. Raphael, that is, corrects and refines Adam's criticism of the heavens by offering a vision of a human-centered universe not linked to the geocentrism of Satan or indeed the lingering geocentrism of some early modern astronomers. The injunction to "[t]hink only what concerns thee and thy being" is not anti-intellectualism. Rather, it recognizes that human beings' place on Earth is the solid foundation for all they will come to know, and that more knowledge yields more praise of the Creator. Adam states the principle when he first asks how the universe came to be: "the more we know," Adam says to Raphael, "the more [we are able]/ To magnify his works" (7.96–97).

The interpretive fruitfulness anticipated in Adam's words has its material parallel in the burgeoning of Creation described by Raphael in Book 7. Generation (expressed by the Hebrew word *toledot*, "generations," as at Genesis 2:4: "These are the generations of the heavens and of the earth when they were created") is the governing principle of the Bible's account of Creation and also of the archangel's brief narration of the work of the Six Days. Its brevity is indeed the most salient feature of Raphael's hexameral poem, which *concisely* depicts abundant generation. The best-known hexameral poem in early modern England, Joshua Sylvester's *The Divine Weeks and Works* (a free translation of the *Semaines* of Guillaume de Saluste, Sieur Du Bartas), is more than five thousand lines long, a sprawling, encyclopedic gathering of common wisdom and marvels about the natural world grouped under the category of each Day's Creation. Milton knew it well. The brevity of Raphael's hexameral poem, at a little more than five hundred lines, constitutes a reformation of the genre. There is no place in it for the unexamined rehearsal of disparate bits of emblematic lore and "theological speculation, contemporary science and pseudo-science, and moral reflection" characteristic of Du Bartas and Sylvester's work (Snyder 1). Rather, Raphael's poem represents the natural world as an organic and conceptual whole in which creatures are at one with the sphere they inhabit, and the elaborating of exotic individuals gives way to the spare, dignified naming of representative kinds. We might regard this as the literary equivalent of a well-tended garden, marked not by rampant unproductive growth but by the pruning that encourages fruitfulness. There is, by implication, room in Milton's reformed hexameral poem for what is yet to be discovered. This amounts to an imperative to continue learning, so that, potentially, the dynamic vitality of Creation is paralleled in the growing wisdom of those who magnify it.

Form that contains while encouraging growth is the controlling figure of Creation in *Paradise Lost*. This is made evident when the Son is sent out in his chariot to create the universe out of Chaos. As Raphael explains, the Son, standing "[o]n Heav'nly ground,"

> took the golden compasses, prepared
> In God's eternal store, to circumscribe
> This universe, and all created things:
> One foot he centered, and the other turned
> Round through the vast profundity obscure,
> And said, "Thus far extend, thus far thy bounds,
> This be thy just circumference, O world." (7.210, 225–31)

"O world" captures the sense of a universe whole, unified, and complete. Within this little O, creatures from stars to creeping things praise God by being and moving as themselves. This is not equivalent to the socially conservative notion that each creature has its place; "place" is too static for the dynamic Creation depicted in Raphael's hexameral poem. A rich variety of verbs is, arguably, its most notable linguistic feature and constitutes a lesson on how to magnify God's works: freshly articulating the wonders of Creation, Raphael's very language is fruitfully re-creative.

In the "Heav'nly ground" on which the Son stands in order to circumscribe the universe we glimpse something from which that universe is being differentiated. The new-created universe contains everything spatialized and temporal. In so far as it defines what is "outside" of itself, this other can only be that which has no spatial or temporal extent. Let us call it a nonspatialized, nontemporal totality, or, better, an uncircumscribed totality. Human beings have no access to it, except through accommodated language or the occasional angelic visitor who comes from and goes back into it. Its most recognizable aspect is Heaven, the "empyreal" or "highest" Heaven. The two modifiers are often taken as equivalents, but etymologically "empyreal" means fiery or incandescent, which sits ill with the notion of Heaven either as the "dwelling place" of God or as the location of his throne. This is not of course a literal throne, for the God of *Paradise Lost* has no body. He "is light,/ And never but in unapproachèd light/ Dwelt from eternity" (3.3–5). In whatever sense God dwells in light, or has his dwelling place in the empyreal Heaven, neither "dwell" nor "place" can have anything like ordinary human meaning. Satan, having made his way from Hell, "behold[s]/ Far off th' empyreal Heav'n, extended wide/ In circuit, undetermined square or round" (2.1046–48). Editorial annotations consistently explain this phrase as meaning that the size of Heaven is so great that its shape is impossible for an archangel, although admittedly a fallen one, to ascertain. But "undetermined" may equally signify that Heaven's circuit is "not restrained within limits" (*OED* sense 4), which means that Satan cannot determine its shape because it has no shape. What Milton says of God in *DDC* may be said of Heaven: "a consequence of his infinity, is that God is present everywhere" (*YP* 6:144). Michael makes this clear in Book 11, when he explains to Adam that God's presence is not confined to the Garden of Eden:

> Adam, thou know'st Heav'n his, and all the Earth,
> Not this rock only; his omnipresence fills
> Land, sea, and air, and every kind that lives,
> Fomented by his virtual power and warmed… (*PL* 11.335–38)

The "Heav'n" of line 335 may refer to the heavens of the spatialized universe, or to the uncircumscribed Heaven, or both, which may partly be Michael's point. Indeed, the fact that the poem uses the same name for both the uncircumscribed and the circumscribed heaven(s) hints at, without insisting on, inaccessibility in the latter, though for reasons of distance that are irrelevant to the former.

Paradise Lost allows us to think of the uncircumscribed Heaven as a place with "opal tow'rs and battlements" (2.1049) and simultaneously indicates that it cannot be a place. The paradox is demonstrated with particular clarity when Satan, having emerged from Chaos, sees "his native seat," Heaven, and

> fast by hanging in a golden chain
> This pendant world, in bigness as a star
> Of smallest magnitude close by the moon. (2.1050–53)

These lines have led scholars to produce diagrams of a globe-like universe hanging by a chain from a huge walled Heaven (as in Hughes's edition 180). A vast Chaos is depicted below the tiny universe, and below Chaos, Hell. It is true that "hanging" and "pendant," especially, encourage such a picture. But what Satan sees is the universe hanging not *by* a golden chain but *in* a golden chain, a phrase that evokes (as Alastair Fowler suggests) what the young Milton calls that "universal concord and sweet union of all things which Pythagoras poetically figures as harmony" (*YP* 1:236; Fowler *PL* 2.1051n). Moreover, "pendant" may mean "pending" as well as "suspended," that is, "hanging in the balance" as well as "hanging" (*OED* senses 1a and 4). We may think of the Son's action of circumscribing not as separating the universe from Chaos but as instituting a coherently conceived differentiation in the uncircumscribed totality. It is the antithesis of the incoherent acts of distancing and differentiation on the part of the rebel angels, as when they move to the "north" of Heaven. Of course Hell and "the vast abrupt" of Chaos (2.409) – an abrupt or abyss that is itself "Wide interrupt[ed]" by Satan (3.84) – are the poem's most profound figures for the distancing and differentiation that break the golden chain of concord. Chaos views the golden linking of Heaven and Earth as an encroachment, while the fallen angels are spiritually bound by Hell's "adamantine chains" (1.48). We need to think of Hell and Chaos in terms of logical rather than geographical or geometric space.

These are matters that Raphael and Adam do not broach directly, nor is the reader of *Paradise Lost* encouraged to worry about them. When Raphael says to Adam, "heav'n is for thee too high/ To know what passes there; be lowly wise" (8.172–73), we may wonder, briefly, which heaven he means. But the point in either case, as the dialogue in Book 8 demonstrates, is that knowledge, human knowledge, comes from the world of near and far, up and down, before and after. Is there a parallel lesson for the reader of *Paradise Lost* in Adam's perception that "the prime wisdom" is "not to know at large of things remote/ From use, obscure and subtle, but to know/ That which before us lies in daily life" (8.191–94)? Perhaps something like this: be resolute against erudite and incomprehensible explanations of Renaissance cosmology; read what is in front of you, the poem itself.

NOTES

1 I am grateful to my friend and colleague, Charles Page, for generously sharing ideas about Milton's cosmology and for his guidance as this essay developed. I would also like to thank Louis Schwartz for commenting on drafts of the essay and for his insight about the conjugal delight with which Eve associates cosmology.

Further Reading

Augustine, *The Literal Meaning of Genesis*, ed. and trans. John Hammond Taylor, 2 vols. (New York, 1982).

Benin, Stephen D., *The Footprints of God: Divine Accommodation in Jewish and Christian Thought* (Albany, 1993).

Blackwell, Richard J., *Galileo, Bellarmine, and the Bible: Including a Translation of Foscarini's Letter on the Motion of the Earth* (Notre Dame, IN, 1991).

Boesky, Amy, "Milton, Galileo, and Sunspots: Optics and Certainty in *Paradise Lost*," *MS* 34 (1997), 23–43.

Campanella, Tommaso, *A Defense of Galileo, the Mathematician from Florence*, ed. and trans. Richard J. Blackwell (Notre Dame, IN, 1994).

Drake, Stillman, ed. and trans., *Discoveries and Opinions of Galileo* (Garden City, NY, 1957).

Fowler, Alastair, ed., *John Milton: "Paradise Lost,"* 2nd ed. (London, 1998).

Haskin, Dayton, *Milton's Burden of Interpretation* (Philadelphia, 1994).

Howell, Kenneth J., *God's Two Books: Copernican Cosmology and Biblical Interpretation in Early Modern Science* (Notre Dame, IN, 2002).

Hughes, Merritt Y., ed., *John Milton: Complete Poems and Major Prose* (New York, 1957).

Kepler, Johannes, *New Astronomy*, trans. William H. Donahue (Cambridge, UK, 1992).

Leonard, John, *Faithful Labourers: A Reception History of "Paradise Lost," 1667–1970*, 2 vols. (Oxford, 2013).

McGrath, Alister E., *Science and Religion: An Introduction* (Oxford, 1999).

Ravetz, J. R., "The Copernican Revolution," in *Companion to the History of Modern Science*, ed. R. C. Olby, G. N. Cantor, J. R. R. Christie, and M. J. S. Hodge (London, 1990), 201–16.

Snobelen, Stephen D., "'In the Language of Men': The Hermeneutics of Accommodation in the Scientific Revolution," in *Nature and Scripture in the Abrahamic Religions: Up to 1700*, ed. Jitse M. van der Meer and Scott Mandelbrote, 2 vols. (Leiden, 2008), 2:691–732.

Snyder, Susan, ed., *The Divine Weeks and Works of Guillaume de Saluste*, trans. Joshuah Sylvester, 2 vols. (Oxford, 1979).

Toulmin, Stephen, and J. Goodfield, *The Fabric of the Heavens* (London, 1961).

PART III

10

WILLIAM SHULLENBERGER

Imagining Eden

In his waking words to Eve after their first bout of postlapsarian lovemaking, Adam recognizes the drastic change in human knowing that has befallen them with their tasting of the prohibited Fruit of the Tree of Knowledge:

> our eyes
> Opened we find indeed, and find we know
> Both good and evil, good lost, and evil got,
> Bad fruit of knowledge, if this be to know,
> Which leaves us naked thus, of honor void,
> Of innocence, of faith, of purity... (9.1070–75)

Eden seems irrecoverable after the Fall, but the good that it represents is not. Milton acknowledged this paradox of postlapsarian knowledge in his early pamphlet *Areopagitica*:

> Good and evil we know in the field of this world grow up together almost inseparably; and the knowledge of the good is so involved and interwoven with the knowledge of evil, and in so many cunning resemblances hardly to be discerned, that those confused seeds which were imposed on Psyche as an incessant labor to cull out and sort asunder, were not more intermixed. It was out of the rind of one apple tasted, that the knowledge of good and evil, as two twins cleaving together, leaped forth into the world. And perhaps this is that doom which Adam fell into of knowing good and evil, that is to say, of knowing good by evil. (*MLM* 938–9)

Milton's prescription in *Areopagitica* for living out the ethical challenges of discernment in a fallen world of intermingled good and evil "resemblances" is not to retreat from but to enter into those challenges: "Assuredly we bring not innocence into the world, we bring impurity much rather: that which purifies us is trial, and trial is by what is contrary" (939). The reading of *Paradise Lost* is such a trial. It entails a hard series of acts of discernment, at the heart of which we discover the flickering idea and real hope of a return to a good and delightful human condition, for which everything in us still yearns, in spite of everything that appears to stand between us and its realization.

The tragic narrative of *Paradise Lost* acknowledges that the Fall has exiled us from the original form of that hope, a garden space of boundless fruitfulness and joy, which is washed out and lost at sea with the Flood (11.829–34). But the poem also gives us glimpses and tastes of the many ways in which we can still apprehend and aspire to the paradisal life. The archangel Michael explains to Adam near the end of the poem that this blessing will be present in the inward experience of grace: "then wilt thou not be loath/ To leave this Paradise, but shalt possess/ A paradise within thee, happier far" (12.585–87). We discover that "paradise within" through the reordering of our relations to one another and the world. "[A]dd/ Deeds to thy knowledge answerable," he says. "Add virtue, patience, temperance, add love" (12.581–83). Michael seems to distinguish the "paradise within," a subjective sense of security, sustained by faith and love, from the earthly Paradise forever lost. But his comparison sets them in suggestive relation to one another as much as it sets them apart.

Michael's "paradise within" climaxes a series of analogies in the poem. Indeed, the unfallen Eden seems itself to be a state of felicitous analogies (Swaim 168–75). For example, Eve exercises a capacity for making analogies when she describes to Adam her first moments of waking consciousness. She finds herself drawn by water sounds to a lake into which she gazes, and she discovers there a pure expanse that resembles Heaven and "seem[s] another sky" (4.456–59). She intuitively joins Heaven and Earth in her analogy, and learns something about each of them in the process. Then she discovers, and plays peekaboo with, a mirror image of herself (4.460–65). A voice, presumably the Creator's, interrupts her potentially narcissistic reverie and, enriching the analogical process, promises: "follow me,/ And I will bring thee where no shadow stays/ Thy coming, and thy soft imbraces, he/ Whose image thou art, him thou shalt enjoy/ Inseparably thine, to him shalt bear/ Multitudes like thyself, and thence be called/ Mother of human Race" (4.469–74). This suggests that knowledge and identity in Eden are fashioned analogically: Eve will be related to both her partner and her children by image and similitude. Later, Raphael will alert them to the necessity as well as the uncertainty of analogy between things knowable on Earth and otherwise unknowable of Heaven. As a preface to his brief epic of the War in Heaven, he explains,

> what surmounts the reach
> Of human sense, I shall delineate so,
> By likening spiritual to corporal forms,
> As may express them best, though what if earth

> Be but the shadow of heaven, and things therein
> Each to other like, more than on earth is thought? (5.571–76)

The contrast that Michael proposes at the end of the poem, between the prelapsarian earthly Paradise and the postlapsarian "paradise within," works the same way. The postlapsarian "paradise within" evokes and substantiates the original Eden, and the things that conjoin the two paradises by analogy are more like one another than different. Indeed, we can only imagine that original template of human delight and creative possibility by the things and relations between them of this fallen world. Milton thus cultivates in his readers a double vision of Eden. Even as the poem obliges us to acknowledge the original's irrevocable lostness, it saturates us with a sense of its presence, not only as a memory trace, but as a possibility to be inspired by and live for.

This flickering of likeness and unlikeness between the world we live in and the perfect one that Milton invites us to imagine may seem a roundabout way to approach that archetypal garden space, but Milton's narrative unfolds itself by indirection. In *Paradise Lost*, we approach and enter Eden piggybacking, as it were, on Satan, the solitary scout and outrider from Hell:

> So on he fares, and to the border comes
> Of Eden, where delicious Paradise,
> Now nearer, crowns with her enclosure green,
> As with a rural mound the champaign head
> Of a steep wilderness ...
>   And of pure now purer air
> Meets his approach, and to the heart inspires
> Vernal delight and joy, able to drive
> All sadness but despair... (4.131–35, 153–56)

There is a narrative logic to this point of entry, and to the traveling shot that Satan's point of view provides us of the verdant and unspoiled landscape of the "delicious Paradise." Inheritors of the human condition begotten by Adam and Eve's failures of patience and trust, we, like Satan, carry our sense of fallenness, including its alienating habits of doubt and suspicion, wherever we go, including into an imagined space that Milton insists is unspoiled by them. Yet as Milton keys in the sensory registers of sight and smell, we are already being challenged and encouraged to differentiate between our own and Satan's responses to the offered delight. Unlike the despair driven Satan, we can still experience the wonder and refreshment of fine spring air "that carries the breath of millions of things" returning to life.[1]

If the alignment of points of view acknowledges the fallenness we appear to share with Satan, the differentiation of points of view sharpens our recognition of the realizable possibilities of a condition of wholeness and delight that is lost to Satan. As he describes Eden and provides us imaginative entry into it, Milton deploys a twofold rhetorical and representational strategy. He immerses us in a deep dream of realizable pleasure, but he also alerts us to, and disarms us of, our ingrained suspicions and refusals of it. He makes us face how we assume, like the fallen Satan does, that it's too good to be true, and look for flaws in the original design, both of the Garden's landscape and of its human occupants. The poet seems to provide "ah ha!" moments to encourage such suspicions. But whenever ambiguity of language or episode seems to alert us to potential flaws in the paradisal state, the larger design of such passages challenges us to acknowledge and bracket our suspicions, and to consider how the potential "flaw" we think we have found discovers its place in a more complex verbal and natural economy.

For instance, we may suspect that the "crisped brooks" of the Edenic meadows, "Rolling on orient pearl and sands of gold,/ With *mazy error* under pendant shades" (4.237–39; my emphasis; viz. Fish 135–6), hint at flaws in the design of the paradisal water system. But what first might appear as errancy in this description looks quite different in the larger ecology of the sentence in which it takes its course:

> But rather to tell how, if art could tell,
> How from that sapphire fount the crisped brooks,
> Rolling on orient pearl and sands of gold,
> With *mazy error* under pendant shades
> Ran nectar, visiting each plant, and fed
> Flowers worthy of paradise which not nice art
> In beds and curious knots, but nature boon
> Poured forth profuse on hill and dale and plain,
> Both where the morning sun first warmly smote
> The open field, and where the unpierced shade
> Imbrowned the noontide bow'rs... (4.236–46; my emphasis)

In this context, we can see how the seemingly aimless "mazy error" of the brooks actually serves the nutritive function of a complex environmental dynamic that integrates several specific ecosystems and feeds flora of all kinds, from the "pendant shades" of the forest edge and glades, to meadow flowers of the open field, to the massy tree-sentinels of the climax forest that impenetrably shades the "noontide bowers."

Twice in this passage, Milton confesses the inadequacy of art even to represent, much less to improve upon, this profuse, dynamic, and unpolluted system of mutually nourishing elements and life forms. Here he is playing on the important Renaissance *topos* of nature and art. He seems to be claiming that art, at its best, whether as poetic representation, as in this poem, or as the human shaping of landscape, follows nature, respects its rhythms and designs, and the integrity of its multitudinous forms. Yet the poem cannot be anything but artful, and the poet calls attention to its supreme artfulness even as he expresses aesthetic modesty about art's limits. Milton thus shows how the artist's work contributes the human part to the reciprocities that make the Edenic ecosystem so dynamic. The passage we are reading begins with bejewelled landscape elements that seem very beautiful but highly artificial. "Sapphire fount," "crisped brooks," "orient pearl," "sands of gold:" these noun phrases share the otherworldly rhetoric by which Milton elsewhere tries to evoke the landscapes of Heaven. Perhaps he wants to remind his readers of the otherness of this terrestrial paradise in its as yet unspoiled state. Yet in the course of the clause, this stylized and seemingly static vision of nature dissolves into dynamic nutritive flow, and to an aesthetic that prefigures Romantic naturalism. "Hill and dale and plain," "open field" and "noontide bowers" (and, if we read forward, "lawns, or level downs," "palmy hillock," "irriguous valley," "umbrageous grots and caves/ Of cool recess"): these phrases represent a Wordsworthian nature that we can recognize, for it seems very much like ours. The clause itself is not set off and self-enclosed, but embedded in a spectacularly long complex compound sentence of forty-one lines (4.223–63), all of whose topographical particularities are woven together by the description of the water flow. The sentence surges and meanders, reproducing the flow of the complex water system Milton is describing in the very course and pulse of his syntax. He thus indicates the mutual, eco-linguistic dissolve of the work of artistic representation into the world it tries to evoke, and the emergence of that world, now beheld, as only art can reveal it, in both its dynamism and its design.

The fecund wildness of this space impresses itself upon the archangel Raphael as he takes his first steps on Earth, striding through the "spicy forest" to meet and forewarn Adam and Eve of Satan's dangerous presence in their Garden home:

> [he] now is come
> Into the blissful field, through groves of myrrh,
> And flowering odors, cassia, nard, and balm;
> A wilderness of sweets; for nature here
> Wantoned as in her prime, and played at will
> Her virgin fancies, pouring forth more sweet,
> Wild above rule or art, enormous bliss. (5.291–97)

In contrast to our first approach to Eden, accompanying the fallen Satan, in this passage we share the first impressions of Raphael, in his own unfallen beauty, amazed at a green and burgeoning environment quite different from, but no less beautiful than, the celestial one that he calls home. Here again Milton plays on the art and nature *topos*. Yet the texture and effect of this sentence is quite different. Whereas the riverine sentence, like its subject, flowed through integrated, contiguous, yet self-contained, ecosystems, this sentence evokes both density and the uncontainable outbursting of vegetative energy. The flora intimate the fragrant delights of the Bible's Song of Songs, yet the sensations that this "wilderness of sweets" evokes are not merely literary, but visual, tactile, and olfactory, as the sentence – burgeoning and branching with its flexible, loosely joined phrases and clauses, its propulsive reiterations and alliterations, its lip-pursing semi-vowels and open vowels – enacts what it describes. "Wild above rule or art," the sentence bursts free of the neoclassical poetic standards of proportion, tact, and reasonableness, that were being formalized by Milton's contemporaries in England's Restoration period. It throbs instead with the generative pulse of life that God in the Bible ordained and sanctified with the reiterated imperative, "be fruitful and multiply" (Genesis 1:22, 28). Here again, Milton seems to favor natural spontaneity, energy, and flexibility over the ordering and containing patterns of art (4.241). But he renders this sense of naturalistic respect, indeed awe, through an art that seems to go beyond its own rules, to suggest that in the poem, ecological vision and poetic vision are so reciprocal to one another that they can't be disentangled.

The passage seems to point us in two directions: first, to the origins of this "Wilderness of sweets," and of all of nature, terrestrial and cosmic, in Chaos, the "wild abyss" (2.217) of warring elements, its inexhaustible supply of raw materials ever open and subject to the Creator's intentions; and second, to the analogous transformation of portions of the "wilderness of sweets," of Eden's first growth forest, into a garden space cultivated by the humans to whom God has assigned the "dominion," and with it the responsibility, of earth-care. In Raphael's epic account of the Creation of the Universe, God the Father assigns the joyful labor of Creation, the separation and transformation of portions of Chaos, into the lightsome and fertile orders of nature (7.162–632), to the "begotten Son" (163) whom he praises as "My word, my wisdom, and effectual might" (3.170). In turn he places in the hands of his terrestrial son and daughter, Adam and Eve, also namers and creators by the word, the "pleasant labor" (4.624) of husbandry, of transforming portions of the wilderness of Eden into a Garden even more beautiful, efficiently fruitful, and pleasant.

Milton indicates in several ways that it is the human presence that makes the Garden of Eden what it is, the "crown" (4.133) of terrestrial creation. Although Milton overlays his dynamic and naturalized garden with images and evocations of more stylized, static eternal gardens, principally drawn from classical mythology and literature, and from Dante's *Purgatorio*, Milton's Garden is a working garden of this Earth. Its vegetative fecundity requires care and cultivation, which is the distinctly human opportunity provided by God to Adam and Eve, and a sign of their God-instilled sense of ethical responsibility toward, and delight in, their environment. In the first exchange between the human couple that Satan overhears in his shape-shifting concealment, Adam declares to Eve that the Creator requires nothing of them other than respecting his "one easy prohibition" (4.433) against tasting the Fruit of the Tree of Knowledge, "The only sign of our obedience left/ Among so many signs of power and rule/ Conferr'd upon us, and dominion giv'n/ Over all other creatures that possess/ Earth, air, and sea" (4.428–32). Adam ends this speech to Eve by celebrating "our delightful task/ To prune these growing plants, and tend these flowers,/ which were it toilsome, yet with thee were sweet" (4.436–39).

This moment is quietly startling. Most readers of the biblical account of Eden, from patristic and medieval interpreters to the present, have presumed that Adam and Eve had nothing to do in the unfallen Garden other than pleasure themselves, as if the Garden were the original Club Med, a perfectly groomed and God-manicured leisure resort for consenting adults. Milton dignifies the original humans by showing them discovering for themselves "delightful" work to do, in extending the Creator's impulse toward order, beauty, and fertility through the arts of gardening. This shaping project is one that Adam and Eve are working out for themselves, evidence of their creative and ethical autonomy. God has not assigned to them compulsory labor, nor has he provided a gardening guide or set of tools. He has left them to figure out what it means to exercise "dominion" in their particular domain of the created order, and they have decided that the transformation of some portions of the "wilderness of sweets" into a sustainable garden would be good work to do. They exercise human "dominion" not as domination and exploitation of other creatures, but as nurturing and shaping the network of creaturely interdependencies, of which humans are a uniquely self-conscious and intentional part.

We think too small, if we imagine Adam and Eve's gardening as the weekend upkeep of a suburban vegetable or flower garden, rather than the immense georgic project of turning wilderness into a sustainable and habitable environment (Lewalski 1971; Hiltner 2003). Adam hints at how overwhelming this task must seem, when he expresses some discouragement about the job they have before themselves:

> With first approach of light, we must be risen,
> And at our pleasant labor, to reform
> Yon flowery arbors, yonder allies green,

> Our walk at noon, with branches overgrown,
> That mock our scant manuring, and require
> More hands than ours to lop their wanton growth:
> Those blossoms also, and those dropping gums,
> That lie bestrown unsightly and unsmooth,
> Ask riddance, if we mean to tread with ease;
> Meanwhile, as nature wills, night bids us rest. (4.624–33)

This sounds familiar to postlapsarian readers trying to get to sleep early while already anxious about their next days' workloads. In his phrases expressing irritation and complaint, we can sense Adam's mood souring. The erotic anticipation of the night's pleasures with Eve dissipates in the monitory shrug of the curt final clause, which might be paraphrased, "Come on, honey, we've got a lot of work to do tomorrow, so let's try to get a good night's sleep."

Eve's response, however, wonderfully interrupts and transforms Adam's emerging gloom. First, she tactfully reminds him, in terms that initially may unsettle our modern assumptions about gender equality in marriage, that he is her superior, and that she delights in his authority over her: "God is thy law, thou mine: to know no more/ Is woman's happiest knowledge and her praise" (4.637–38). Sincere as this expression of love is on Eve's part, it is also a good disarming tactic. Adam is bound to receive both the gesture of submission and the compliment, as he has earlier, "in delight/ Both of her beauty and submissive charms" (4.498–99). But there is more to Eve than ritual gestures of obeisance like this one indicate, and more to her effect on Adam. She spontaneously composes for him a rhapsodic love song that reveals her excitement about their life together (4.641–56). The opening nine lines enumerate the sensory and creaturely delights of Eden (4.641–49), and her closing sequence reiterates this catalog of delights in a suspenseful series of negations (650–55) decorously closing with a double negative that weaves all the wonders of Eden into the loving partnership of the pair to whom it has been entrusted: "… Nor grateful evening mild, nor silent night/ With this her solemn bird, nor walk by moon,/ Or glittering starlight without thee is sweet" (4.650–56). Adam has stressed the work ethic by which they are learning to organize and inform their lives, but Eve reminds him of the sweetness of Eden, and of how it is in the mutual partnership of their love for one another that these Edenic blessings have their fulfillment.

Milton periodically genders their contributions to this partnership in ways that seem to privilege Adam. But when Milton dramatizes the lovers engaging with each other, the process of relationship complicates gendered character design and nominal male hierarchy. From our first view of them, Eve and Adam are works in progress, as is their relationship. They learn and grow from one another, discovering who they are in the give-and-take of committed relationship. We see this process of self-giving, mutual enlargement, and transformation in virtually every exchange between Adam and Eve in the middle books of the epic. Thus, the self-appointed labor of cultivating the Garden is analogous with and integral to the ongoing project of cultivating their relationship (Lewalski 1971). There is nothing, indeed, that Adam and Eve can't think and talk about, in shaping their relationships to one another, to their world, and to their Creator. In his treatment of the accelerating growth curve of their knowledge, Milton challenges another traditional and still widely held assumption about the original Garden state of humanity: that knowledge itself is forbidden, and that Edenic bliss is founded on ignorance. Milton represents the Garden as a challenging domain for significant choices, and shows how those choices are informed by dynamic and ever-unfolding thought – thought that is formed in "sweet converse" (9.909).

Sexuality seals and sanctifies the transformative reciprocities between Adam and Eve. One of Milton's most startling inventions in *Paradise Lost* is the fullness and frankness of their erotic delight. Traditional readings of the Creation and Fall in Genesis introduced suspicions of sexuality, and conditioned – and still condition – readers and interpreters of those narratives to presume that the tasting of the forbidden fruit was synonymous with the discovery of sexual desire: sexuality was accused as the cause as well as the immediate consequence of the Fall, the destroyer of innocence and the sign of its destruction. But Milton challenges this understanding by embodying the erotic promise of Edenic life embedded in the first two chapters of Genesis. Although the Genesis authors and editors are discreet about the erotics of unfallen Eden, Milton develops their cue that it is perhaps the greatest of Edenic blessings, a perfecting of human existence. Surprisingly, it is Satan, their voyeuristic stalker and would-be destroyer, who makes explicit the connection between environment and mind:

> Sight-hateful, sight tormenting! Thus these two
> Imparadised in one another's arms
> The happier Eden, shall enjoy their fill
> Of bliss on bliss, while I to Hell am thrust,
> Where neither joy nor love, but fierce desire,
> Among our other torments not the least
> Still unfulfilled with pain of longing pines… (4.505–11)

Satan is stunned into admission of truth in this moment, testifying that Edenic delight is consummated in the human embrace, which torments him into a deeper realization of his own alienation and despair, fueled by a desire that can only gratify itself by trying to destroy what has awakened it.

How, then, does the prohibited Fruit of the Tree of Knowledge of Good and Evil figure in the dense organic, intellectual, and moral ecosystems that constitute Edenic existence? Overhearing Adam's explanation of the "One easy prohibition" among the "choice/ Unlimited of manifold delights" (4.433–35), Satan concludes that this is a sign of God's oppressive injustice: "knowledge forbidden?/ Suspicious, reasonless. Why should their Lord/ Envy them that? .../ ... do they only stand/ By ignorance, is that their happy state,/ The proof of their obedience and their faith?" (4.513–20). Milton cannily lets Satan give voice to our own likely skeptical responses to the prohibition. Satan's response to Adam's explanation overlooks Adam's original understanding of the Fruit as a symbol, "the only sign of our obedience left/ Among so many signs of power and rule/ Conferred upon us" (4.428–30). As a "sign of obedience," the Fruit signifies that humans, sovereigns over all else in the world, are creatures like the other "living souls" (7.388, 451, 528) they share that world with. Their being is not "self-begot, self-raised/ By [their] own quickening power," as Satan deludes himself into claiming (5.860), but a gift. By abstaining from eating the Fruit, Eve and Adam signal their recognition of this gift, and of its Giver, which in turn orders all the relations of Eden rightly, investing the created goodness of the world with the distinctive ethical goodness of human intention. It follows from this recognition that nothing else need be forbidden, for the ordering of their relations to God rightly ensures that Adam and Eve would not take their dominion on Earth as a license for domination or exploitation, but as an opportunity for cultivation and creation.

How swiftly it all seems to collapse, this flourishing, self-sustaining vision of human and natural possibility that Milton evokes through more than five books of his twelve-book epic. The swiftness of their Fall seems to suggest Eve and Adam have not been as capable or prepared to confront temptation as Raphael had insisted: "stand fast; to stand or fall/ Free in thine own arbitrement it lies./ Perfect within, no outward aid require" (8.640–42). Eve's fall is an intellectual collapse, an apparent weakness in reasoning power that Satan spots and exploits; Adam's seems a consequence of excessive love, the emotional vulnerability for which Raphael had scolded him (8.588–94). But Milton makes us think twice about presuming previous flaws from the negative outcomes of decisions and actions. Eve has shown intelligence and resolve in persuading her husband to agree to the division of their labor (9.205–384). In response to Raphael, Adam has defended and refined his understanding of how human love is different from the "carnal pleasure" enjoyed by other creatures, a life-giving source of their "Union of mind," "one soul" (8.604). Milton's invocation to Book 9 frames its tragic action by contrasting the "tedious havoc" (9.30) of warrior-heroism celebrated in traditional epics to "the better fortitude/ Of patience and heroic martyrdom/ Unsung" (9.31–33). "Patience and heroic martyrdom" will be necessary virtues in the postlapsarian world, as the archangel Michael instructs Adam in spiritual warfare. Milton's foregrounding of these previously unsung virtues prior to their Fall anticipates where Eve and Adam go wrong: not through the inevitable consequence of some internal "flaw," but through failures of patience and the capacity to love selflessly rather than possessively.

In the devastating impact of this pair of human choices upon Eden itself, Milton shows how human fallenness first manifests itself in exploiting and destroying the natural world. Given that it's not just an apple that she plucks, but the symbol of people's right relations to one another, their environing world, and their Creator, Eve's initial transgression sets in motion the sorry history of aggressive human despoliation of nature:

> her rash hand in evil hour
> Forth reaching to the Fruit, she pluck'd, she eat:
> Earth felt the wound, and nature from her seat
> Sighing through all her works gave signs of woe,
> That all was lost. (9.780–84)

Adam's impulsive participation in Eve's rash choice completes "the mortal Sin/ Original," and the immediate response of all Creation is the "groan" of painfully permanent organic rupture between nature and her human caretakers (9.1000–04).

> Earth trembl'd from her entrails, as again
> In pangs, and nature gave a second groan,
> Sky low'r'd, and muttering thunder, some sad drops
> Wept at completing of the mortal sin
> Original. (9.1000–04)

Perhaps there is a slightly hopeful suggestiveness in the birth pangs here, but poor Earth is bearing sin and death now, materializing the monstrous world of pain, death, and guilt, whose allegorical generation Sin recounted so vividly to her father Satan in Book 2 (2.777–89).

"All was lost" – yet was it? Eve's last lines in the poem – the last human words spoken in Eden – revive and play on the word "all," taking responsibility for the irreversible finality of her transgression, yet also intimating the regeneration of hope, and the will to realize that hope, of such a Garden as she and Adam must leave behind:

> thou to mee
> Art *all* things under Heav'n, *all* places thou,
> Who for my willful crime art banisht hence.
> This further consolation yet secure

> I carry hence; though *all* by mee is lost,
> Such favor I unworthy am voutsaf't,
> By mee the Promis'd Seed shall *all* restore.
>
> (12.622–23; my emphasis)

In acknowledging the loss, and her responsibility for it, she paradoxically perceives the providential opportunity for restoration, through the exercise of the love toward others, and toward the world, that a regenerated faith in providence makes newly possible.

And so, although it seems that the Fall exiles us forever from the possibilities of full and integrated humanity enjoyed by our "Grand Parents" (1.29), Milton's poem suggests that we can intimate, and enact, the paradisal life for which humans were created, even in the painful and divisive conditions of the fallen world. The very fact of the poem itself, the visionary testimony of a blind and politically defeated but unbroken man, is evidence of this promissory opportunity. From the archaic text of Genesis, Milton recovers and revivifies the idea of a garden state that fosters work, knowledge, and love. His vision challenges his readers to take up the responsibility and hard work of shaping the fallen world we inhabit into a life-surround that is truly habitable and friendly to human works of creativity and sociability. Michael's envisioning for Adam of a "Paradise within" (12.587) does not promise a private interior happiness, sequestered from the world, but a spiritual condition that is at once personal and political, lived out in the demanding exercise of freedom: we might yet be living in Eden, if we are willing to take the risk of understanding who we are meant to be. We know from the momentary fullness of our experiences of pleasure, discovery, justice, and love how near at hand that may be, even as it emerges from the daily knowledge of what human beings can be capable, desirous, and willing to do to one another, and to the world we share. We may find ourselves so moved by the reading of Eden in *Paradise Lost* as to live toward it, wherever we find ourselves in this fallen world. To try to do so would be to raise, as Milton puts it in his epic sequel, *Paradise Regained*, "Eden ... in the waste Wilderness" (*PR* 1.7).

NOTES

1 Thanks to Clare Follmann, email to author, 9/24/2012.

Further Reading

Fenton, Mary C., *Milton's Places of Hope: Spiritual and Political Connections of Hope with Land* (Aldershot, UK, 2003).
Fish, Stanley, *Surprised by Sin: The Reader in "Paradise Lost"* (New York, 1967).
Hiltner, Ken, *Milton and Ecology* (Cambridge, UK, 2003).
Kermode, Frank, "Adam Unparadised," in *The Living Milton: Essays by Various Hands*, ed. Frank Kermode (London, 1960) 85–123.
Lewalski, Barbara, "Innocence and Experience in Milton's Eden," in *New Essays on "Paradise Lost,"* ed. Thomas Kranidas (Berkeley, CA, 1971) 86–117.
McColley, Diane K., *Milton's Eve* (Urbana, IL, 1983).
  Poetry and Ecology in the Age of Milton and Marvell (Aldershot, UK, 2007).
Swaim, Kathleen, *Before and After the Fall: Contrasting Modes in "Paradise Lost"* (Amherst, MA, 1986).

11

JOAD RAYMOND

Milton's Angels

Good and Bad Angels

Milton's Satan is the disturbingly human embodiment of metaphysical evil, but he is also an angel. He has to do as angels do, see as angels see, move as angels move. Milton does not release him from the conditions of angelic being, and this makes his struggle and his decisions and decision making all the more directly pertinent to Milton's human readers: and this is one reason why some of those readers, seeing themselves reflected in God's antagonist, have declared him the hero of the poem. There are few moments in Western literature as sublime, shocking, dizzying, discomforting as the opening sequence of *Paradise Lost*, following its invocation:

> Hurled headlong flaming from th' ethereal sky
> With hideous ruin and combustion down
> To bottomless perdition, there to dwell
> In adamantine chains and penal fire,
> Who durst defy th' Omnipotent to arms. (3.45–49)

That Satan is a conscious being who feels gravity and heat, and a moral being aware of his own growing depravity, is essential to his suffering.

In addition to his structural role in Milton's plot, Satan also plays an aesthetic and ethical role, the latter as an exemplar not only of evil but also of poor decision making. Satan falls through pride; characteristically Milton uses pride as the foundation and connecting point of a plethora of sins, including but not limited to ambition, hate, vanity, and desire for revenge. This matches traditions of Christian exegesis dating at least as far back as Origen (Raymond 2010, 73–8). Milton, however, shows – imaginatively explores – how that pride infects Satan's perceptions and his determinations. He "thought himself impaired" (5.665) at the Son's promotion (and this is not a commonplace of Christian exegesis), responds with contempt, refuses to worship, and seduces through persuasion those who are already under his command (thus betraying the responsibilities of leadership). Satan's foil in this is a lowly angel under his command: Abdiel. Satan, at the end of Book 5 and at his most heroic, gorgeous, and defiant, tempts his subordinates with a speech about freedom and equality. His subordinates listen: "Thus far his bold discourse without control/ Had audience" (5.803–04). Notice how "without control" refers *both* to his discourse and to the having of an audience; Abdiel *is* Satan's control. A single angel stands against him fortified by zealous adoration of God. Abdiel matches Satan's sophisticated rhetorications with solid arguments about the nature of Heaven, but no one supports him. He thus becomes the paragon of *virtuous* choice.

Abdiel alone makes the right decision when his peers and superiors fail. They judge his words as "out of season ... / Or singular or rash" (5.850–51). His arguments are founded on reason, and experience (of God's goodness) insofar as it supports the conclusions of reason, although they seem to a modern reader to be intuitive, to rest on what he already knows. This need not represent a contradiction: Raphael has already explained to Adam that while humans rely on discursive reason, angelic reason is intuitive, hence their reason might seem like intuition to the human reader (5.487–90). Most important, however, are the circumstances of choosing. Abdiel sticks to his arguments even when "Encompassed round with foes" (5.876), he ignores their "hostile scorn," and the fact that he is in a minority of one does not lure him "To swerve from truth, or change his constant mind/ Though single" (5.902–03).

To treat these angels as human characters, and to apply to them modes of character criticism associated with nineteenth-century novels, in which stories are translated into ethical guides to conduct, is to miss the interesting twist: to understand the angels as humanlike characters is to efface the gulf between us and them, and this gulf is one of the things that Milton brings into focus at moments throughout the poem. Angels and humans are not the same (and the illumination of species-difference should also problematize the moral judgments that critics offer on Adam and Eve). While they have much in common, and while Milton envisages future human growth so that they will have even more in common (5.493–500), the foundations of angelic being are different: they are sempiternal and incorporeal, created rather than born, and created free from sin (prelapsarian Adam and Eve are nearer to angels than are subsequent humans). Angelic and human ontology – the foundations of their being – are different. Abdiel is a pattern of correct decision making, and Satan of flawed, but their actions cannot be simply translated to human equivalents. To read and fully appreciate the poem we need to grasp the distinctiveness of Milton's angelology.

Reformation

A brief note on the word "angelology" is necessary. Strictly speaking it is an anachronism: Milton's contemporaries did not commonly use the word, and they did not think of it as a conceptually distinct mode of writing or group of texts. This was because writing about the doctrine, nature, offices, and being of angels was seldom distinct: instead it thoroughly interpenetrated other forms of writing, from poetry through theology to journalism. I will use the term to designate understandings of the doctrine, nature, offices, and being of angels, even though to Milton's contemporaries angels did not inhabit a "–logy" but were everywhere.

In 1500, Christian doctrine concerning angels was extensive and elaborate. The dominant exegetical tradition extended back through Aquinas, and the Parisian universities in the thirteenth and fourteenth centuries, through Bonaventure and Peter Lombard, through pseudo-Dionysius and Augustine to the Church Fathers, including Justin Martyr, Tertullian, Cyprian, Irenaeus, and Origen. Their writings were themselves influenced by various non-Christian traditions: ancient Egyptians, Assyrians, Zoroastrians, and Judaism. Much Christian exegesis was not, or was only loosely, based on Scripture. Pseudo-Dionysius, whose *Celestial Hierarchy* is one of the most profoundly influential accounts of angels, describes personal visions of Heaven. He also presents himself as a first-century convert, although as early as the mid-fifteenth century Lorenzo Valla and others demonstrated that this was untrue: in fact his treatises were written in the fifth or sixth centuries. He is unique in his authority and in the elaborate detail of his pronouncements, but he is also representative of the tendency within the Church to accept non-scriptural doctrines, and to build further structures on those doctrines. It was against this that later Protestants so vehemently reacted, and John Calvin singled out pseudo-Dionysius for particular scorn: "If one should read that booke, he would thinke that the man were slipped downe from heauen, and did tell of things not that he had learned by hearesay, but that he had seene with his eyes" (Calvin 1611, 65). Might the same not be said of Milton? Other exegetes would inform interpretation of Scripture with other authorities and sources of information: for Bonaventure and Aquinas, Aristotle was especially useful. Both asked questions about the angels of Scripture that could be answered through examining angels as beings within the purview of natural philosophy. How did angels move? How fast did they move? How did they speak? How much might they know? Milton, though no admirer of Aquinas, was sympathetic to this approach. While his theological treatise *De Doctrina Christiana* is reserved in its opinions, and is based on Scripture rather than later traditions, *Paradise Lost* ventures opinions on angels that extend far beyond what the Bible authorizes, and appears to use reason and natural philosophy to think about them.

But the Reformers of the sixteenth and seventeenth centuries reacted against the extra-scriptural expanses of pre-Reformation angel doctrine, and set about stripping it down, through iconoclasm and an iconoclastic scriptural minimalism. The Protestant Bible (which rejects as apocryphal twelve books that appear in Catholic bibles) contains almost three hundred references to angels. These, indirect and slight as many of them are on the material facts that many Christians sought, are extraordinarily slim foundations for the capacious body of doctrine that Protestants came to reject. Again, the quotable Calvin wrote: "if we will be rightly wise, we must leaue those vanities that idle men haue taught without warrant of the word of God, concerning the nature, degree, and multitude of Angels" (Calvin 1611, 65). Protestants challenged a number of central doctrines of Roman Catholic angelology: individual Guardian angels, the pseudo-Dionysian hierarchies (Mohamed 2008), the efficacy (and legitimacy) of prayers to and invocation of angels, the insight of angels into human souls and thoughts, the continuing intercession of angels and their appearance to humans (which most Protestants thought ended with the Apostolic age). Milton takes a broadly reformed position on all of these, but the complexities of doctrine and debate meant that in practice the dividing lines were neither absolute nor always clear: many Protestants diverged and shared beliefs with Roman Catholics, while Roman Catholics pruned some of the overgrown doctrines of the Church. Counter-Reformation theologians made Roman Catholic doctrine more rigorous, and corrected the looseness with which support had been found in Scripture and tradition; they also adapted angelology to more up-to-date humanist and natural-philosophical scholarship. Simultaneously Protestant theologians began to explore, in scriptural commentaries, systematic theologies (of which DDC is one), and sermons, many of the same questions that a previous generation had dismissed or ignored: when were angels created, when and why did they fall, how do they know things, do they have bodies, do they make noise, how do they sense things, do they have free-will, do they have individual names or names of offices, what are their purposes in creation? Scholastic angelologists had never actually debated how many angels could dance on a pinhead: that was a slur cast upon them by seventeenth-century Protestants. However, Protestants opened up the same questions about angels and the physics of place that would have made such a question meaningful (West 1955; Raymond 2010, 48–88; Raymond 2011). Many of these questions are implicitly answered in Milton's poetic narrative.

In sum, angels offered a rich and dense cluster of topics in various modes of religious writing when Milton wrote his epic. Their immediate soteriological relevance had, moreover, been enhanced in the 1640s, when civil war and political revolution made them more immediate: people had visions of angels, prophets claimed to have been inspired by them, and swelling millenarianism brought them into closer contact with human experience. Radical writers discovered angels everywhere, but other, non-enthusiast and non-antiformalist writers also wrote about them more frequently, exploring angelological issues and using them in metaphors or rhetorical devices (Raymond 2010, 89–124). Some who saw and conversed with actual, creaturely angels actively sought to summon them by ritual magic. Among these was the Behmenist John Pordage, a minister in Berkshire (ejected in 1654) who gathered a church around him, had conversations with angels in his kitchen, and was a charismatic leader in the 1640s through the 1670s; his son Samuel proceeded to write an epic poem that describes a voyage around inner and outer universes in the company of a guardian angel. This poem, *Mundorum Explicatio* (1661), offers a striking and underexplored parallel with *Paradise Lost* (Raymond 2010, 125–61). Others also explored angels in epic poetry around this time: Phineas Fletcher's *Locustae, vel Pietas Jesuitica* (1627), Thomas Heywood's *Hierarchie of the Blessed Angels* (1635), Abraham Cowley's *Davideis* (1656), and, exactly contemporary with Milton, Lucy Hutchinson's *Order and Disorder* (written 1660–79), not to mention others, such as George Wither, who used angels in narrative poems. Poets explored angels partly because angels (and especially theories of angelic apparitions and assumed bodies) provided a means of meditating on literary representation and inspiration. Far from consigning angels to pre-Reformation foolishness and excess, Protestants wrote about angels extensively and imaginatively. Angels were used to understand and explain the universe, to organize knowledge, to describe spiritual experience, to bring ineffable truths within the compass of human understanding and imagination.

Milton was thus, concerning his interest in angels, in some respects typical of his age – typical of Reformation theologians and of seventeenth-century vernacular poets. Despite his emphasis on the primacy of Scripture, and his rejection of much unsupported patristic doctrine, he used angels imaginatively and exploratively. He did so on the basis of extended reflection on their place in creation and their soteriological significance. But having reflected on this, and unlike other writers, Protestant and Roman Catholic, he absorbed it into his storytelling, and through his storytelling was able to explore, develop, and extend what he believed. From this arises the peculiar intensity of his angelology and its poetry.

Angelic Ontology

Milton draws attention to the disparity between humans and angels implicitly throughout the poem (as when the angels throw mountains and fly through space), but also explicitly in Book 8, toward the close of the conversation between Raphael and Adam. Adam tries to explain his feelings for Eve and the "Commotion strange" (5.531) he experiences when looking at her, the lack and vulnerability he feels in the shadow of her beauty, and he muses on his sense of imperfection, notwithstanding his conscious understanding of his actual superiority in things that matter. Raphael responds censoriously and didactically: angels do not understand that kind of love. "Half abashed" at Raphael's response, Adam must explain to the angel what he understands by love:

> Neither her outside formed so fair, nor aught
> In procreation common to all kinds
> (Though higher of the genial beds by far,
> And with mysterious reverence I deem)
> So much delights me, as those graceful acts,
> Those thousand decencies that daily flow
> From all her words and actions, mixed with love
> And sweet compliance, which declare unfeigned
> Union of mind, or in us both one soul ... (8.596–604)

Love, Adam reminds the angel, leads up to Heaven. Yet angels do not experience love in this way, so Adam's description of what it feels like to miss a rib is quite alien to Raphael.

This subtle failure in interspecies communication builds up to one of the passages in the epic in which the strangeness of angels is brought into the foreground. Adam asks Raphael if angels love, and how they express that love, by looking or touching. He receives a warm description of what sounds like angelic sexual intercourse:

> Whatever pure thou in the body enjoyst
> (And pure thou wert created) we enjoy
> In eminence, and obstacle find none
> Of membrane, joint, or limb, exclusive bars:
> Easier than air with air, if spirits embrace,
> Total they mix, union of pure with pure
> Desiring; nor restrained conveyance need
> As flesh to mix with flesh, or soul with soul. (8.622–29)

It necessarily sounds like intercourse, because that is how we (humans) must receive and understand a description of penetrative amatory pleasures. Angels are material beings, composed of a tenuous form of matter. They are incorporeal, but assume bodies at will as their purposes necessitate (Fallon 1991, 137–67). Substantial yet without determined bodies, they are not limited by sexual difference, as a resonant passage in Book 1 asserts:

> spirits when they please
> Can either sex assume, or both; so soft
> And uncompounded is their essence pure … (1.423–25)

By "uncompounded" the narrator means not made from elements, or from mixed elements; a characteristic Miltonic negative that renders mysterious the undefinable, divine matter from which spirits are made. This is all conducive to physical gratification. This sex is also apparently thoroughly promiscuous; there is no marriage in Heaven, according to Matthew 22:30.

Angels are different from humans, but the two species have much in common. This is partly because they share the foundations of a narrative poem, in which characters move through time and space, exchange words, and perform actions that have consequences; but also because they are material, created beings who operate through reason, have finite knowledge and senses, and follow the commands of God through freewill. If we think of angels as distinct, carefully imagined and constructed beings, rather than humans with additions, their realization and their roles in the epic appear all the more significant and striking.

Aspects of angelic life and being in the poem demand attentive reading. Angels not only sing as Adam and Eve approach their bed; they sing through the night while humans sleep – just as nightingales do (4.602–03) – and they sing in Heaven and in Hell for recreation. They do not sing for humans, but because music is part of their being. Theirs is a noisy universe: Adam and Eve can hear their songs from Earth, as Adam describes:

> … how often from the steep
> Of echoing hill or thicket have we heard
> Celestial voices to the midnight air,
> Sole, or responsive each to other's note
> Singing their great Creator: oft in bands
> While they keep watch, or nightly rounding walk
> With Heav'nly touch of instrumental sounds
> In full harmonic number joined, their songs
> Divide the night, and lift our thoughts to heaven. (4.680–88)

The image emerges from traditional iconography (Frye), but Milton characteristically follows it through and imagines its implications for the universe, and for the angels themselves. Celestial music shapes the universe, but it also is audible to humans, which means that angels must make noise of a conventional (and not purely symbolic) kind. Book 8 begins, with lines added in 1674:

> The angel ended, and in Adam's ear
> So charming left his voice, that he awhile
> Thought him still speaking, still stood fixed to hear... (8.1–3)

While many Christian exegetes described ways in which angels could project thoughts into the human mind, Milton's angels are simply but intoxicatingly audible. This means, presumably, that they also play actual instruments – harps in fact (3.366). Even the fallen angels perform, to console their loss (2.547–52). And when Satan, disguised as a serpent, tempts Eve, the narrator pauses to consider the mechanics of speech:

> glad
> Of her attention gained, with serpent tongue
> Organic, or impulse of vocal air,
> His fraudulent temptation thus began. (9.528–31)

Or is one of the most consequential words in *Paradise Lost*. Here it signals a strangely and significantly superfluous consideration. Does Satan manipulate the serpent's tongue (as angels can when they possess bodies, according to some commentaries on angels), or does he use his own being to produce sound directly though incorporeally in the air (as other authorities suggest)? It scarcely matters (and surely the narrator knows the answer in any case?), yet the narrator discreetly alludes to this dichotomy in lines that might easily be passed over as insignificant. Why? To draw attention to Satan's endless duplicity? To ask readers to unpick the significance of each alternative? To remind readers of the non-definitive nature of contemporary angelology? To mock angelological debates that look for answers regardless of the relevance of the answers?

A similar exercise – unpicking the material basis of Milton's narrative – can be undertaken for his accounts of motion, material form, names, taste, sight, the identity of the angels in Revelation, their day of creation, and other aspects of angelic ontology. One becomes evident in Book 4, when the angels, including Ithuriel, discover Satan disguised as a toad whispering in Eve's ear. Initially the phrase "Squat like a toad" (4.800) might be interpreted as a pure simile, indicating that Satan is like a toad in the way he squats; yet subsequent events suggest that he is squatting in the assumed form of a toad. Ithuriel touches Satan with his spear, and, because "no falsehood can endure/ Touch of celestial temper, but returns/ Of force to its own likeness: up he starts," returning to his own shape (4.811–19).

Symbolically and allegorically the passage signifies the power of frail purity over mighty corruption, the affinity between fraud and disguise, the final account to which evil will always be brought. These meanings might be sufficient to overshadow the curious detail that Satan has his *own shape*. Can Milton mean this? After all, as we have seen, the incorporeality of angels permits them to change shape at will. Yet Milton does mean this, as he repeats this phrase, and similar words, through the poem: while angels are incorporeal, and thus have no fixed form, and can thus assume shapes as they choose, they are nonetheless material, and have a form that reflects who they are. Fallen angels seem to be less able to change form at will – although Satan is the most prolific shape-shifter, as Book 4 reveals – and this "proper shape" represents the limitations of the will, and is associated with some of the limitations of having a body (though none of the pleasures). In Book 10 God punishes the fallen angels by transforming them into serpents. The proper shape is a potential for corporeality as beings descend the hierarchy of nature; Adam is correspondingly promised a sublimation of his body, so that one day he will be able to share the food of angels (5.493–95). Conversely, when Satan returns to his "proper shape" at the touch of Ithuriel's spear, he is not immediately recognized, as his "lustre" is "visibly impaired" (4.850); his brightness is diminished. His shape has deteriorated with his fall from perfection.

The capacity to change shape is integral to the fallen angels' ability to deceive humans. Yet even unfallen angels have an implicit shape. When Raphael flies to Earth he travels – or seems as he travels – as a phoenix. Thus he appears to the birds he passes as he flies: "to all the Fowles he seems/ A *Phœnix*" (5.271–72). The phrase perhaps only conveys that he looks *like* a phoenix, a mere similitude that is emphasized by the choice of a mythological bird (one can be like, but not actually be, something that is not real), a bird associated, as the development of the simile (5.272–74) notes, with pagan, and therefore spurious, religion. Yet when Raphael lands, he actually transforms:

> He lights, and to his proper shape returns
> A seraph winged; six wings he wore, to shade
> His lineaments divine ... (5.276–78)

The transformation is both literal and metaphorical. The wings are in part symbolic, signifying speed, as Milton writes in his *DDC* (*YP* 6:315), and the difficulty of traveling at finite speeds, but they are also real. Wings belonging to the fallen angels rustle; Raphael's shed a "heavenly fragrance" (*PL* 1.768; 5.286). They are part of his visible brilliance (defined by his closeness to and ardor for God, rather than the hierarchical status in much traditional angelology) and simultaneously prevent that brilliance from blinding the humans. While Raphael can freely present other forms, this is his proper shape, and significantly he assumes this, and not a disguise, when conversing with Adam and Eve. In a departure from Isaiah 6:2, one source for this passage, the first pair of wings covers his shoulders rather than his face: so he communicates with the humans face to face, unmasked, unshaded. The proper shape of angels is also an incidental detail that determines the narrative during the war in heaven in Book 6. The unfallen angels dress in "arms" of "golden panoply" (6.527) (panoply derives from a Greek word for full body armor, and was used in a spiritual sense in several seventeenth-century English sermons; the Son also wears "celestial panoply" at 6.760). Because they are armed (by which the poet means furnished with both arms and armor), they find themselves unable to avoid their enemies canon shot "By quick contraction or remove" (6.597). The consequences are worse for the fallen angels when the unfallen angels respond by throwing hills at them (one of the earliest literary representations of the dangers of military escalation), as their spiritual being has (already) grown gross through sin:

> Their armour helped their harm, crushed in and bruised
> Into their substance pent, which wrought them pain (6.656–57)

Dressed in armor, neither fallen nor unfallen angels can alter their shape, or alter it swiftly enough to wriggle out and avoid projectiles; and the fallen can experience pain. Yet why should angels of any sort choose to wear armor when they are incorporeal and, when unfallen, invulnerable? To some early readers this seemed nonsensical or even absurd. These readers were perhaps less than attentive to the question of angelic substance, and to Milton's subtle yet persistent distinction between matter and bodies. The armor of angels is one of the seemingly intractable critical puzzles surrounding *Paradise Lost*, and a source of the earliest complaints about its representational mode. Yet is actual armor entirely implausible? It fits the martial-ceremonial theme of Heaven, and angels are potentially susceptible to bleeding ("a Nectarous humor .../ Sanguin, such as Celestial Spirits may bleed" [6.332–33]) and wounds. Were the spirits of humans entirely separate from their substance (as opposed to their bodies), they might not need material armor. Angels wear full body armor, a panoply, because it protects the spirit; yet angels are wholly spirits (and wholly material spirits), and it is their spiritual substance that needs protection. As spirit is substantial, so should be spiritual armor. The problem is an intricate one, but it is not unreasonable that the armor is both literal and symbolic.

There is also the problem of travel. While others' angels traveled by instant transport, or, following Thomas Aquinas, through discontinuous time, Milton's labor through time and space. Abdiel flies across Heaven

through a whole night, arriving at dawn (the episode extends across the
boundary between Books 5 and 6). Even in terrestrial creation traveling
is time consuming. In his journey from Heaven to Earth Raphael sets out
at "the morning hour," and arrives "ere mid-day" (8.811–12). Uriel rides
a sunbeam (4.555–56). When Satan flies from the Gates of Hell he initially soars through space by the power of his great wings, but when he
unexpectedly meets

> A vast vacuity: all unawares
> Fluttering his pennons vain plumb down he drops
> Ten thousand fathom deep ... (2.932–34)

A fiery, nitric cloud rebuffs his fall. A fallen angel cannot fly in a vacuum;
even though Raphael can apparently fly to the gates of Hell (he tells Adam
that he and a legion of angels inspected them on the day that Adam was
created; 8.229–33). Angelic flight is burdensome, fast but finite, sensitive to
terrain. This is not merely decorative, but carefully worked into the plot; the
otherness of angels is not incidental, but integral to the poem.

Digestion

It is in Raphael's discussion of digestion that Milton foregrounds his engagement with other, non-scriptural writing about angels. Digestion was a common
topic in scriptural commentary because of Genesis 18, when Abraham eats a
meal with two disguised angelic visitors. Some commentators suggested that
the assumed bodies of the angels digested the food, others that the apparition
of eating was miraculous, and the food simply vanished. Milton's Raphael,
emphasising angel-human sociability, articulates a different elucidation:

> Therefore what he gives
> (Whose praise be ever sung) to man in part
> Spiritual, may of purest spirits be found
> No ingrateful food; and food alike those pure
> Intelligential substances require
> As doth your rational; and both contain
> Within them every lower faculty
> Of sense, whereby they hear, see, smell, touch, taste,
> Tasting concoct, digest, assimilate,
> And corporeal to incorporeal turn.
> For know, whatever was created, needs
> To be sustained and fed ... (5.404–15)

Milton's angels actually need sustenance (in Heaven they eat "ambrosial
fruitage" [5.427]), and their digestive processes are sufficiently robust to

deal with human food. Instead of presenting a semblance or apparition of eating to Adam and Eve, Raphael actually eats, converting the corporeal matter to incorporeal matter (glossing Genesis 18:8: "they did eat"). Milton uses the narrative moment as an occasion to explicate his theory of matter: all of creation is substantial, but there is a hierarchy from corporeal to spiritual/incorporeal, a hierarchy that permits movement through a process that is very much like digestion. It is an expansive pun in a poem that is centered on an act of dietary transgression. This is a rare moment in which the poem becomes didactic about angels – its standard mode of conveying an understanding of angels is through narrative – and shortly thereafter the narrator puts aside theological abstractions, further emphasizing Milton's engagement with non-scriptural writing here:

> So down they sat,
> And to their viands fell, nor seemingly
> The angel, nor in mist, the common gloss
> Of theologians, but with keen despatch
> Of real hunger, and concoctive heat
> To transubstantiate ... (5.433–38)

The reference to the "common gloss/ Of theologians" seems dismissive, yet the deeper interest in questions of angelic being and action indicates that Milton's attitude is far from contempt. Milton is working through his own angels-on-a-pinhead question: his theory of material angels resolves what happens in Genesis 18, and his narrative provides an occasion for presenting this account. The poetry and the theology feed into each other. Milton's resolution to the question is characteristically literal-minded.

Another passage in which Milton's views on angels are manifestly heterodox enough to have attracted attention and comment is Raphael's account of angelic sexual intercourse, quoted and discussed earlier. Yet, digestion and sex are only two aspects of Milton's more extensive angelology (and there is much more not explored here). We know that Milton held some of these tenets from his unpublished and incomplete *DDC*, much of which was written contemporaneously with *Paradise Lost*, and we regard a systematic statement of doctrine as closer to personal beliefs than an imaginative poem. But in the case of *Paradise Lost*, a poem underpinned by the theory of accommodation (a Christian doctrine of representation, in which the ineffable is lowered and human understanding lifted so that they meet without misrepresentation) and a strong sense of prophetic inspiration, imaginative narrative and theological reason can work in unison in order to challenge the dichotomy between the two. I would suggest that Milton did not think that *Paradise Lost* was fiction in any limited sense of that word.

Conclusions

One of the angels' most prolific activities in *Paradise Lost* is talking. Angels converse with each other and with humans. Angels narrate much of the poem. They enjoy explaining. Angels are sociable beings, especially the "social spirit" Raphael (5.221). They seem to take as much pleasure from language and communication as from singing. Perhaps the matter of angelic sexual intercourse should be reconsidered in the light of this. Critics have seized upon it as a moment of daring imagination, in which Milton challenged conventions to make something strange and new. But why should we think of the pleasure of sex as self-evident? What the passage also uncovers for the reader is that angels are beings who, like humans, incline to pleasure, and who experience the world as something full of wonder and sublimity. They are not cogs in the cosmos, beatific lights and mere messengers in the service of humanity, but beings who have an intellectual, sociable, sensual life.

The angels of *Paradise Lost* serve several functions. They provide a means of telling the story; they are the plot's machinery and architecture; they interact with and inform humans; their fall presents a parallel with Adam and Eve's, but is also causally connected to it; they make decisions, and make mistakes; they offer a bridge between Heaven and Earth. The epic has humanity at its center, but angels provide a frame through which the tragedy of Adam and Eve, their domestic relationship and poignant sin, are given cosmic significance.

Early readers of Milton were fascinated and dazzled by his angels. The first critical annotator of the poem (Patrick Hume in 1695) was captivated by them; their armor was much regretted by others; eighteenth-century epics borrowed heavily (and often cumbersomely) from Milton's angelic machinery. Angels were central to the way in which William Blake engaged with and interpreted and adapted Milton, as he made plain in *The Marriage of Heaven and Hell* (1790), and to Philip Pullman's (mis-) reading of Milton in his brilliant *His Dark Materials* trilogy (1995–2000). Somehow modern criticism has seldom focused on Milton's angels, at least collectively, perhaps because they are so ubiquitous, perhaps because ancient and early-modern angelology is so bewildering and extensive. Yet, in a very real sense, *Paradise Lost* is a poem made from angels.[1]

NOTES

1 I would like to dedicate this essay to David Aers.

Further Reading

Calvin, John, *The Institution of Christian Religion*, trans. Thomas Norton (London, 1611).

Fallon, Stephen M., *Milton among the Philosophers: Poetry and Materialism in Seventeenth-Century England* (Ithaca, NY, 1991).

Frye, Roland Mushat, *Milton's Imagery and the Visual Arts: Iconographic Tradition in the Epic Poems* (Princeton, NJ, 1978).

Hume, Patrick, *Annotations on Milton's "Paradise Lost"* (London, 1695).

Mohamed, Feisal G., *In the Anteroom of Divinity: The Reformation of the Angels from Colet to Milton* (Toronto, 2008).

Raymond, Joad, ed., *Conversations with Angels: Essays Towards a History of Spiritual Communication, 1100–1700* (Basingstoke, UK, 2011).

Milton's Angels: The Early Modern Imagination (Oxford, 2010).

West, Philip, *Milton and the Angels* (Athens, GA, 1955).

12

SHANNON MILLER

Gender

Paradise Lost is Milton's most sustained attempt to represent in poetry gender roles, relations, and hierarchy. In the course of his introduction of Adam and Eve in Book 4, the (divergent) stories of creation they relate there and in Book 8 (along with that Book's debates over gender hierarchy and desire), and finally in the way Milton presents the consequences of the Fall, we observe the process by which gender is constructed as a cultural category. This process, nonetheless, is heavily contested, as the poem raises, rather than always answers, questions about matters like Adam's primacy, Eve's sufficiency, and the role of gender hierarchy within the household. Division marks Milton's attempts to stabilize the poem's presentation of gender, and while the poem may effectively stabilize its categories in its last four Books, the questions it raises – even for critics quite divided over the poem's representation of gender and of Eve – show it actively participating in a seventeenth-century cultural debate about the status of women that continues to resonate even today.

Obviously primary to the narrative of *Paradise Lost*, the Genesis account of Adam and Eve's creation establishes that clear gender roles were a result of the Fall: husbands "shall rule" over their wives while men will labor on the land and women will suffer pain in childbirth. The familial hierarchy established in this account was central to seventeenth-century political theory, organizing both the domestic and the public spheres. Husbands were considered the rulers of the household, while the household provided an analog for the commonwealth. As Gordon Schochet and Rachel Weil have observed, seventeenth-century patriarchalist political thought grounded its claims about kingship on the biblical authority granted to husbands over wives. The effect of these biblical strictures was felt at every level in the culture. Yet the hierarchy they prescribed is actually challenged by the compositional practices of the Bible. As scholars have shown, the opening books of Genesis are a fusion of two distinct accounts: Genesis 1, the Priestly (P) account, differs dramatically from Genesis 2, the Yahwist (J) account. As

Mary Nyquist has succinctly outlined, a potential vision of equality between man and woman appears in Genesis 1's "male and female created he them," while Genesis 2 inscribes Adam's superiority over Eve because she is created second and made from Adam himself. Nyquist has argued that Milton, recognizing that the biblical text allowed for readings more complex than conventional understanding of them allowed, attempted in *Paradise Lost* to knit the two accounts together, allowing their divergence to resonate throughout the poem.

In doing so, Milton was responding to the cultural dynamics of his time. The literary and cultural texts of the early and middle seventeenth century suggest that traditional gender roles were under significant pressure. Such texts present us with, for example, the active involvement of powerful wives in the English Civil War, women prophets predicting England's future, and female petitioners challenging Parliamentary decisions: these women defied cultural expectations that they be "chaste, silent, and obedient." Discourses meant to instantiate and maintain women's roles, such as domestic manuals, religious sermons, and antifeminist attacks, shared bookstall space with responses defending women. Although this antifeminist tradition reached back to the Medieval period, it became reenergized in the late sixteenth and early seventeenth century. Defenses of women, some even authored by women themselves, returned to Genesis and the portrait of Eve to elevate her and all women, often through a reconsideration of the divergence between the P and J texts. Rachel Speght's and Esther Sowernam's 1617 texts, *A Mouzell for Melastomus* and *Esther hath hang'd Haman*, for example, drew directly on that divergence, inverting some of the key terms of the antifeminist rhetoric. Sowernam uses the primacy of Adam's creation in the J text to transform Eve into the purer creation: Adam was made of earth, she notes, but Eve was made from the more refined material of man himself. And while Adam may have been made first, Eve's secondariness actually makes her, to use the words Milton would later use, "Heav'n's last best gift" (*PL* 5.19).

Milton's response to such cultural pressures and reconsiderations doesn't unfold so simply as a defense of Eve and womankind. The Book 2 portrayal of Sin as a serpentine female, for example, draws on a motif common in antifeminist accounts, and it creates a context for viewing women that can never be fully forgotten as one enters into Eden in Book 4. The opening description of Adam and Eve probably reenvisions our encounter with Sin: the first couple is unquestionably idealized. Yet this account simultaneously stresses that subordination follows from the differences between the genders:

> Two of far nobler shape erect and tall,
> Godlike erect, with native honor clad
> In naked majesty seemed lords of all,

> And worthy seemed, for in their looks divine
> The image of their glorious Maker shone,
> Truth, wisdom, sanctitude severe and pure,
> Severe but in true filial freedom placed;
> Whence true authority in men; though both
> Not equal, as their sex not equal seemed;
> For contemplation he and valor formed,
> For softness she and sweet attractive grace,
> He for God only, she for God in him ... (4.288–99)

The description fuses Genesis 1 and 2, initially offering an account of Adam and Eve as co-equal by granting them both "naked majesty" such that they "seemed lords of all," much as Genesis 1 grants mankind dominion: "let *them* have dominion over" the world (1:26; my emphasis). Yet at line 295, Milton's assertion that "true authority" resides "in men" initiates a gender specific differentiation of Adam and Eve that reflects the creation narrative in Genesis 2 and some of its more traditional implications. Milton further underscores the difference that gender differences make, repeating "not equal" twice in line 296 and elaborating on Adam's contemplative nature and his "valor," which are contrasted with Eve's "softness" and "sweet attractive grace" (297–98). The line "He for God only, she for God in him" further invokes the process of Adam's initial creation and Eve as a product of Adam's rib; if Adam is once removed from divinity, she is twice removed. The twelve lines that follow, which describe their bodies in some detail, then fully inscribe the secondary status of Eve.

Milton's seeming reconciliation of the divergent accounts of creation in Genesis 1 and 2 is immediately repeated, but then subsequently challenged by the succeeding scenes in Book 4. In his opening speech, Adam invokes a Genesis 1-like account of their creation and the prohibition of the fruit, while Eve narrates her status, her creation, and the initiation of her relationship with Adam in language consistent with Genesis 2. The divergent biblical source texts thus sustain *Paradise Lost*'s conflicted portrait of gender. Following the transformation of their joint "naked majesty" into a status described as "not equal" at line 296, Adam registers Genesis 1's collective assignment of their "dominion" in their first conversation. In describing "so many signs of power and rule/ Conferred upon us, and dominion giv'n/ Over all other creatures," Adam echoes the sentimental account of Eve that he gave at the beginning of his speech (his first in the poem), when he called her his "Sole *partner* and sole part of all these joys" (4.429–31; 411; my emphasis). Although Adam avoids establishing his priority at line 411, Eve ventriloquizes aspects of the Genesis 2 account of her creation. Her line, "O thou for whom/ And from whom I was formed flesh of thy flesh,/ And without whom am to no end, my guide/ And head"

(4.440–43), effectively underscores her secondary status. Eve's subsequent recollection of her creation will dramatize aspects of Genesis 2 while qualifying
her descriptor of Adam as "my guide/ And head."

Eve's account is particularly complicated in this regard. Following her
creation, Eve tells us, she was attracted to her own image, which she saw
reflected in the water of a lake near the place where she first woke up. After
God "invisibly" leads Eve away from that image to her mate, she initially
rejects Adam: "back I turn'd," she tells us, preferring "the smooth wat'ry
image" (4.476; 480). She is only turned around again by Adam's sudden
seizure of her hand. Christine Froula argues that Eve, in the course of this
sequence, is schooled in the cultural elevation of Adam's "manly grace/ And
wisdom" over her mere "beauty" and a narcissistic tendency toward self-
love (4.490–91). For Froula, Eve demonstrates that she has learned to speak
the patriarchalist message of hierarchy, one that disputes the "dominion"
that Adam and Eve both were given "Over all other creatures that possess/
Earth, air, and sea" (4.430–32). Ventriloquizing Adam, she recounts the climactic moment of the sequence:

> "... Part of my soul I seek thee, and thee claim
> My other half." With that thy gentle hand
> Seized mine, I yielded, and from that time see
> How beauty is excelled by manly grace
> And wisdom, which alone is truly fair. (4.487–91)

Adam's language of possession – here recounted by Eve – modifies the portrait of shared "dominion" that characterized the opening seven lines of
their Book 4 description and Adam's speech preceding Eve's creation narrative. In repeating Adam's "claim" on her, Eve supports the traditional reading of Genesis 2's account of gender distinction and validates the post-fall
authority granted to Adam in Genesis 3, supplanting the joint dominion first
awarded to both of them.

This process continues when we later hear Adam's version of these same
events, part of the long account he gives to the archangel Raphael of his own
creation and early experiences in Book 8. His account structures the whole
of the book, which unfolds in three distinct movements. In the opening
sequence, Adam asks and Raphael responds to questions about the structure
of the cosmos. In the second, Adam relates the story of his own creation,
including his memory of Eve's creation, and in the final sequence, Raphael
admonishes Adam, insisting upon the necessity of a gendered hierarchy. In
the book's middle movement, Adam's account of his creation starkly differs from Eve's. Adam is created under an open sky, Eve "Under a shade"
(4.451). After her creation, Eve looks downward toward her reflection in

the lake, but in Book 8 Adam turns his "wond'ring eyes" "Straight toward heav'n" (8.257). Adam immediately assumes "some great Maker" has created him, while Eve is drawn into a narcissistic reverie (8.278). Even more significant are their unaligned memories of their first meeting. In Eve's version, Adam asserts his authority through his "claim" and "Seiz[ing]" of Eve's hand, but in Adam's account Eve "turned" from him because she "would be wooed, and not unsought be won" (4.487, 489; 8.507, 503).

These distinct, even competing, memories return us to the competition between equality and hierarchy recorded in Book 4. Among the most interesting passages in the account are lines 8.494–98, where Adam echoes the language designating marriage from Genesis 2:23–24: "I now see/ Bone of my bone, flesh of my flesh, my self/ Before me; woman is her name, of man/ Extracted; for this cause he shall forgo/ Father and mother, and to his wife adhere." Milton adds "my self/ Before me" to this echo of Genesis. This addition recalls the language of equality between Adam and Eve, but the description of Eve's secondary creation, especially her naming as a being "extracted" from man, resurrects the secondariness that the Genesis 2 account was traditionally understood to assert. Phrasing that invokes hierarchy and equality simultaneously continues in Adam's portrait of the courtship he claims followed as he deploys the language of political authority: "I followed her, she what was honor knew,/ And with *obsequious majesty* approved/ My pleaded reason" (8.508–10; my emphasis). If in her memory she "yielded" to his seizure of her hand, in Adam's memory her courtly response seems to elevate her in his mind (4.489). His linking of "majesty" to the oxymoronic descriptor "obsequious" grants Eve a moment of "dominion," while at the same time accounting for her submission to his grabbing her hand. Sustaining, rather than shifting away from, the tension between the two Genesis accounts, Milton alternately introduces and attempts to silence the political implications of Genesis 1.

Milton's ordering of these two accounts is also significant. By putting Eve's narrative first, the poem reverses the more hierarchical creation order of Genesis 2. By positioning the better creation – supposedly Adam's – second in the sequence, the poem illustrates for us the somewhat subversive possibility that Heaven's last gift is the "best gift." Adam occupies, by narrative if not biblical sequence, the position of the second creation, and this opens up the intellectual possibility of defining Eve as in some sense primary. Adam's later descriptions of her "complete[ness]," her "absolute[ness]," and "As one intended first," then resonate with that possibility. I am not suggesting that a genuinely subversive, feminist inversion of the gender hierarchy exists within *Paradise Lost*; the poem will increasingly assert that Eve must "acknowledge [Adam] her head" (8.574), a continuity with Book 4's

"He for God only, she for God in him" that extends through to the epic's final books (4.299). But the poem introduces a structural irony, offering a reworked narrative of creation that highlights Eve's primacy while working in other ways to assert Eve's secondary status. This structural enactment of a gender hierarchy inversion resonates with Adam's description of Eve in the closing lines of Book 8, one that will trigger Raphael's admonishment.

In that final discussion, Adam describes the power of the "passion" he first felt on seeing Eve, which made him "weak/ Against the charm of beauty's powerful glance" (8.530, 532–33). Critics have frequently noted the danger Adam's uxoriousness poses to Adam and Eve's unfallen state, but the key threat is his willingness to imagine the inversion of the very hierarchy Eve articulated in Book 4. As Adam tries to account for how he feels in Eve's presence, he seems able to outline to Raphael what the hierarchy should be. Yet that does not describe Adam's experience of Eve:

> For well I understand in the prime end
> Of nature her th' inferior, in the mind
> And inward faculties, which most excel,
> In outward also her resembling less
> His image who made both, and less expressing
> The character of that dominion giv'n
> O'er other creatures; yet when I approach
> Her loveliness, so absolute she seems
> And in herself complete, so well to know
> Her own, that what she wills to do or say,
> Seems wisest, virtuousest, discreetest, best;
> All higher knowledge in her presence falls
> Degraded, wisdom in discourse with her
> Loses discount'nanced, and like folly shows;
> Authority and reason on her wait,
> As one intended first, not after made
> Occasionally … (8:540–56)

Eve's narrative of her creation illustrated problems – she is first attracted to herself and initially turns away from Adam – that are resolved through her ultimate elevation of masculine grace and wisdom over female beauty. Adam's speech works inversely. He can articulate the party line about male authority: she is less like God, made as she is from Adam; she illustrates less "dominion" over other creatures, recalling Book 4's assertion that "true authority" exists "in men" (4.295). But these traditional distinctions collapse within his speech. Adam proceeds to elevate her over himself, granting her the "majesty" he recalls from her creation: Eve becomes "wisest, virtuousest, discreetest, best" and, in a phrase that rewrites her previously limited "dominion," she seems "absolute." A parallel to Milton's ordering of the distinct creation stories, Adam inverts the very creation stories that had been integrated in Book 4's description of the first couple. Instead of asserting the secondary nature of Eve's creation in Genesis 2 and echoed in his creation narrative, Adam now challenges that status all together, saying she seems "As one intended first, not after made/ Occasionally" (8.556–57). Earlier in his speech to Raphael, Adam mused that God "from my side subducting, took perhaps/ More than enough" (8.536–37). The very elements of Eve's inferiority, including that she was made from Adam and thus owes her creation to him, become transformed into an argument about her "complete[ness]." Here, Adam seems influenced by arguments, made earlier by Agrippa and female defenders such as Rachel Speght and Ester Sowernam, that stress Eve's greater refinement: as the last creation, she is the better creation.

Raphael, however, attempts to reassert the proper gender hierarchy disrupted by Adam's speech: "with contracted brow" he insists that Adam not attribute "overmuch to things/ Less excellent," since it is only "An outside" to which Adam is responding (8.560, 565–66, 568). Adam's response to Raphael emphasizes the domestic context of his love for Eve, listing at line 596 the same lovely traits that prompted him to call Eve "absolute" and "complete." Yet while Adam asserts "these subject [me] not" (8.607), his invocation of political subjection simultaneously recalls the "majesty" accorded to Eve only lines before. Additionally, Adam can only assert his own control through the use of negative grammatical constructions within this sequence: he is "not therefore foiled," or overcome by the emotional power exerted by Eve (8.608). He opens his defense with just such a linguistic contortion: "Neither her outside formed so fair, nor aught/ In procreation common to all kinds .../ So much delights me ..." (596–97, 600). Adam's subsequent turn to angelic sex parallels his use of evasive language in response to Raphael. But in having Adam ask about the ungendered, as well as non-material, sexual activities of the angels, Milton indirectly focuses our attention on the gendered nature of the human condition, and the accompanying problem of gendered hierarchy that resonates throughout Book 8. Adam can't succeed in explicitly remapping his earlier "problematic" inversion of hierarchy, as he neither fully defends it nor reestablishes the more traditional order. Further, his inquiry about relationships that evade the challenges of gender exposes the elusiveness of a proper and stable gender hierarchy as we enter Book 9.

As readers, we have experienced structural and thematic challenges to such a hierarchy, challenges sustained through a motif of division. One might expect destabilizing narratives to recede in Book 9. Yet this motif of division continues in a series of "pre-falls" as the story unfolds. As Adam and Eve prepare for the day's labor in the Garden, Eve's practical but also highly inventive suggestion of dividing their labor prompts Adam's condescending response: "nothing lovelier can be found/ In woman, than to study household good,/ And good works in her husband to promote" (9.232–34). Adam's statement reasserts the hierarchy on which Raphael had insisted in Book 8, but the effect instead sustains and extends the motif of division introduced by Eve. Adam has linked her to "household good" as well as defined her as the helpmeet who promotes good works in her husband. But this division of the household from a larger public sphere – which David Norbrook has seen modeled in the all-male discussion between Raphael and Adam (115) – will result in the very language of political authority from which Eve has been at times distanced and at other times associated.

Division consequently becomes a major theme of the book: the idea of division of labor prompts Adam's division between household and public spheres. Adam and Eve's resulting spat creates physical and emotional division between the couple that predicts their division from God as a consequence of the Fall. The very questions of gendered hierarchy and gendered identities continue to put pressure on, possibly even create, these divisions. Eve's suggestion that they separate in order to maximize their gardening labor prompts Adam's concern that Eve not be exposed to their "foe" alone (9.253). As their debate continues, Adam asserts the kind of authority on which Raphael had insisted: "The wife .../ Safest and seemliest by her husband stays" (9.267–68). But Eve, who experiences this as "unkindness," ultimately seizes on Adam's words that "trial unsought" may find them both "securer," or less on guard than Eve is likely to be when she's alone, expecting an attack (9.271; 370–71). Her response, "our trial, when least sought,/ May find us both perhaps far less prepared" (380–81), sustains the upending of a strictly maintained gender hierarchy. Any exclusive male access to "wisdom" and intellectual capacity is challenged by Eve's own arguments echoing *Areopagitica*'s rejection of "a fugitive and cloistered virtue ... that never sallies out and sees her adversary" (*MLM* 939). It may be "seemliest" for a "submiss" wife to remain with her husband, but Eve suspends this hierarchy by deploying Adam's response to her thoughts about individual trial, and invoking Milton's own language, to justify her departure (8.377).

Milton's representation of Eve's fall emphasizes the effect of these discussions – between Adam and Raphael, and between Adam and Eve – about a gendered hierarchy. Eve's seduction into eating the apple obviously has many components: the sensuousness of the fruit encourages her in the final moment, invoking a cultural association between women and the physical senses; Satan appeals to her curiosity and vanity, both considered traditional female weaknesses. As Diane McColley has noted, these conventional female traits are present in Milton's representation of Eve, although they do not negate what is largely still – in the course of the poem – a positive view of her. Analogs of the Fall story, for example, (like those by Hugo Grotius and Serafino della Salandra) stress Eve's immediate curiosity or her fetishistic obsession with the fruit. Another of Milton's notable divergences from the analogs is the sequence's emphasis on forms of political authority. Eve engages the issue of hierarchy immediately after the Fall, wondering whether the fruit could "render [her] more equal, and perhaps,/ A thing not undesirable, sometime/ Superior; for inferior who is free?" (9.823–25). Satan's own process of seduction has clearly shaped her musings; he has centered his temptation on issues of political authority from which the poem, Raphael, and, most recently, Adam have tried to distance Eve. In the course of his temptation, Satan deploys a series of political titles for Eve: "sovereign mistress," "Empress of this fair world," "Sov'reign of creatures, universal dame," "Queen of this universe," and finally "Goddess humane" as he draws Eve to the final "rash" taking of the fruit (9.532; 568; 612; 684; 732; 780).

In addition to disobeying God, Eve actively contemplates the meaning and implications of "equal," a word on which so much emphasis has been placed since Book 4's introduction of Adam and Eve as "Not equal, as their sex not equal seemed" (296). Eve appeals to Adam to taste of the fruit through the language of equality: "Thou therefore also taste, that equal lot/ May join us, equal joy, as equal love;/ Lest thou not tasting, different degree/ Disjoin us ..." (9.881–84). Eve now imagines herself in an elevated state to which she can bring Adam. As her argument inverts the distance to divinity asserted in "He for God only, she for God in him," Eve is looking to reclaim the "dominion" initially granted to both of them in Genesis 1 but gradually relocated onto only Adam. This impulse works hand in hand with the larger issues of primacy and secondariness that Genesis 1 and 2 introduce, and which the poem has engaged continually. After her fall, but before his, Adam describes her as "fairest of creation, last and best/ Of all God's works" (9.896–97). Now explicitly reinforcing his Book 5 description of Eve as "Heav'n's last best gift," Adam engages the problem of the sequence of the creation, articulating what the poem's structuring of their creation narratives has suggested. All of the efforts to stabilize these categories have failed as Eve beseeches Adam to follow her into disobedience, and he, for fear of losing her, does.

Yet Eve has also rebelled against her secondary position as articulated by Raphael and the construction of a gender hierarchy the poem attempts to model. *Paradise Lost*'s ability to simultaneously describe Eve as the "best" creation and as the lesser creation only ends at the Fall and the consequent biblical injunction from Genesis: "thy desire shall be for thy husband, and he shall rule over thee" (3:16). The assertion of authority after the Fall is equally clear in the Son's admonition to Adam: "Was she thy God, that her thou didst obey/ Before his voice, or was she made thy guide,/ Superior, or but equal, that to her/ Thou didst resign thy manhood, and the place/ Wherein God set thee above her made of thee,/ And for thee" (10.145–50). All of the certainty established in Book 4's first description of them, but then challenged as the epic moved forward, is now reasserted by God: Eve was "lovely to attract/ Thy love, not thy subjection." (10.152–53). "[H]er gifts" were appropriately, or "well seemed" "under [Adam's] government," but it was "Unseemly" for her "to bear rule, which was thy part" (10.153–55). Echoing the language of "seemed" in the Book 4 description, but now clarifying this gendered authority to be suitable or seemly, this passage reasserts the hierarchy sketched in our opening view of Adam and Eve. These injunctions now follow Genesis 3's explicit statement, "to thy husband's will/ Thine shall submit, he over thee shall rule" (*PL* 10.195–96).

This assertion of gendered roles seemingly accomplished, Book 10's final section shows Adam's and Eve's responses to God's punishments for the Fall. Adam's politically-articulated authority will no longer be challenged, either by him, Eve, or the structure of the text. And yet his responses both reflect and expose the social construction of this language of hierarchy. Critics are routinely critical of Adam's Book 10 antifeminist attack on Eve, a forty-line diatribe against all women that begins "Out of my sight, thou serpent" (10.867). As Adam invokes traditional motifs about women, casting Eve as the "last" creation that is a "defect/ Of nature" (10.890–92), he no longer will question the issues of primacy and secondariness their respective creation stories introduced into the poem. In fact, Adam attacks Eve for all of the weaknesses of women chronicled in antifeminist tracts: she is aligned with the serpent, cast as inherently bad, attacked for pride and vanity, and accused of sexually manipulating men. In other words, Adam recites, but also creates, these cultural stereotypes before any other people or even communities exist.

The attack becomes a self-conscious acknowledgement of the tradition's faulty representation of women, but also an illustration of the tradition's effectiveness. Eve's response confirms this, as her submission is complete as well as visually enacted for us. She falls "humble" at Adam's feet (9.911–12), where she is "... *submissive* in distress" (10.942; my emphasis). She further confirms her necessary submission by revising line 299 of Book 4 ("He for God only, she for God in him"). "[T]hou/ Against God only, I against God and thee" have sinned, Eve says, accepting Adam's authority over her along with his blame (10.930–31). Her gracious acceptance of that blame does not validate his diatribe, nor the antifeminist tradition that he anticipates, even creates in this moment. The untraditionally positive portrayal of Eve is, in fact, clearest at this point in the text, where her submission is presented as a Christ-like willingness to accept *all* the blame: "Me me only just object of his ire" (10.936). Through her actions, then, Eve turns the emotional tide of Book 10, and Adam's "heart relent[s]/ Towards her" (10.940–41). She also models an acceptance of the gender roles that have gradually solidified in the course of the text. Book 10 will still remind us of an Eve who can act in defiance of the plan. Her proposal for suicide, for example, shows the same innovation as her Book 9 idea for the division of labor. But after the Fall, commandments are followed, as the previously innovative Eve accedes to the cultural dictum that it is "Unseemly to bear rule" as a woman.

In the course of reading *Paradise Lost*, my students have often cited, and agreed with, a bumper sticker that reads, "Eve was framed." The assignment of guilt that the slogan resists joins a second and more resonant meaning: that the cultural framing of gender itself is one of *Paradise Lost*'s more astonishing contributions to both Milton's period and our own. By exploring and exposing the process by which a gendered hierarchy is created and then naturalized in the seventeenth century, the poem may uphold its own cultural views of women's secondary status. But its disputes – with Genesis, within itself, and between individual reader's responses to Adam and Eve – expose the problems presented by a stable gender hierarchy. Twenty-first-century students, male and female, most likely will resist the resulting hierarchy that the poem ultimately articulates, but its origins are perhaps the most important element of the epic for them to encounter and, like the poem itself and its long tradition of critics, to dispute.

Further Reading

Froula, Christine, "When Eve Reads Milton: Undoing the Canonical Economy," *Critical Inquiry* 10, 2 (1983), 321–47.

Grotius, Hugo, *Adamus Exul, in The Celestial Cycle: The Theme of "Paradise Lost" in World Literature, with Translations of the Major Analogues*, ed. Watson Kirkconnell (Toronto, 1952), 96–220.

Guillory, John, "From the Superfluous to the Supernumerary: Reading Gender into *Paradise Lost*," in *Soliciting Interpretation: Literary Theory and Seventeenth-Century English Poetry*, ed. Elizabeth D. Harvey and Katharine Eisaman Maus (Chicago, 1990), 68–88.

McBride, Kari Boyd and John C. Ulreich, "'Eves Apologie': Agrippa, Lanyer, and Milton," in *"All in All": Unity, Diversity, and the Miltonic Perspective*, ed. Charles W. Durham and Kristen A. Pruitt (Selingsgrove, PA, 1999), 100–11.

McColley, Diane Kelsey, *Milton's Eve* (Urbana, IL, 1983).

Miller, Shannon, *Engendering the Fall: John Milton and Seventeenth-Century Women Writers* (Philadelphia, 2008).

Norbrook, David, *Writing the English Republic: Poetry, Rhetoric and Politics, 1627–1660* (Cambridge, UK, 1998).

Nyquist, Mary, "The Genesis of Gendered Subjectivity in the Divorce Tracts and in *Paradise Lost*," in *Re-Membering Milton: Essays on the Texts and Traditions*, ed. Mary Nyquist and Margaret W. Ferguson (New York, 1988), 99–127.

Polydorou, Desma, "Gender and Spiritual Equality in Marriage: A Dialogic Reading of Rachel Speght and John Milton," *MQ* 35, 1 (2001), 22–32.

Salandra, Serafino della, *Adamo Caduto*, in *The Celestial Cycle: The Theme of "Paradise Lost" in World Literature, with Translations of the Major Analogues*, ed. Watson Kirkconnell (Toronto, 1952), 290–349.

Schochet, Gordon J., *Patriarchalism in Political Thought: The Authoritarian Family and Political Speculation and Attitudes, Especially in Seventeenth-Century England* (New York, 1975).

Speght, Rachel, *A Mouzell for Melastomus* (London, 1617).

Sowernam, Ester, *Ester hath hang'd Haman: or An Answer to a lewd Pamphlet* (London, 1617).

Sumers, Alinda, "Milton's Mat(t)erology: Paradise Lost and the Seventeenth-Century Querelle des Femmes," *MQ* 38, 4 (2004), 200–25.

Turner, James Grantham, *One Flesh: Paradisal Marriage and Sexual Relations in the Age of Milton* (Oxford, 1994).

Weil, Rachel, *Political Passions: Gender, the Family, and Political Argument in England, 1680–1714* (Manchester, 1999).

Wilding, Michael, "'Their Sex Not Equal Seemed': Equality and Hierarchy in John Milton's *Paradise Lost*," in *The Epic in History*, ed. Lola Davidson, et al. (Sydney, 1994), 176–92.

13

W. GARDNER CAMPBELL

Temptation

"Of Man's first disobedience, and the fruit/ Of that forbidden tree." *Paradise Lost*'s ringing first lines toll the occasion and disastrous outcome of the poem's climactic temptation: "death ... and all our woe." Even an initial reading of *Paradise Lost*, however, reveals that scenes of temptation are everywhere in the poem. Temptation is as abundant as the vegetation in Eden, which Milton calls "a wilderness of sweets ... wild above rule or art" (5.294–98). Throughout the epic, Adam and Eve struggle to understand their role as gardeners in a Paradise of such abundance, where the very act of gardening stimulates even more abundance (Campbell 1997). Similarly, we as readers must constantly struggle to understand the profusion of temptations in the setting, action, and theology of the poem, temptations that seem to be inherent in the Garden itself, the setting of the poem's central action, long before a specific tempter named Satan enters it.

At times, depending on our perspective as readers, Milton can seem almost willful in the way he presents these scenes of temptation, provoking us to ask questions that could lead us to accept Satan's bitter conclusion about the angelic temptation that precedes the human one in the timeline of the poem, that the God who created him and all the fallen angels also tricked them into sinning by withholding unambiguous signs of the extent of his divine power. To his fallen companions, Satan denounces their creator as a liar, a devil in disguise, one who "tempted our attempt [i.e., their rebellion in the War in Heaven], and wrought our fall" (1.642). It is indeed hard to imagine how one could justify the ways of a God who provokes through trickery the very sin he then punishes. St. Paul (especially in his letter to the Romans) and a long tradition of Christian theologians recoil in horror from the idea that God constantly entraps us and thus in effect becomes the author of sin itself. In the context of Milton's epic, we may reject Satan's conclusion, of course – he is Satan, after all, rallying his troops and justifying his own ways – but then we soon find we are asked to make such decisions again and again in this poem. Such wearyingly repetitive reaffirmations may inspire the very doubts they strive to eliminate, the way (for example) endless theatrical declarations of love and devotion may cause one to suspect that they hide a lack of love, a lack that is being suppressed or denied. Why does Milton take such risks, creating continual dis-ease where other writers might have been more cautious and more protective of their God?

William Blake and, much later, William Empson both thought that Milton consciously or unconsciously meant us to come to Satan's side. To agree with Blake and Empson, however, is to read Milton's stated purpose ironically. This is difficult to do when Milton states his purpose so directly and urgently – when the blind poet, knowing what lies ahead in his story, writes this heartrending prayer:

> what in me is dark
> Illumine, what is low raise and support;
> That to the highth of this great argument
> I may assert eternal providence
> And justify the ways of God to men. (1.22–26)

Dennis Danielson argues that Milton faces three principal difficulties in achieving such a purpose: the Fall must be credible, the Fall must not be inevitable, the Fall must not be desirable:

> To put the matter technically, Milton had to build into his narrative both the necessary conditions for Adam and Eve's falling *and* the necessary conditions for their standing. One of the main ways he does this is to expose Adam and Eve to some kind of trial or temptation before they must face *the* temptation. (152)

Yet what distinguishes "some kind of" temptation from "the" temptation? Proximity to the forbidden fruit? The Garden makes that proximity perilously easy, even in a way ubiquitous. The Forbidden Fruit hangs from the Tree of the Knowledge of Good and Evil, next to the Tree of Life at the center of Paradise, a center defined by a wall that appears ineffectual (it does not keep Satan out, after all) except as a means of defining the center of that space. *Intellectual* proximity, then? Ease or readiness of consideration? Degree of desire? Our inquiry spreads and grows even as we try to define its boundaries.

The most influential solution to the problem of God's tempting his own creation is offered in Stanley Fish's *Surprised by Sin*. Fish believes that *Paradise Lost* is a kind of dramatic catechism, a moral education by means of temptation not only for Adam and Eve, but also for the reader. As we read the epic, according to Fish, we ourselves are tempted by the complexities of Milton's portrayal of temptation in ways that, if we are attentive to the bedrock assertions of Milton's theology, demonstrate to us again and again the realities of own fallenness. For Fish, the fact that we find Milton's temptations problematic is the most compelling evidence possible that we are fallen ourselves; and Milton has structured his poem to bring us face-to-face with that compelling evidence over and over, thus continually surprising us with the irreducible sinfulness of our own fallen sensibilities. Unlike Blake or Empson, Fish offers us a remarkably consistent Milton, so consistent that Fish could confidently title an anthology of his own Milton criticism *How Milton Works*, a title suggesting an exhaustive and definitive answer to our many questions.

Yet our many questions remain. *Paradise Lost* is a poem, and poetry is a web of symbols mediated within a network of layered associations, rhymes, rhythms, and narrative traditions. Within a poem, no single utterance becomes merely definitive or denotative. Even the normative words of Milton's God must be understood in a discourse mediated by complexly crafted symbols. At times the words and actions of this God become riddling, mysterious, or even apparently cruel. Fish's argument solves this problem by creating a Milton who tutors us primarily or exclusively in self-correction (Rumrich 1996). But as William Kerrigan points out, Fish's argument makes *Paradise Lost* into something other than a poem. By contrast, Kerrigan insists that Milton's choice of poetry is essential to his purpose:

> *Paradise Lost* combines mythopoetic narrative with rational theodicy. Its rhythmic interplay of discursive and symbolic representation is ... constant and various... [T]he overall effect of [Fish's] reading is to promulgate a tyrannical notion of aesthetic unity at the expense of introducing, without overt recognition, a new and unheard-of flaw in the poem: the alarming idea that its mythopoesis is not generative but repetitive, that its similes, metaphors, and symbols tell us nothing about Christianity that the dogmatizing and sermonizing passages of the poem have not told us already. (Kerrigan 98–9)

As Kerrigan notes, symbols do not simply transmit information or enforce obedience to prior structures of meaning-making. For Kerrigan, "good symbols are a home" (298) not because they are dogmatically prescriptive, but because they are doctrinally freeing, demonstrating and inspiring the sacred activity of complex meaning-making that defines our humanity. Interestingly, however, temptation in Milton's work sometimes brings Kerrigan close to Fish's catechistical dogmatics. When he treats the temptation of ambition, for example, Kerrigan argues that Adam and Eve must desire angelhood without being motivated by that desire, as if appetite itself is to blame for the Fall (228–9). Unfortunately, such an argument leads us back to where we started, and the questions arise again. Is desire somehow a trap? If the answer is always the same – find a way to "just say no" – are the questions always the same as well? What could curiosity or discovery mean in such a world? The anthropologist Gregory Bateson defines the "double bind" as "an experience of being punished precisely for being right in one's own view of the context" (236). Is the unbounded human capacity Milton celebrates in *Areopagitica* – "minds that can wander beyond all limit and satiety" – the condition of just such a double bind in Paradise, an unboundedness granted us by a God who then punishes us for the ambitious energies that unboundedness generates (*YP* 2:528)?

These questions in *Paradise Lost* are awesome and dreadful, and they revolve around scenes of temptation. Could Satan have climbed the stairway to heaven in a moment of temptation that inspires the narrator himself to wonder about God's motives and the purpose of the trial: "whether to dare/ The fiend by easy ascent, or aggravate/ His sad exclusion from the doors of bliss" (3.523–25)? Perhaps Satan was right that God "tempted his attempt" in the War in Heaven, for God seems to do the very same thing as soon as the now fallen angel lands on the rim of our universe. However quickly we rush to excuse this God and explain away the ugly spectacle, we may hear a voice whispering, "what kind of God would taunt one of his own creations with a false opportunity for repentance?" We may hear an even louder voice of doubt inside us at the beginning of Book 4, when Satan utters his famous soliloquy on the top of Mt. Niphates. Is Satan's inner torment merely for our benefit, to demonstrate the way in which he finally rejects God and thus justifies God's damnation of him? As Satan's recriminations lead to self-incrimination, we may wonder if his "say I could repent" (4.93) has any moral force at all. Should we simply reject everything he says as untrue, even from his own point of view, as C. S. Lewis urges? If so, why the overwhelming pathos here? Is our feeling our failure? Or could Satan really decide to repent? When he is struck "stupidly good" (9.465) by the sight of Eve just before he begins the climactic temptation, was there still a chance he could turn around? Might we say that Eve in this moment tempts Satan to goodness, surprising him with his own remaining capacity for virtue, blessing him unawares? Or is this one more taunting moment of sad exclusion from the doors of bliss?

Adam and Eve undergo even more frequent and subtle temptations in *Paradise Lost* than Satan does. Although the temptation of Eve at the Tree is the poem's dramatic climax, many temptations precede this moment, so much so that Milton warns us at 7.59–69 that an increasingly inquisitive Adam is "yet sinless," and that Eve is "yet sinless" even as she pursues conversation with the serpent who has led her to the forbidden fruit (9.659). These warnings emphasize the complexity of temptation in these unfallen human lives. Were the human beings God created really "sufficient to have stood, though free to fall," as Milton's God insists (3.99)? Does Eve's "sweet, reluctant, amorous delay" (4.311) not only increase the couple's shared desire but also inevitably lead to Adam's uxoriousness? When in the same book Eve tells the story of awakening next to the lake and pining, Narcissus-like, for her own reflection, is the temptation also an indication of an insufficiency, a fatal flaw? When Eve has her bad dream in Book 5, does she yield to what we might call a "virtual" temptation in ways that also signal – or create – a propensity to sin that makes the test unfair, especially given that Satan himself is whispering in her ear? (McColley 1983 and 1999).

These questions become even more poignant as one considers that a dramatically interesting portrayal of temptation need not engage with such complications. Take for example the visual depiction of temptation in paintings of the era. A favorite subject is the temptation of St. Anthony. One particularly vivid rendering of this temptation was painted sometime around 1540 by Flemish artist Pieter Coecke Van Aelst. On the left side of the image, St. Anthony is praying in his hermitage, presumably imploring God to protect him from the temptations that threaten his sanctity and disturb his spiritual retreat. In the rest of the painting we see a lovely young naked woman proffering a golden urn, small devils tugging at St. Anthony's hair and clothing, and in a tiny detail in the center of the painting, a companionable devil who stands next to a presumably drunken man who bends over the wall of a bridge to vomit into the river below. (In a perversely fraternal gesture, the devil holds onto the man's arm to keep him from tumbling in.) We see in the painting a catalog of the three traditional categories – the world, the flesh, and the devil – that populate much of the discourse around temptation. But while our sympathies are engaged, and our own susceptibilities to temptation are perhaps tested, the judgment we are called to make is clear – as indeed it must be, lest the *portrayal* of temptation become an *occasion* of temptation, ironically undercutting the moral lesson the portrayal is presumably designed to deliver.

St. Anthony's temptation cannot be Milton's, however, for in Milton's mind, temptation must not be avoided by retreating from experience, but rather sought within the hurly-burly of a teeming world. In *Areopagitica* Milton insists he cannot praise "a fugitive and cloister'd vertue, unexercis'd & unbreath'd, that never sallies out and sees her adversary, but slinks out of the race ..." (*YP* 2:515). One might argue with Milton's judgment, claiming that St. Anthony does not need to sally out and see his adversary when a whole swarm of adversaries is obviously sallying out to see him. Milton's Adam, in fact, makes that very argument to Eve in the separation scene in Book 9 of *Paradise Lost*, and it's fair to say that we are tempted to agree with Adam's judgment at that moment, given the perilous circumstances. Yet Milton has Eve respond with words that sound just like Milton's in

Areopagitica, and again our critical difficulties multiply. Edward LeComte observes that "both *Areopagitica* and *Paradise Lost* deal with the limits of freedom, which was always Milton's subject. Both works portray temptation" (71) – to which we might add that temptation itself powerfully explores the limits of freedom.

Indeed, the more we look at Milton's portrayal of temptation in *Paradise Lost*, particularly through the lens of *Areopagitica*, his greatest sustained treatment of the philosophy and theology of temptation, the more it looks as if temptation is not a set of events, but a condition of being, the engine of freedom and reason itself. Milton appears to embrace a view of freedom that includes desire triggered not only by prohibition – I mustn't, so I want to – but desire triggered by abundance – I have much, yet I want more: more knowledge, more conversation, more questions, more challenges, more amplitude of being. For Milton, this *wanting more* is the "dear might" of intimate, profuse, creative power we experience within a context of obedience. Milton's characters, and his own narrative voice – by turns plaintive, thundering, and tender – are constantly stimulated and bewildered by the pressures of abundance, the paradoxical sense, as Adam puts it, that we are "happier than [we] know" (8.282). And for Milton, temptation is typically the medium in which we experience both the pressure of abundance, and the full and growing measure of our created capacities.

We can see Milton exploring this idea repeatedly throughout *Areopagitica* in ways that prepare us for the fuller experience of *Paradise Lost*. For example, in *Areopagitica* Milton defends his freedom to read "promiscuously," that is, without prepublication censorship that (at least purportedly) aims to keep dangerous books from doing damage to their readers (YP 2:517). For Milton, however, this immediate context quickly expands to a consideration of the very grounds of our created being. Danielson identifies this part of Milton's project as "what is sometimes called a 'soul-making' theodicy, one that in part explains possibilities of both natural and moral evil as necessary ingredients in an environment for what Milton elsewhere in *Areopagitica* calls 'the constituting of human vertue' (YP 2:516)" (Danielson 153). To support his point, Danielson quotes another famous passage from *Areopagitica*:

> Wherefore did [God] creat passions within us, pleasures round about us, but that these rightly temper'd are the very ingredients of vertu? They are not skillfull considerers of human things, who imagin to remove sin by removing the matter of sin … *This justifies the high providence of God*, who though he command us temperance, justice, continence, yet powrs out befor us ev'n to a profuseness all desirable things, and gives us minds that can wander beyond all limit and satiety. Why should we then affect a rigor contrary to the manner of God and of nature, by abridging or scanting those means, which books

> freely permitted are, both to the *triall of virtue*, and the exercise of truth …
> Were I the chooser, a dram of well-doing should be preferr'd before many
> times as much the forcible hindrance of evill-doing. For God sure esteems the
> *growth and compleatng* of one virtuous person, more then the restraint of ten
> vitious. (*YP* 2:527–8, quoted in Danielson 153; Danielson's italics)

Although he praises the "conspicuous richness of life that such an environment makes possible" in *Paradise Lost*, Danielson also admits that the trials
of Adam and Eve are "interesting, challenging, even at times frightening"
(153). That last word is especially interesting, and introduces yet another
set of complexities into our consideration of temptation. What is this fear?
Where does it come from? What should we learn from it? In Book 5, Adam
reassures Eve that when "damp horror chilled" her during her dream of eating the fruit, her fear indicated she would never "consent to do" this sinful
act while awake (5.65, 121). His explanation is loving, but it also seems a
little strained, even a little pat, and is finally shown to be false in Book 9. But
what if Adam were right? If fear is an effective deterrent, does it become the
coercion that for Milton makes obedience meaningless? Again the puzzles
multiply, and we are left to wonder why they should.

For Milton not only dwells *on* the complexities of temptation within all
his mature poetry and throughout much of his career, but dwells *within*
them, and argues for their necessity:

> He that can apprehend and consider vice with all her baits and seeming plea-
> sures, and yet abstain, and yet distinguish, and yet prefer that which is truly
> better, he is the true warfaring Christian. (*YP* 2:514–15)

This passage contains one of the more famous textual cruxes in all of Milton's
prose. The editor's note in the Yale edition tells us "The printed text has *wayfaring.* All four presentations copies and 'F' have the y crossed through in ink
and an r written above it… It can scarcely be doubted … that the change has
Milton's authority, and was made, if not by himself, by the printer or book-
seller after the error was discovered" (*YP* 2:515, n. 102). An error it may
be, and Milton's correction it may be, but the complexities emerging at this
moment in *Areopagitica* are enormous, for given Milton's description of the
process of temptation, "wayfaring" works just as well as "warfaring."

A number of fascinating complications at this wayfaring moment in
Areopagitica may indicate a certain heated process within Milton himself. A few lines later, Milton makes one of his most famous *uncorrected*
errors. As Milton tries to illustrate his idea of temptation, he invokes the
"sage and serious Spenser," whose allegorical romance *The Faerie Queene*
explored the winding paths of knights as they develop their capacities for
the virtues they represent. Describing a scene from Book 2 of *The Faerie*

Queene, Milton makes his crucial error. In Milton's account, Sir Guyon, the allegorical representation of the virtue of Temperance, is accompanied by the Palmer, representing Sir Guyon's powers of reason, into the cave of Mammon, where Sir Guyon is tempted. Unfortunately, this is not what Spenser wrote. The whole point of the cave of Mammon episode in Spenser is that reason does *not* accompany Guyon into that scene of temptation. As the Yale Prose editor notes, "before confronting [Guyon] with Mammon Spenser separates him from the Palmer, partly to show that the mere habit of temperance is sufficient to withstand the solicitations of that god [i.e., Mammon]" (*YP* 2:516, n. 108). Milton, however, is not merely "less disposed [than Spenser] to rely on the security of habit" (*YP* 2:516, n. 108). Milton strenuously insists throughout his work that habit alone can never constitute virtue or, for that matter, knowledge. (Fish's argument, by contrast, often seems to be that *Paradise Lost* inculcates little *besides* "mere habit.") For Milton, the experience of temptation is incomplete, and the arts of freedom unlearned, unless one is led to "see and know, and yet abstain" (*YP* 2:516). Let us look again at the "wayfaring/warfaring" passage. Observe how Milton creates the effect of lingering within a complex multistage process. Notice how he includes both "apprehend" *and* "consider," then dallies with "yet," and "yet," and "yet." See *and* know, and *yet* abstain, Milton tells us. Not "*see* and thus *abstain*," or even "see and know, and *then* abstain." The knowing is in exquisite and ongoing tension with the abstaining. "Yet" suggests both exception and duration.

Throughout his work, Milton sought and engaged with such tensions, and he did so consciously within a Christian tradition he frequently thought "fugitive and cloistered" in its willingness simply to explain those tensions away. To take but one powerful example of such fugitive explanations, there is considerable discussion of temptation within the commentaries on Scripture that flourished during the Reformation as a growing cadre of literate worshippers engaged with a Bible newly translated into their own language. Among these commentators, the Lord's Prayer generated considerable interest, as it was one of the very few examples of Jesus himself prescribing a form of worship or devotion. More than forty of these published commentaries on the Lord's Prayer were in English and thus available to a wide reading public by the time Milton came to write *Areopagitica*. King James I of England himself wrote one, as did many famous preachers of the day. Some of them are quite lengthy, running more than three hundred quarto pages. A keen student of Scripture and scriptural commentary, Milton doubtless read some, perhaps many, himself. They provide a fascinating context for apprehending and considering the productive possibilities Milton saw in the tension that arises in knowing and yet abstaining from vice.

Here is the Lord's Prayer as it is found in the Gospel of Matthew. The numerals here indicate not verses, but "petitions," as they are described in most of the English commentaries:

1. Our Father which art in heaven, Hallowed be thy name.
2. Thy kingdom come,
3. Thy will be done in earth, as it is in heaven.
4. Give us this day our daily bread.
5. And forgive us our debts, as we forgive our debtors.
6. And lead us not into temptation,
7. but deliver us from evil: For thine is the kingdom, and the power, and the glory, for ever. Amen.

For our purposes, the most interesting petition is, of course, the sixth. Commentators sometimes spend as many as one hundred pages or more on this petition alone, for the more one considers the petition, the stranger it appears. If temptation is harmful, why would we need to ask God not to harm us? On the other hand, if temptation is not harmful but potentially "soul-making," to use Danielson's term, why would we ask God *not* to lead us into it? What should we make of this petition coming from the mouth of the Son of God when he himself was led (or "driven," as Mark's Gospel has it) by the Spirit of God into the wilderness specifically "to be tempted of the devil" (Matthew 4:1)? (This temptation will be the subject of Milton's *Paradise Regained*.)

With this context in mind, let us look at the way Milton presents a crucial turning point in Book 9. Satan in the serpent speaks blithely to Eve:

> "Empress, the way is ready, and not long,
> Beyond a row of myrtles, on a flat,
> Fast by a fountain, one small thicket past
> Of blowing myrrh and balm, if thou accept
> My conduct, I can bring thee thither soon."
>   "Lead then," said Eve. He leading swiftly rolled
> In tangles, and made intricate seem straight... (9.626–32)

The words "lead" and "leading" conduct us directly back to that sixth petition, "lead us not into temptation," and strangely so. Eve does not know that she is inviting the serpent to lead her into temptation, but before we accept this as simple dramatic irony we may hear an echo of her final words to Adam before the separation, "that our trial, when least sought,/ May find us both perhaps far less prepared ..." (9.380–81). Eve is enacting for us her own irony; she knows and yet does not know, seeks trial, and is yet sinless. This is an example of what Kerrigan terms the "*nunc stans* of fateful decision" (19), strangely liminal, known and provisionally denied: an implausible paradox, yet one that every human being experiences.

Milton understands this strange liminality, and we see this understanding in the semantic abundance of his verse. Adam falsely believed that physical togetherness with Eve would be a more secure retreat. At that very moment in the separation scene, a key word becomes what Freud called a "primal" word, a word that means one thing and also its opposite. A tangle and a tension emerge in the couple's conversation, as for the first time in human experience they truly discuss the ethics of temptation, working these matters out, assaying and revising their thoughts in response to one another. Adam says to Eve:

> Seek not temptation then, which to avoid
> Were better, and most likely if from me
> You sever not: trial will come unsought.
> Would thou approve thy constancy, approve
> First thy obedience; th' other who can know,
> Not seeing thee attempted, who attest? (9.364–69)

The waywardness of the argument snares Adam in a thicket of contradictions: he appears to argue that temptation should not be sought, that it can be avoided, and yet that it will come of its own accord regardless. More interestingly, he seems to be claiming that neither sufficiency nor freedom can be known unless one is tempted – but how can that happen if temptation is avoided? Yet Adam may hear the strained notes in his own voice, and grow in the hearing. He certainly recalls that he knows better when he immediately corrects himself:

> But if thou think, trial unsought may find
> Us both securer than thus warned thou seem'st,
> Go; for thy stay, not free, absents thee more (9.370–73)

Now Adam's words echo *Areopagitica*, too, just as Eve's did earlier in this scene, and primal meaning arrives at our listening ears in the word "securer," which in Milton's day could mean either "safer" or "more careless." The Modern Library edition (2007) offers the latter gloss, which makes sense. In the context of Adam's struggles, however, the moment is confusing. For an instant, we recognize both meanings of "securer," and we bring Adam's error and his more gracious recollection into our minds at once.

A similar thing happens when Eve says to the serpent "Lead then." We remember the Lord's Prayer, *Areopagitica*, and the recent separation scene. We apprehend and consider, and we find clear distinctions become increasingly difficult to make. Such difficulty may conduce to good, as the narrator's subsequent description of the serpent's movement suggests. If the way is intricate, it is dishonest to pretend otherwise. Rather than make "intricate seem straight," as Satan is trying to do with all his might, Milton's mythopoesis creates and inspires "sense variously drawn out," as he describes his poetics in the epic's headnote on "The Verse." We remain entangled in a complex knot of meanings. If we are to abstain from anything it is from the decision to ignore or deny this complexity, to yield to the temptation to simplify. There are moments in the course of an existence governed by this dynamic of temptation when it is necessary to recall and act on the simple requirement to obey, but the pressure of that requirement is generative, not repetitive. For Milton, the meaning and value of living in that pressure – the pressure at work within and among "apprehend," "consider," "abstain," "yet distinguish," and "yet abstain" – is in the abundance that can develop only if one welcomes the intricacies of that pressured position. "Intricacies" is word that suggests both complexity and perplexity, difficulties and tricks, and Milton uses it to describe not only the movements of Satan in the serpent, but also the locking mechanisms of the Gates of Hell and the "intricate mazes" of angelic dance (2.877; 5.622). Adam and Eve's soul building, and the reader's, depends on seeking and dwelling within those intricacies, as do the meaning and value of any choices made along the way. Even at so crucial a point as the moment in which Eve grasps the fruit in her hand (literally "apprehending" it) and considers that fatal bite, she has done nothing more than amplify her existence. Should she have then abstained, that would have been a grand thing, but even that cannot be thought of as settling the matter. The Tree and the temptation it represents would remain.

This crowning strangeness is made clearest by Milton in another passage of *Areopagitica* that describes the forbidden Tree itself. The passage stands in direct contradiction to the swiftly rolling commentaries on the Lord's Prayer that make the intricate, puzzling matter of temptation seem straight. To solve the ironies and apparent contradictions in Scripture, commentators almost invariably argue that there are two forms of temptation: *probative* temptations that prove our faith, and *provocative* temptations that entice us to sin. The poet Henry King's magisterial 365-page commentary (1628) exemplifies this analytical strategy:

> As God is not the Author of sinne, so neither of Temptation, which in the definition of the Schooles [i.e., the Church Fathers] is ... [a] motive or provocation to ill... The end [goal or purpose] of a Tempter is to seduce and make ill. How then can it stand with his goodnesse to be a Factor for reprobation, or a Confederate in that Act which he abhorres? ... There is one kinde of temptation wherein God proves and makes trial of the faith of his servants, and this himself sometimes vouchsafes to owne; and there is another temptation of deceit, which allures men to sinne, whereof He is by no means the Author. (King 428, 432)

Temptation as "provocation" (awakening, literally "calling forth" the desire to sin) versus temptation as "probation" (testing, examining, trying, from the same root from which we get "probe" and "prove"): the contrast, in these very words or forms of them, is reiterated throughout these commentaries. Bishop George Downame's *The Doctrine of Practicall Praying: Together With a Learned Exposition on the LORDS PRAYER* (1656), for example, states that "Temptations are of two sorts: 1. Probation; 2. Provocations to evil" (394). Even closer to Milton, witness Herbert Palmer, the priest who attacked Milton in Parliament for his arguments in *The Doctrine and Discipline of Divorce*. Palmer's *An Endeavor of Making the Principles of Christian Religion, namely the Creed, the ten Commandements, the LORDS Prayer, and the Sacraments, plaine and easie"* (1645) glosses the sixth petition, "lead us not into temptation," directly and succinctly: "*Q: What are we taught to pray for, saying, Lead us not into temptation? A.* When wee say, *Lead us not into temptation,* we beg of God that we may not meet with any provocation to sinne, and have all helps to grace" (37). Milton's *DDC,* an extended prose treatise on theology, makes a superficially similar distinction, arguing that "God tempts no one in the sense of enticing or persuading him to sin" (*YP* 6:338–9).

When we turn from the strenuous logic of *DDC* to the far more poetic work *Areopagitica,* however, we find the striking passage that evokes more deeply the soul-making tangles of Milton's intricate imagining of temptation in *Paradise Lost.* The passage comes just after the discussion of reason, choosing, obedience, love, and giving.

> God therefore left him [Adam] free, set before him a provoking object, ever almost in his eyes; herein consisted his merit, herein the right of his reward, the praise of his abstinence. (*YP* 2:527)

Not a probative object, but a provoking object, one so provocative that this passage is rarely glossed and sometimes (as in Danielson's analysis) omitted altogether. Here we recognize Milton's bold tangles, the mythopoesis Kerrigan rightly praises as going beyond mere dogmatizing and sermonizing into the realm of meaning-generating, indeed meaning-provoking, symbol. For other writers, provocative temptation is simply enticing, and comes from the devil. For Milton, the provocation is complex; it performs its etymology. The provoking object of the fruit and the Tree from which it hangs represent a calling forth, an ever-almost. Like freedom, this ever-almost offers a generative (not merely probative) discipline as well as an intricate expansion of being. This is a different sort of soul-making, where strength lies less in resistance than in extent and capacity, boundaries that Milton also complicates beautifully in his account of angelic eating in the Heaven of Book 5, "where full measure only bounds/ Excess" (5.639–40). As we consider the ever-almost of provocative temptation Milton imagines, we may find that many episodes within the poem surprise us not with sin, but with complexly mythopoeic energies.

Two concluding examples may illustrate these possibilities of energetic mythopoetic surprise. First, consider Adam's story of his first entry into his garden home. Adam has awakened, full of wonder and curiosity, and in naming the elements of his natal environment he is simultaneously drawn to ask them "how came I thus, how here?" (8.278). Unsurprisingly, Adam receives no answer from the animals, plants, hills, or dales. He then undergoes his own dream, eerily similar to Eve's, although it is the deity, not the devil, who leads him on. Leads him on, and immediately leads him into temptation:

> ... by the hand he [God] took me raised,
> And over fields and waters, as in air
> Smooth sliding without step, last led me up
> A woody mountain, whose high top was plain,
> A circuit wide, enclosed, with goodliest trees
> Planted, with walks, and bowers, that what I saw
> Of Earth before scarce pleasant seemed. Each tree
> Loaden with fairest fruit, that hung to the eye
> Tempting, stirred in me sudden appetite
> To pluck and eat... (8.300–09)

Adam is asked to cultivate whole groves of fruit trees that yield not only nourishment but "sudden appetite." Appetite itself becomes a tempting fruit, part of *human* nature that follows nature itself as it "multiplies ... which instructs us not to spare" (5.318–20). Both Adam and Eve have their trials before the trees. Adam's temptation clearly comes from God. Perhaps Eve's does as well.

Later in Book 8, when Adam is only "half abashed" after being chided by Raphael for his tangled, enthusiastic relating of the "vehement desire" he feels for Eve, we see how the "sudden appetite" Adam has narrated is also strangely linked to his insatiable desire for the angel's conversation, and how both intense desires lead him into a deepened understanding of the nature and potential sanctity of desiring without satiety:

> To love thou blam'st me not, for love thou say'st
> Leads up to Heav'n, is both the way and guide;
> Bear with me then, if lawful what I ask;
> Love not the Heav'nly spirits, and how their love
> Express they, by looks only, or do they mix
> Irradiance, virtual or immediate touch? (8.612–17)

Bear with me then: Adam manages the difficult feat of at once rebuking the angel, demonstrating his own maturing powers of reason and expression, enticing the angel into further conversation, and causing the angel to glow with the light of desire. Adam's ever-almost of exorbitant desire for Eve is also a provocative ever-almost of comprehensive understanding that can, in this instance, quickly surpass an angel's. These are dramatically fascinating moments in the epic, and they both yield and stimulate varieties of sense, yet sinless, and an ever-developing sense of what is true. Such is the weight of meaning we bear in colloquy with this provoking epic.

Milton uses two striking images in *Areopagitica* to illustrate the post-lapsarian recovery of Truth he seeks from his reading. One is that of a re-membering. Like puzzle-workers trying to reassemble a unity in which each unique part has one unique place and no more, those who seek Truth are its "sad friends" who, "imitating the careful search that *Isis* made for the mangl'd body of *Osiris*, went up and down gathering up limb by limb still as they could find them" (*YP* 2:549). In this analogy, to love Truth is to patiently experience a sequence of yes-no moments: this part goes here, not there. The experience is varied, but always binary, tending toward a total-izing unity. This is the essence of Fish's understanding of temptation's role in Milton. And as we can see, there is warrant for Fish's position.

Yet this re-membering is only part of the story. For the mythopoetic and generative part, where we may see Milton with his "singing robes" about him, we need another image, one that leads not to a single unity but to growth diverging along many wandering and mazy paths:

> Truth is compar'd in Scripture to a streaming fountain; if her waters flow not in a perpetuall progression, they sick'n into a muddy pool of conformity and tradition. A man may be a heretick in the truth; and if he believe things only because his Pastor sayes so, or the Assembly so determins, without knowing other reason, though his belief be true, yet the very truth he holds, becomes his heresie. There is not any burden that som would gladlier post off to another, then the charge and care of their Religion. (*YP* 2:543)

Perhaps the provoking object is the source of the "perpetuall fountain" of streaming Truth. For from those provocations, those temptations ever almost in our eyes, Milton urges us to learn that one cannot post the charge and care of one's religion to anyone, not even to God himself. That stream-ing fountain, like "the perpetual fountain of domestic sweets" (4.760) that Milton calls the act of love between Adam and Eve, is a mode of being, a renewing delight. Our temptations, the provoking objects we see before us, are also our nourishments, the last best gifts of a providential universe, for only by them do we find the liberties that infuse meaning into our love and obedience.

Further Reading

Bateson, Gregory, *Steps to an Ecology of Mind* (Chicago, 1972; rev. ed. 2000).

Campbell, Gardner, "Paradisal Appetite and Cusan Food in *Paradise Lost*," in *Arenas of Conflict: Milton and the Unfettered Mind*, ed. Kristin Pruitt McColgan and Charles W. Durham (Susquehanna, PA, 1997), 239–50.

Danielson, Dennis, "The Fall and Milton's Theodicy," in *The Cambridge Companion to Milton*, 2nd ed., ed. Dennis Danielson (Cambridge, UK, 1999), 144–59.

Fish, Stanley, *How Milton Works* (Cambridge, MA, 2001).

Surprised by Sin: The Reader in "Paradise Lost," 2nd ed. (Cambridge, MA, 1997).

Kerrigan, William, *The Sacred Complex: On the Psychogenesis of "Paradise Lost"* (Cambridge, MA, 1983).

King, Henry, "An Exposition Upon the Lords Prayer," in *A Critical Edition of "An Exposition Upon the Lords Prayer" by Henry King, 1592–1669*, ed. Shirley Anne Rush (Ann Arbor, MI, University Microforms, 1970), 150–520.

LeComte, Edward, "Areopagitica as a Scenario for *Paradise Lost*," in *Milton's Unchanging Mind: Three Essays* (New York and London, 1973), 69–98.

Lewis, C. S., *A Preface to "Paradise Lost"* (Oxford, 1942).

McColley, Diane, "Milton and the Sexes," in *The Cambridge Companion to Milton*, 2nd ed., ed. Dennis Danielson (Cambridge, UK, 1999), 175–92.

Milton's Eve (Urbana, IL, 1983).

Milton, John, *Paradise Lost*, ed. Alastair Fowler, 2nd ed. (London and New York, 1998).

Rumrich, John, *Milton Unbound: Controversy and Reinterpretation* (Cambridge, UK, 1996).

Tanner, John, "Say First What Cause: Ricoeur and the Etiology of Evil in *Paradise Lost*," *PMLA* 103:1 (1988), 45–56.

14

MARY C. FENTON

Regeneration in Books 11 and 12

The final books of *Paradise Lost* show us that when life feels like "endless misery" or a "deathless death," more courage might be required to choose to continue living than to choose to die (10.810; 798). Whatever seemingly unbearable suffering any of us may have to endure, we have the merciful advantage of *not* knowing the future. Unlike Adam, we are not given a time-lapsed vision of futurity that reveals the consequences of our sins rippling forward in time. The gift of not having foreknowledge empowers us with a guaranteed uncertainty about what the future holds, a lack of knowledge that may at times provide hope – the energizing, imaginative, and rejuve-nating strength that elevates the will to carry on living. Deeper than wishful thinking and larger than optimism or idealism, true hope is for the unseen and unknown, and Milton asserts in the last books of the epic that true hope requires faith in God and in the ways of God.

Adam and Eve, knowing what they have done, knowing what they have lost, knowing – even worse – what the future holds because of what *they* have done and lost, must exhibit the profoundest faith and hope, first, in choosing to continue to love one another (10.958–61), then in not committing suicide (10.992–1046), and finally in producing a human race doomed to sin and death. Still, they surmise that self-destruction or "willful barrenness" cuts them "off from hope" (10.1042–43), and they discover the most compelling reason to continue living is to enact the promise that they shall bring forth the "seed [that] shall bruise/ The serpent's head" (10.1031–32). The very thing their knowledge of the future might dissuade them from doing presents itself as the very thing that will bend their sad story to its promised "happy end" (12.605). In living and in creating life, despite inevitable suffering – and in some ways because of suffering – there may yet be joy.

The image of the seed figures both the natural and spiritual process of regeneration, and is both a metaphor and metonymy for Christ, but Adam and Eve do not know this at first (Shullenberger 167). The "mysterious terms" (10.173), "obscurely ... foretold" (12.543) when the Son curses the serpent, will not be understood as referring to the Son's later actions in his role as incarnated Redeemer until the archangel Michael reveals this in the visions to Adam in Book 12. Michael prefaces his exuberant account of the "great Messiah" (12.244) by reiterating the redemptive promise about the seed, the *protevangelium* ("the first prophecy of Christ"). Adam and Eve thus begin their return back to a right relationship with God with faith in the promise that will not only provide some merciful comfort for their personal and immediate future, but the primary source of hope for all humanity: by Eve "Man is to live, and all things live for man" (11.161).

The final books cannot be read in isolation, though, detached from Raphael's earlier teachings, the narrator's commentary, or the epic scenes showing the altogether different worlds of Eden and Heaven. These earlier portions of the epic animate Books 11 and 12 with an aching poignancy, and they help elucidate why Adam and Eve are able to discover resources they have for joy, comfort, and regeneration in the face of the sorrow and loss they will have to bear. The final books resound with the sad, but ultimately hopeful message of the epic, possible only *because* of human anguish and suffering, which, as C. S. Lewis says, is "the very nerve of redemption" (2002, 103).

Regeneration and Suffering

Still, readers have often complained that Books 11 and 12 feel anticlimactic, harsh, depressing, and even poetically disappointing after the psychological drama and invigorating tensions of the first ten books. Even C. S. Lewis himself famously complained that the final books were "inartistic" – an "untransmuted lump of futurity" (1943, 125). Other Milton critics have admitted that sometimes "the episode of Adam's visionary and auditory instruction [is] easier to read about than to read" (Shullenberger 176). The archangel Michael's lessons to Adam from the highest hill of Paradise, the "top/ Of Speculation" (12.588–89), strip human history bare to its iniquities and force us to witness dreadful human suffering – Adam's and humanity's. There seems to be very little goodness, let alone joy, possible in the world, so little that it might be fair to say that although the final books do not focus on Satan himself as a character, they certainly focus on his achievements. Books 11 and 12 raise the provocative question of whether Satan accomplishes what he has set out to do since his own fall from Heaven: "to interrupt [God's] joy" (2.371).

Books 11 and 12 indeed circle back to Book 2 where Beelzebub first publicly proposed the retaliatory plan against God, "first devised/ By Satan," proclaiming that interrupting God's joy would "surpass/ Common revenge"

(379–80; 370–71). This is no insipid, lackluster goal, symptomatic of a weakened, fallen state. Satan and the devil's party aim to do nothing short of "kill[ing] God, as it were in the eye" (*Areopagitica, YP* 2:492). More than simply a state of divine emotion, joy, Satan recognizes, is the manifestation of something essential to God. In this, Milton is following St. Thomas Aquinas's notion of how love and joy exist in God: "love is the origin and joy is the end result," and thus "divine joy is identical with divine being" (*Summa Contra Gentiles* 17 n.19; *Summa Theologiae* I-II, q.3, a.2, ad I). Milton's choice of word is telling. In "interrupting" God's joy, Satan hopes, he will collapse, reverse, or disintegrate God's providential design (the bringing of good out of evil). He hopes he will "grieve" God so deeply as to "disturb/ His inmost counsels from their destined aim" (1.167–68). From the Latin *inter* ("between") and *rumpere* ("break"), "interrupt" means "tear apart," and signifies breaking in, cutting short, even destroying the continuity of something, whether it is time, space, serial order, or action. Satan aims to fracture time itself, or at least the ordered time of the providential narrative: God's will in action, the history of his creation unfolding in and toward joy. Satan believes, in other words, that he has identified joy as a divine vulnerability. Having failed in direct confrontation, he strives with a new method of violence, a subterfuge that intends to collapse the equilibrium, tranquility, and dynamic stability of God's love for his "new created world" (9.937), so that He might "with repenting hand/ Abolish" it (2.369–70).

The critical, if unsettling, question of whether Satan can or does interrupt God's joy centers on the synergetic relationship between suffering and regeneration that Michael's prophetic visions presents. The significance of the final books, then, comes not merely from the relentless spectacle of human faithlessness and its consequences, but from the remarkable possibilities of hope, love, and joy that must be shown to arise from it (either that or Milton's justification fails, and Satan's rupture is all there is).

Milton therefore encloses the visions in Books 11 and 12 within the discourse of regeneration, framing them with a preface and an epilogue, a narrative construction purposeful for two reasons: the prefatory section, describing Adam and Eve's penitential prayer (10.1086–11.21), and God and the Son's subsequent response (11.22–126), serves to "assert eternal providence" and to orient readers to the meaning and purpose of the upcoming visions. The visions' preface emphasizes that suffering is not good for its own sake, but necessary because the human heart "Self-left" without God is "variable and vain," (11.93, 92). Suffering leads to submission of the human will that leads to a return and reorientation to God, which is essential to regeneration (Lieb 1971, 205). Suffering causes Adam to fear, but also to feel pity and compassion, which brings him to a deeper understanding of freedom and love because suffering presents choice: to continue to suffer as a result of being isolated from God, or to return to God in atonement – literally, "at-one-ment," to make as one. As the Son puts it to the Father: "with me/ All my redeemed may dwell in joy and bliss,/ Made one with me as I with thee am one" (11.42–44). The epilogue after Michael's visions, in the final three hundred lines of Book 12, reinforces humanity's *need* for the redemptive, regenerative outcome provided by the Son's human life, death, and resurrection, and provides the assurance that salvation will be delivered for the faithful and obedient.

By the beginning of Book 11, the process of regeneration has already begun for Adam and Eve in their choice to forgive and to love one another (Shullenberger 163–84). It is at the end of Book 10, however, that Milton first sets up the final recurring paradigm of a "world destroyed," followed by a "world restored" (12.3). Book 10 ends with Adam and Eve returning to pray at the very place where God had earlier judged them, verifying that the judgment was right, and Milton's audience would have known well that returning to the physical place of judgment was the proper way to begin the process of atonement and forgiveness.[1] Without hope that God would even receive and listen to their prayers, they would have remained in merely a static state of fear. Instead, they make a leap of faith, trusting in a continued love that might bestow mercy on them after their transgression. Adam first declares what they *will* do:

> What better can we do, than to the place
> Repairing where he judged us, prostrate fall
> Before him reverent, and there confess
> Humbly our faults, and pardon beg. (1086–89)

And the scene concludes with them doing it:

> they forthwith to the place
> Repairing where he judged them prostrate fell
> Before him reverent, and both confessed
> Humbly their faults, and pardon begged. (1098–101)

Book 11, in other words, begins by showing that God's providential intent, stated earlier in Book 3, will be fulfilled:

> To prayer, repentance, and obedience due
> Though but endeavored with sincere intent,
> Mine ear shall not be slow, mine eye not shut. (3.191–93)

Adam's *intent* to pray in Book 10 is followed precisely by his *act* of praying, and Books 10 and 11 duplicate God's Word (*Logos*) as well as the textual words from Book 3. God's intention to soften the stony hearts of sinners (3.188–89) first becomes evident in Adam and Eve's intention to pray, and it is then fulfilled in the prayer itself. This linguistic repetition poetically performs the requisite reorientation to God and the core tenet of regeneration: intention must be renovated into action. Faith must be lived, "Deeds" added "to thy knowledge answerable," as Michael will instruct at the end of the poem (12.582). Further, the suggestive double entendre of "repairing" (to return to and to fix something broken), repeated in the Book 10 scene twice directly after an enjambment at the word "place," suggests a regenerative process, as the poetry's ritualistic, *verbatim* replication again translates Adam and Eve's intentions into deed. Movement through space, externalized action, becomes one with their interior state, first broken then repaired.

Faithful and dependent on God, they pray in a posture of absolute humility – lying on the ground in reverence and need. Their cries of anguish and contrition produce the very source of life and symbol of rebirth – water – as their tears, "Watering the ground" (10.1102), prepare that ground, metaphorically and naturally, for the "INGRAFTING and REGENERATION" that Milton says in his *DDC* produces "NEW LIFE and GROWTH," and "NEW LIFE means that we live 'to God'" (*YP* 7:477). Signifying the promise of a radical change toward something better than the present, regeneration in the Old Testament comes in the form of a new material creation, the land transformed, or the human body freed from suffering as it is newly infused with God's presence. When something becomes consecrated internally by a renewed oneness with God, it may be restored to its original, prelapsarian, perfect condition. In the New Testament, regenerated individuals share "one heart" with God, are given "new flesh and new spirit," as the outcome of the union with Christ, and the faithful will walk and live with God as his people (Revelation 21:1).

The Gospel writers explain regeneration with earthbound metaphors of natural birth and rebirth, organic growth and regrowth of the land, and washing, cleansing, and renewal of the body and spirit. John, for example, describes being born again not as a literal physical return to and from the mother's womb, but as a transcendent unification with God, through the Son of God, which transforms the whole human self, giving new life "in his name" (20:31). In the 1611 King James Version of the New Testament, the word "regeneration" itself occurs only twice, in Matthew 19:28 and Titus 3:5, as a translation of the Greek *paliggenesia*, from *palin* ("again, anew") and *genesis* ("origin, source, existence"). The idea is, however, expressed in several other important places (see Matthew 19:28; Titus 3:3–6; and John 3:3–7). In his letter to the Romans, St. Paul also describes rebirth through water and baptism into Christ, a process uniting humans to Christ's divinity through his death and resurrection (Romans 6:1–5; 6:21–28), and

Peter offers a metaphor for regeneration that connects the life of the spirit with the growth of grass and flowers (1:21–25).

Book 11's very first word, "Thus," signifies not a conclusion but a consequence, a regenerative beginning:

> Thus they in lowliest plight repentant stood
> Praying, for from the mercy-seat above
> Prevenient Grace descending had removed
> The stony from their hearts, and made new flesh
> Regenerate grow instead. (11. 1–5)

DDC's first mention of regeneration states, "Those who are delivered from it [spiritual death] are said to be regenerated and born again and created anew" (*YP* 7:394). Likewise, "Supernatural renovation ... restores man's natural faculties of faultless understanding and of free will more completely than before ... makes the inner man like new and infuses by divine means new and supernatural faculties into the minds of those who are made new. This process is called REGENERATION and INGRAFTING IN CHRIST" (*YP* 7:461). Regeneration may be attributed to faith "because faith is an instrumental and contributing cause of the process of sanctification" (*YP* 7:465). Adam and Eve choose to accept the previously prepared (prevenient) grace God offers, for regeneration depends on both God's original act, which removes the "stony," *and* humanity's corollary, participatory choice to receive the grace offered. The cause of regeneration (God's love and grace) is also its effect (a return to God's love and grace).

But regeneration does not mean Adam and Eve's postlapsarian selves and world will be a replica of their prelapsarian state. Almost immediately after their prayer, Adam feels the new complexity of what it now means to be human. He had already felt and expressed in his long anguished speech in Book 10 how to be human is to suffer. Now he experiences how suffering is necessary for experiencing joy and reunion with God, feeling peace return "Home to [his] breast" (11.153–54). The cycle, however, is not quite over. Almost immediately, he meets the formidable Michael and learns he and Eve must leave Eden:

> to remove thee I am come,
> And send thee from the garden forth to till
> The ground whence thou wast tak'n, fitter soil. (11.259–62)

In Eve's despondent lament when she learns she will be banished from her home (11.268–86), Milton portrays the condition of sheer, ordinary human desolation, magnified by the feeling of losing a beloved, incomparable place in the world. Yet God will separate Adam and Eve only from what Eve calls their "native soil," the local place of Eden, not from the global conditions that define their essential humanness (270; McColley 1994, 231–2). Genesis

2 establishes the initial purposes of human existence – "to till the ground" (2:5), to "dress" and "keep" the Garden of Eden (2:15). Milton combines these in the formula he has God use when he first brings Adam to Eden "to till and keep" it (8.320). When God later says he will remove Adam and Eve from their native soil to "fitter soil," (11.262), he retains their primary human essence, function, and self-worth. Their new place in the world, what the narrator calls "the subjected plain" (12.640), will not just be a place where they will have to labor to grow enough food to live. It will be where they begin a new process of self-cultivation. They learn more fully now some things Adam had intuited in his Book 10 lament: "That dust [they are] and to dust shall return" (10.770), and that dust will become their "final rest" and, in a sense more fundamental and general, their true "native home" (10.1085).

Natural, horticultural imagery of fertility, growth, and vitality suffuses the discourse of regeneration, beginning with the first exchange between the Father and the Son in Book 3. We learn in Book 11 that the Son chooses to live out what God had told him earlier:

> As in [Adam] perish all men, so in thee
> As from a second root shall be restored,
> As many as are restored, without thee none.
> His crime makes guilty all his sons, thy merit
> Imputed shall absolve them who renounce
> Their own both righteous and unrighteous deeds,
> And live in thee transplanted, and from thee
> Receive new life. (3.287–94)

Regeneration preserves the dignity of humanity's origins and purpose as the Son fuses his divine grace with human earthliness, asking the Father, "all his works on mee/ Good or not good ingraft" (11.34–35). In Book 4, in his description of Adam and Eve's bower, Milton's narrator describes God as "the sov'reign planter" (4.691), echoing a biblically based agricultural discourse he also uses in *DDC* saying "the Father plants believers in Christ" (*YP* 7:477). The process of regeneration merges the natural with the spiritual, the divine with the human, and like planting, involves possible loss, alteration, time, renewal, and choice. Seeds must grow in darkness, their places chosen, in order to come to light and life in a new form.

After Adam and Eve's prayer of contrition, "the glad Son" (11.20) acts as humanity's intercessor in his mediatory role as advocate and Redeemer:

> Accept me, and in me from these receive
> The smell of peace toward mankind, let him live
> Before thee reconciled, at least his days
> Numbered, though sad, till death, his doom (which I

> To mitigate thus plead, not to reverse)
> To better life shall yield him, where with me
> All my redeemed may dwell in joy and bliss,
> Made one with me as I with thee am one. (11.37–44)

Both banishment from Eden and death are merciful gifts. Humanity will be sent out of the garden,

> Lest therefore his now bolder hand
> Reach also of the Tree of Life, and eat,
> And live forever, dream at least to live
> Forever, to remove him I decree. (11.93–96)

Michael will be instructed to "all terror hide" about Adam and Eve's "perpetual banishment" from Eden (11.112, 109), another merciful gesture, given what we know from Book 6 about Satan and the rebel angels' expulsion from Heaven, as they were driven out "With terrors and with furies" to meet "the monstrous sight" of Hell that "Strook them with horror backward" (6.859–63). In contrast, Michael's merciful purpose is to "Dismiss them not disconsolate ..." and to

>   ... intermix
> [God's] cov'nant in the woman's seed renewed;
> So send them forth, though sorrowing, yet in peace. (11.113–17)

Regeneration and Joy

As I said earlier, the impact of the final books – in their presentation of both suffering and the power of regeneration – depends on earlier scenes of Heaven and Eden that provide visual, spiritual, and conceptual bedrock for the regenerative spiritual discourse of the final books. Readers are provided with the imaginative possibility that those worlds may be within the sphere of human possibility as "the paradise within .../ happier far" (12.587). Among the most important of these are the scenes of Heavenly joy described in Books 3 and 5 which unfold in a constant dynamic of action, tranquility, concord, and community. Spatially, circles, revolutions, and patterns offer an objective correlative of joy in Heaven, which according to Augustine, results from an unbroken union with God. The angels "Circle [God's] throne rejoicing" (5.163), and when they gather together for the Son's anointing and exultation, "in orbs/ Of circuit inexpressible," they stand "Orb within orb" (5.594–96). The spatial value of the circle registers the moral value of completeness, balance, and fusion, and the dynamism of the circle also enacts the cycle of regeneration, which originates with God and brings about a return to God. Joy, like creation, flows from God and returns.

And joy in Heaven is depicted sensually in sound, smell, and taste. The angels sing "hymns and sacred songs" (3.148), but as they respond to the Son's salvific heroism, "Ambrosial fragrance" fills "all Heav'n," and the angels feel "Sense of new joy ineffable diffused" (3.134–37). The angels enjoy a sumptuous feast and "in communion sweet/ Quaff immortality and joy," before their "all bounteous King" who rejoices in their joy (5.637–41). As the communal activities of singing, eating, drinking, and moving in God's immediate presence express joy, so do rest and repose. Not only are the unfallen angels not unsettled, as the fallen are, by misguided egotism, futile rationalizations, and vain philosophical conjectures about the nature of God, free will, and fate, but they live in a perfect equilibrium of action and peace, service and rest. God has created a realm embodying his own "holy rest" (6.272, 7.91; Knott 490; Lieb 2006, 147–53).

In addition to the images and scenes of joy in Heaven, there is, of course, Hell and the negative example of Satan who, carrying Hell within him, consistently not only misses opportunities for joy, but deliberately, consciously rejects joy. When he first spies Adam and Eve, joyful in Eden, the narrator says he "Saw undelighted all delight" (4.286). Part of the depth of Satan's evil derives from this refusal of a joy that is central to Christian soteriology and belief (Potkay 17), and that Milton makes central to his portrayal of heavenly and Edenic existence. Satan makes clear his rejection of such joy at the Son's exaltation when, unlike the multitude of angels, who sing, dance and "Quaff immortality and joy" at the celebratory banquet, he only *seems* well pleased and conceives "Deep malice" and "disdain," rather than feeling an immediate and joyful acceptance of the Son's sovereignty (5.616–66). Milton's audience would have been familiar with biblical exhortations such as Psalm 100 and St. Paul's fervent call to "Rejoice in the Lord always" (Philippians 4:4). In refusing to rejoice, Satan denies a principle of real joy: the ability and choice to love, and in loving, to create. Satan rejects the creative impetus of joy, choosing not to preserve life, but to destroy it; choosing not to hold creation in wonder and amazement, but to interrupt it. He stands narcissistically detached in joyless, wholesale, adversarial rejection. In Satan's joylessness, Milton shows, on the one hand, its power to destroy and degenerate. On the other hand, in the angels' rejoicing and in Adam and Eve's enjoying their Edenic life, Milton shows the generative source and expressions of joy, and how joy offers the possibility of experiencing true freedom. Joy can mean the opportunity to lose control of the self in either negative ways toward the excessive, misused freedom of detached individualism and self-centeredness, as in the "pleasure" Satan takes in destroying – the only "joy" left to him, he tells us in Book 9, as he prepares to tempt Eve, pointedly and poignantly refusing the compulsion he feels to love her instead

(9.473–93). Or joy can lead in positive ways toward exultant surrender to the God-centered communal, generative divine, in an experience or apprehension of union or fulfillment.

Adam seems to come closest to understanding divine joy when, on awakening from his own creation and intuiting that he must have been created "by some great maker," he asks everything in the surrounding landscape, "Tell me how may I know him, how adore,/ From whom I have that thus I move and live/ And feel that I am happier than I know[?]" (8.281–82). He feels in this moment of awe something inexplicable, some form of human joy, which he consciously recognizes is beyond his ability to comprehend rationally (not known but "felt" in having life and motion). In this moment, Milton depicts most aptly, the overwhelming mindlessness of true rejoicing, a sublime recognition of the divine in creation. Adam experiences an incoherent but prescient verisimilitude of the divine joy that impels God to create. He empathizes with the "sheer joy," that is, according to Aquinas in his *Commentary on the Nicomachean Ethics*, "God's and from which creation happens" (886). In contrast to Satan, Adam knows he did not create himself, but instead feels joy and awe in having been created, and in the creation round about him: his experience of his own origin intimates an experience of divine creativity and joy. He will be able to project this feeling into a future when he learns of the *protevangelium*, knowing then that creation is the emanation of joy, and procreation will move creation forward ("pro") in providential time.

When Raphael delivers his injunction to Adam and Eve, to "Be strong, live happy, and love" (8.633), this final instruction is anchored in their own prior experiences of happiness, but Raphael further grounds their understanding of how to sustain happiness in deepened spirituality, rational choice, and emotion. To "be strong," Adam and Eve must "apprehend and consider vice with all her baits and seeming pleasures, and yet abstain, and yet distinguish, and yet prefer that with is truly better" (*Areopagitica*, YP 2:514–15). To "live happy" enjoins them to exist in a vigorous, dynamic process, not a state of static pleasure, and to subsist in a way that demonstrates they are grateful for their happiness, aware that it is contingent so that evidence of their strength and love stands in their choice to "keep/ His great command" (8.634). "Keep," the same word God uses when he gave Eden to Adam in the first place ("To till and keep"), suggests not only action, but action sustained over time (8.320).[2]

Because "happiness" has its etymological roots in *hap*, in chance and fortune, "happy" emphasizes not only Adam and Eve's mutability, but reinforces the idea that God's grace, although gratuitous, is provisional, requiring choice, obedience, responsibility. And although grace is the primal source of happiness, the feeling of happiness infuses the human heart, soul, and mind only when one chooses to receive that grace, and then act on it. The mandate to "love" means not only to love one another (*amor proximi*) but to love God (*amor dei*), recalling Augustine's teaching that loving another is of no worth without loving God. The union of human and divine love is the basis of true charity, true *caritas*, true joy. Raphael, in so lovingly teaching what it means to "live happy," teaches Adam and Eve to internalize and actively live the divine message he delivers, framing happiness with strength and love in what amounts to a succinct prescription for how choice may open the way for God's prevenient grace, and thus joy.

This brings us back to the meaning of suffering. At the crucial moment of their fall, Adam and Eve will lose the happiness they had known, each of them failing to maintain their strength in the face of temptation to love something – autonomy, a partner – more than God, forgetting that in Milton's Augustinian schema, both derive from putting God first. God's explanation of death and Michael's sad visions teach them, however, how happiness might yet be restored. "[H]appiness/ And immortality" (11.58–59) will not be permanently lost or revoked, but provided in a different form and by a different means. As the Father puts it,

> ... I provided death, so death becomes
> His final remedy, and after life
> Tried in sharp tribulation, and refined
> By faith and faithful works, to second life,
> Waked in the renovation of the just,
> Resigns him up with heav'n and Earth renewed. (11.61–66)

Such "Second life" can only be gained through suffering, and thus, much of the purpose and impact of the final books comes from the anguish Michael makes Adam – and all Milton's readers – witness and experience. Adam asks the question all humans likely ask: "But is there yet no other way, besides/ These painful passages, how we may come/ To death, and mix with our connatural dust?" (11.527–29). Michael assures him suffering is not a good in itself, but now necessary to redirect the will toward God, toward a renewal of the self in "service of God, and the performance of good works" (*YP* 7:461). Death will become humanity's "final remedy" (11.62), because in the wake of the fall, immortality would serve only to "eternize woe" (11.60), and death marks the moment of transition to a happy second life earned through a proper confrontation with that woe.

Adam, therefore, does not respond to human suffering with detached, sentimental pity, but enters into it fully with dismay, despair, submission, a sense of bereavement, and true *pathos*, indeed with a sense of "compassion," (11.496) – of being one-with (*com-passio*) those who suffer. He recognizes both his own potential for suffering and "Th'effects which [his] original crime hath wrought/ In some to spring from him" (11.424).

Although the Son's human suffering may not be accentuated in the epic's final books, the Passion and Crucifixion are nonetheless crucial in the regenerative process (Chaplin 2010). Suffering and compassion lead Adam to the epiphany "Of utmost hope" that "one man found so perfect and so just" will "raise another world" (12.376; 11.876–77), and to the understanding of how his own regenerated life will be lived through paradoxes rightly understood. Bound by faith in God's "eternal providence" (1.25), Adam claims to have internalized the lessons of humanity's suffering (Swaim 236), which may be redeemed by the Savior's suffering:

> Henceforth I learn, that to obey is best,
> And love with fear the only God, to walk
> As in his presence, ever to observe
> His providence, and on him sole depend,
> Merciful over all his works, with good
> Still overcoming evil, and by small
> Accomplishing great things, by things deemed weak
> Subverting worldly strong, and worldly wise
> By simply meek; that suffering for truth's sake
> Is fortitude to highest victory,
> And, to the faithful, death the gate of life. (12.561–71)

At this point, he provides the poem with a climactic acknowledgement: "Taught this by his example," Adam now comprehends the Son as his "Redeemer ever blest" (12.572–73). Yet in his moment of appreciative amazement and gratitude, Michael immediately corrects him, reiterating Raphael's earlier lessons, emphatically inserting "add" four times to Adam's summary of insights. Michael stresses, with terse firmness, that Adam must externalize the internal, actualize understanding into lived reality: "add/ Deeds to thy knowledge answerable, add faith/ Add virtue, patience, temperance, add love" (12.582–83). Michael's message has certainly not been one of naïve optimism about humanity's future; nor does he present the way back to God as easy or effortless, for the work of "keeping" is ongoing. Yet because of "The great deliverance" by Eve's "seed to come" (600), he assures Adam there is reason to live out their "many days" as they meditate on "the happy end" (602; 605), with the assurance that in distant time their actions will "bring forth fruits, joy and eternal Bliss" (551), at some eschatological moment when, as the creator puts it in Book 7, humans will "open to themselves at length the way/ Up hither …/ And Earth be chang'd to Heav'n and Heav'n to Earth/ One kingdom, joy and union without end" (7.157–61), a circle of perfection, a union with the source of life, and a return to the source.

The epic elucidates a wholistic vision of joy past, and of joy possible in an eternal future. Memory of the past and hope for the future, anchored in faith, enable joy to remain active in the present "transient world," even after it is ruined by sin (12.554). Michael's visions and lessons, infused as they are with the human suffering that makes joy possible, conclude with the promise of regeneration, "of some great good/ Presaging" (12.612–13). The *protevangelium*, and what it will mean – the Son's human life and his teachings, his "cursèd death," Resurrection, and return to "his seat at God's right hand" (12.386–465) – manifests divine joy, the means to human joy, and the lived example of it. Thus Adam can stand, as he says, "Replete with joy and wonder" (12.468), and Eve can be awakened from her dream renewed with vitality and faith, certain of her will to live. They choose to keep creating – to move creation forward, to preserve life and the capacity for life and new things. Their human joy and the desire to create is the image of God pouring out existence itself and giving being to hope.

NOTES

1 Suggested by Alison Chapman's forthcoming essay, "Satan's Pardon: The Forms of Judicial Mercy in *Paradise Lost*," which she kindly shared with me.
2 I am grateful to Louis Schwartz for this observation and the earlier one about Milton's use of the word, also for his helpful editorial comments throughout.

Further Reading

Aquinas, St. Thomas, *Commentary on the Nicomachean Ethics*, trans. C. I. Litzinger, 2 vols. (Chicago, 1964).
  Summa Contra Gentiles, trans. Anton C. Pegis, et al., 4 vols. (Notre Dame, IN, 1975).
  Summa Theologiae, trans. Fathers of the English Dominican Province, 3 vols. (New York, 1947).
Chaplin, Gregory, "Beyond Sacrifice: Milton and the Atonement," *PMLA* 125 (2010), 354–69.
DuRocher, Richard J., "'Tears Such as Angels Weep': Passion and Allusion in *Paradise Lost*," in *Their Maker's Image: New Essays on Milton*, ed. Mary C. Fenton and Louis Schwartz (Selinsgrove, PA, 2011), 23–45.
Fox, Matthew, *Sheer Joy: Conversations with Thomas Aquinas on Creation Spirituality* (New York, 1992).
Hillier, Russell M., *Milton's Messiah: The Son of God in the Works of John Milton* (Oxford, 2011).
John, Donald, "They Became What They Beheld: Theodicy and Regeneration in Milton, Law and Blake," in *Radicalism in British Literary Culture, 1650–1830: From Revolution to Revolution*, ed. Timothy Morton and Nigel Smith (Cambridge, UK, 2002), 86–100.
Knott, John R., Jr., "Milton's Heaven," *PMLA* 85 (1970), 487–95.
Lewalski, Barbara, "Structure and Symbolism of Vision in Michael's Prophecy, *Paradise Lost*, Books XI–XII," *Philological Quarterly* 42 (1963), 25–35.

Lewis, C. S., *The Problem of Pain* (London, 2002).
  A Preface to "Paradise Lost" (London, 1943).
  Surprised by Joy (London, 1955).
Lieb, Michael, *Dialectics of Creation: Patterns of Birth and Regeneration in "Paradise Lost"* (Amherst, MA, 1970).
  Poetics of the Holy: A Reading of "Paradise Lost" (Chapel Hill, NC, 1981).
  Theological Milton: Deity, Discourse, and Heresy in the Miltonic Canon (Pittsburgh, PA, 2006).
McColley, Diane, "Beneficent Hierarchies: Reading Milton Greenly," in *Spokesperson Milton: Voices in Contemporary Criticism*, ed. Charles W. Durham and Kristin Pruitt McColgan (Selinsgrove, PA, 1994), 239–49.
  A Gust for Eden: Milton's Eden and the Visual Arts (Urbana, IL, 1993).
Myers, Benjamin, "Prevenient Grace and Conversion in Paradise Lost" *MQ* 40.1 (2006), 20–36.
Poole, William, *Milton and the Idea of the Fall* (Cambridge, UK, 2005).
Potkay, Adam, *The Story of Joy: From the Bible to Late Romanticism* (Cambridge, NY, 2007).
Schwartz, Regina, *Remembering and Repeating: On Milton's Theology and Poetics* (Chicago 1993).
Shullenberger, William, "Sorting the Seeds: Regeneration of Love in *Paradise Lost*," *MS* 28 (1992), 163–84.
Swaim, Kathleen, *Before and After the Fall: Contrasting Modes in "Paradise Lost"* (Amherst, MA, (1986), 163–84.
Tanner, John, *Anxiety in Eden: A Kierkegaardian Reading of "Paradise Lost"* (Oxford, 1992).

PART IV

15

WILLIAM KOLBRENER

Reception

In "The Moses of Michelangelo," Sigmund Freud wonders whether "the master hand" of the Italian sculptor "indeed traced such a vague or ambiguous script in the stone," that "so many readings of it are possible" (13, 17). Freud faults interpreters who fail to convey Michelangelo's "magical appeal," while also considering that perhaps the responsibility lies with the artist himself. "We may be allowed to point out," he writes, "that the artist is no less responsible for ... the obscurity which surrounds his work." "In his creations," Freud concludes, "Michelangelo has often enough gone to the utmost limit of what is expressible in art" (40–1).

Freud's ambivalent figure of the artist, at once creating "obscurity" and producing works surpassing categories of understanding, and thus eliciting multiple perspectives and interpretations, serves as a model for reading the critical history of *Paradise Lost*. Indeed critics throughout the centuries have lamented the contradictions inherent in the poet's work. For this reason perhaps, Milton, more than any other figure in literary history, has elicited divergent, radically opposed readings, producing what Freud calls "differing and contradictory interpretive events." He is certainly one of the "figures of cultural significance" – perhaps the paradigm example – who has acquired, as Steven Marcus and Charles Taylor write, a "dichotomous image" (6). The dichotomous Milton, although transforming over the generations, emerges in relation to what a critic more than half a century ago called "two schools" of reading *Paradise Lost*: one so "impressed" by the epic's heresies as to lose sight of its "fundamental Christianity," and the other insisting on the "traditional character" of both poet and poem (Woodhouse 211). So, in a complicated and sometimes polemical critical history, *Paradise Lost* stands as a testament to Milton's critical orthodoxy, as well as his radical heresy.

The engagements, indeed investments, of Miltonic readers – editors, poets, and literary critics – are immense, and *Paradise Lost* only emerges through an encounter with responses to Milton's poem, in all of their divergent differences, and sometimes antagonisms. As Harold Bloom writes, the literary method of *Paradise Lost* is "transumptive," appropriating and transforming much of precedent literary history, from Homer and Virgil to Spenser and Shakespeare (9). But more than that, the epic becomes through its celebration or repression, its praise or condemnation, the means by which later writers will define not only Milton, but themselves and their own relationships to politics, theology, and the writing of poetry.

William Blake, aware of the energies of a poem that has elicited so many differing interpretations, wrote, "I saw Milton in imagination and he told me to be aware of being misled by his *Paradise Lost*" (Wittreich 96). In the readings that I survey here, it is not Milton's epic that misleads, but those readings that claim to fully define it. Indeed, some of Milton's most insightful and influential critics reveal the power of Milton's poem in their very acts of appropriation, as much for what they leave out as for what they reveal. In some sense, Milton criticism becomes, in its various forms, ways of confronting the "wild work" that is *Paradise Lost* (6.698): the wildness manifesting itself sometimes in a political radicalism, either marginalized or celebrated, or in theological heresy, similarly celebrated or downplayed as irrelevant to the artistic sublimity of the epic. This history focuses on constellations of engagements at key turning points in the reception of the epic: in its early editions, in eighteenth-century efforts at canonization, in romantic recastings of the poem, and in early twentieth-century critical controversies, ending with a survey of Milton Studies at the current critical moment. This admittedly distilled and unconventional account shows how readings of the epic – even as they most succeed by either repressing or promoting the "wild" Milton – always engender, indeed require, further readings and interpretations.

A Classic in the Making: Early Editions of Paradise Lost

Starting in the seventeenth century, the reputation of *Paradise Lost* was a matter of contention, Milton's epic a classic in the making. Indeed, Milton's precedent reputation as a revolutionary and regicide threatened to occlude his poetic achievement. Reflecting Milton's political legacy, William Winstanley wrote in 1687 that while *Paradise Lost* "might deservedly give [Milton] a place amongst the principal of our English Poets," his "Fame is gone out like a Candle in Snuff." The "Memory" of the poet, for having "impiously and villanously bely'd that blessed Martyr King *Charles*," Winstanley continues, "will always stink, which might have ever lived in honourable Repute" (Shawcross 1970, 97). In 1698, Thomas Yalden also registers the disjunction between the experience of reading Milton the political radical and the poet of *Paradise Lost*. Yalden distinguishes between the "sacred lines," which "with wonder we peruse," and the "seditious prose," which "provokes our rage" (122). Already in the late seventeenth century, the image of Milton the man, the political radical and regicide, rescued from almost certain execution at the Restoration by the intervention of fellow poets Dryden and Marvell, threatens to occlude the poem.

Tonson's 1688 edition, which, as Nicholas von Maltzahn notes, helped make Milton more appealing by hiding his politics behind a new image of the poet as a "classic," contributed more than any other early publication to Milton's rehabilitation (Armitage 253). The edition, the work of Whigs and Tories alike (the latter, inheritors of royalist ideology and thus Milton's natural political enemies), includes an ornate frontispiece, with John Dryden's now famous epigram:

> Three poets, in three distant ages born,
> Greece, Italy, and England did adorn.
> The first in loftiness of thought surpassed;
> The next in Majesty; in both the last.
> The force of nature could no further go:
> To make a third she joined the former two. (Shawcross 1970, 97)

"Patrick Hume's *Annotations*" (1695) goes even farther, giving the poem a critical apparatus that provides references to "the Texts of Sacred Writ" relevant to it as well as "the Parallel Places and Imitations of the most Excellent Homer and Virgil." By rendering "All the Obscure Parts ... in Phrases more Familiar," the "Old and Obsolete Words ... Explain'd and made Easie to the English Reader," Hume also situates *Paradise Lost* in a distinctly English tradition of sacred epic. He makes the poet the author of an English classic: not just Milton, but, as Hume writes, "our Milton" (Walsh 54).

In 1698, John Toland, the radical republican and theist, published Milton's complete prose, emphasizing a part of the Miltonic legacy that many would have rather left forgotten. While the Tonson edition presented the somber visage of an established poet, the inheritor of a life beyond such messy things as radical politics, Toland insisted on telling the story of Milton's earthly life. In his *Amyntor*, a "defense of Milton's Life," Toland was both defending his own work and Milton's life against those claiming that the Milton of his account "was not the true MILTON" (5, 6). Toland may not have published an edition of the epic, but the publication of the prose and the foregrounding of the actual life of the poet provided an explicit counterpart to the life-beyond-life of the Milton canonized in the Tonson edition, foregrounding instead the radical Milton that others would later find in the epic. The late seventeenth century in this sense saw an argument about the provenance of *Paradise Lost*, not in the conventional sense of whether Milton was its author, but rather in asking the question: which Milton wrote it?

Milton in Good Taste: The Eighteenth-Century Orthodox Milton

Joseph Addison devoted eighteen of his *Spectator* papers written from 1711 to 1713 to *Paradise Lost*, including one on each of the books, attempting to make the epic suitable for a canon corresponding to the new tastes of eighteenth-century polite society. "Those," he writes, "who know how many Volumes have been written on the Poems of *Homer* and *Virgil*, will easily pardon the Length of my Discourse upon *Milton*." But for Addison, *Paradise Lost* is a poem that resists his critical categories, even as he insists on their application. Addison's determination to "examine" *Paradise Lost* by "the Rules of Epic Poetry," the sometimes seemingly obsessive resolve to apply "*Aristotle's* Method of considering," testifies not only to his anxiety that Milton may have produced an epic falling "short of the *Iliad* or *Odyssey*," but that the poem refuses *any* conventional rules or expectations (Shawcross 1970, 151). His concern over whether the poem evidences the "Beauties which are essential" to the "kind of writing" pursued by Homer and Virgil betrays his unease about whether *Paradise Lost* could be accommodated within his canon of politeness. The "beautiful," as Joseph Wittreich writes, was a means by which *Paradise Lost* might be sanitized of its more radical political and theological tendencies (Moore 177).

Excess, however, may be said to find expression in what Addison describes as the "sublime" element in the poem, which he calls "astonishingly great and wild." John Dennis had already in 1704 noted that although Milton "had a desire to give the World something like an Epick Poem," he had "resolv'd to break thro' the Rules of Aristotle," producing a "most lofty, but most irregular Poem" (Shawcross 1970, 128). Addison, committed to a work that presents the "Mysteries of Christianity" that were "drawn from the Books of the most Orthodox Divines," displaces his discomfort with the poem's "irregularity" onto the sublime, in particular onto the figure of Satan who is able "to raise and terrifie the Reader's Imagination" (168, 70, 51). There is no "single Passage in the whole Poem worked up to a greater Sublimity," Addison writes, than that of Satan, "celebrated" in the lines, "... He above the rest/ In shape and gesture proudly eminent/ Stood like a tower ..." (52). Addison may have served in the making of the canonical poet, a figure of politeness, and *Paradise Lost*, as Jonathan Richardson later put it, a poem "to Calm and Purify the Mind ... to a State of Tranquility and Happiness" (163). But in the category of the sublime associated with Satan – Dennis saw the "tower" simile as condensing terror, fear, *and* admiration – Addison acknowledges a set of poetically "wild" energies, however consciously, not to be contained either by classical strictures or standards of taste, anticipating a different Milton, not just the radical political figure, but a radical *poet* of excess as well (Moore 101–9).

More so than the *Spectator* Essays, the 1732 edition of *Paradise Lost* brings to the forefront the very wild energies – theological, political, and poetic – that the edition's editor, Richard Bentley, seeks to repress. Although Bentley, classicist and lecturer at the Royal Society, sought to provide a *Paradise Lost* safe for contemporary political and theological orthodoxy, he gives voice to the very heterodoxy his edition explicitly seeks to exclude. In the trope that governs Bentley's edition, an unscrupulous printer or editor has foisted lines onto the poem, and Bentley's own "Sagacity" and "happy Conjecture" restores the poet's intentions (a2v). In the creation of this nefarious editor or incompetent printer, Bentley creates a figure embodying the heresies of his day: a radical republican in politics, a materialist and freethinker in religion who managed to slip his influence into a poem otherwise suitable for eighteenth-century polite society. Addison registers the presence of a Milton who fit uneasily within classicist strictures; the hyper-orthodox Bentley, by contrast, locates the heterodoxies of the poem, and then displaces them through his figure of the editor/printer.

So Bentley, inheriting a spirit of dualism from philosophical and scientific antecedents, notably Descartes and Newton, creates a Milton in his own orthodox image, excising any hints of the radical heresy that he senses in the poem. Bentley thus objects to the notion that Milton's angels have physical qualities and perform physical functions – including eating and sex. To Milton's description of angelic eating, Bentley "snorted" (as William Empson describes it): "If the angels want *feeding*, our Author made poor Provision for them in his Second Book; where they have nothing to eat but *Hell-fire*" (Empson 1974, 153; Bentley 162). Bentley rejects not only the equating of spirit and matter, but also "Divine Narratives" and classical mythology (what he calls "Fable and Lye") (152). The poet would not, Bentley affirms, "have clogged" his poem with such "Romantic trash," risking the identification of his scriptural story with "Fabulous" legend (26). To those who emphasized Milton's political radicalism and heresies, Bentley countered with a unified and sacred poem, not just externally sanitized through critical interpretation, but more brazenly through a rewriting of the poem itself. Almost by virtue of an obsessive desire to maintain *Paradise Lost* as a poem of orthodoxy, Bentley gives lessons in how to see *Paradise Lost* as a manual of heresies.

In claiming the poet for orthodoxy, Bentley reinforces the trend of distancing *Paradise Lost* from the actualities of Milton's life of radical politics, in the process, not only concocting a fictional editor, but also a fictional Milton. Bentley's Milton, no longer the "Monster of a regicide," as he was called by the High Church polemicist William Baron, was able to "abstract his Thoughts from his own Troubles" and consider "all Periods of Time from before the Creation to the Consummation of all Things" (Baron 27; Bentley a3v). The 1732 edition claims to restore *Paradise Lost* to its "native, unextinguishable beauty" – divorced from the details of Milton's personal history (a3r). Bentley's domestication of *Paradise Lost* for orthodoxy moreover, attended not only to Milton's politics and theology, but also to his poetry, as when Bentley changes Milton's suggestive and ambiguous identification of Mount Sinai, the place of divine revelation, as the "secret top of Oreb" to the theologically more benign and poetically neutral "sacred top."

Although before Addison's *Spectator* essays the Dean of Westminster had refused to allow Milton's name to appear on a statue commemorating another poet in Poet's Corner, by 1737, after Bentley's makeover, Milton "was respectable enough to have a monument erected in that venerable repository of Kings and Prelates" (Griffin 151). From the eighteenth-century's respectable and orthodox *Paradise Lost* emerges the epic of the nineteenth century, canonized for a middle-class reading public to be read, after Church, with *Robinson Crusoe* and *Pilgrim's Progress* as "Sunday-Books" (Sharrat 35). It was finally the achievement of the eighteenth century to separate *Paradise Lost*, which Dr. Johnson called the "book of universal knowledge" exciting "reverence" and confirming "piety," from the life and energies of its "acrimonious and surly republican" author (Johnson 192).

The Romantic Milton: The "Power" of Paradise Lost

It was the *Paradise Lost* that had become a mere token of cultural and religious orthodoxy, domesticated as a distinctly theological work, to which William Wordsworth and other romantics poets objected. "People for their own credit must now have it," but Wordsworth goes on to lament, "how few, how very few, read it." And those who do read *Paradise Lost*, the "multitude" as he terms them, read it "almost exclusively not as a poem, but a religious Book" (Wittreich 14). Samuel Taylor Coleridge similarly acknowledges the cultural currency of *Paradise Lost* but writes, "I wish the Paradise Lost were more carefully read and studied than I can see any grounds for believing it is" (Wittreich 245). Eighteenth-century critics sanitized Milton the man of his political and theological energies, taming his wildness, but the romantics lamented the lost legacy and attempted to revitalize it. To restore the epic to its place as an "immortal book" – Dr. Johnson's "unrelenting malignity" was, to Thomas De Quincy, the reason it had "slumbered for a generation" – the romantics put their focus back on Milton the man (Wittreich 506).

Although Coleridge credits the "character of the times," he also assumes that Milton's "original genius" was the "immediate agent and efficient cause of the epic" (Wittreich 240). For Coleridge, the man leads back to the poetry, or in some sense *is* the poetry. In *Paradise Lost*, "it is Milton himself whom you see; his Satan, his Adam, his Raphael, almost his Eve – are all John Milton" (Wittreich 277). In an age celebrating individual "Genius," Coleridge finds in Milton the apotheosis of a new and now sacred self: "the egotism of such a man is a revelation" (Wittreich 277). Keats distilled a romantic view of Milton whose poetic powers were both inevitable and unavoidable: "life to him would be death to me," he once lamented, although also admitting that Milton's "spirit" "rolls about ... for ever and for ever" (Wittreich 562). In this way, Keats and his contemporaries, unlike his eighteenth-century predecessors, faced up to the power of the poet whom they both dreaded and revered.

Moreover, the "wild" sublimity that Addison acknowledged, but never allowed himself to explore fully, shows itself among the romantics who, in the early decades of the nineteenth century, rejoice in the sublime, sometimes even, Satanic Milton. For De Quincy, "there is no human composition ... as uniformly sublime from first to last" as *Paradise Lost*, in which Milton's "great agency" can be seen to "blaze and glow as a furnace kept to white heat." "If the man had failed," De Quincy affirms, "the power would have failed" (Wittreich 478–80). For Coleridge, sublimity is at once associated, as in De Quincy, with the "grandeur and purity" of Milton's blazing soul, but also with Satan. "Around this character," he writes of Milton's archangel, the poet "has thrown a singularity of daring, a grandeur of sufferance, and a ruined splendor, which constitute the very height of poetic sublimity" (Wittreich 244). Echoing the tower metaphor that so stirred Addison, Coleridge associates Satan's sublimity with the poet himself. "In the Paradise Lost," Coleridge writes, "the sublimest parts are the revelations of Milton's own mind" (Wittreich 245). To be sure, for Coleridge, Milton's "grandeur," unlike Satan's, is pure, but their shared suffering and egotism assert a resemblance between them (Wittreich 177). More so in Percy Bysshe Shelley's account, which asserts a near identification between the two, Satan figured, like the poet, as one "who perseveres in some purpose which he has conceived to be excellent in spite of adversity and torture" (Wittreich 534–5).

Blake, like Coleridge and Shelley, highlights Satan's tortured magnificence, not only in his *Marriage of Heaven and Hell* (1793), but in three separate sets of illustrations. Milton, Shelley had written, "divested" Satan of "a sting, hoofs, and horns" (Wittreich 535). Indeed, in Blake's illustrations, both celestial and infernal spirits are noble and divine, and so are Adam and Eve, who in the illustration to Book 5, though sleeping, mirror the

Figure 1 William Blake (1757–1827), *Adam and Eve Asleep* (Museum of
Fine Arts, Boston).

looks of the archangels Ithuriel and Zephon hovering above (see Figure 1).
Blake's Milton is one for whom matter and spirit – the divine and the human –
not only mix but overlap and interfuse such that the human becomes angelic,
divine. Man, Blake wrote, in the section of the *Marriage of Heaven and
Hell* entitled the "Voice of the Devil," "has no Body distinct from his Soul"
(34). The romantics gave voice to a *Paradise Lost* whose center of gravity,
sanctity, and sublimity is as much the human as the divine. Even more so,

the divinity of the human, as Empson's *Milton's God* will read the romantics, rises with a concomitant distaste for God himself. (Empson would go even farther than the romantics, comparing Milton's divinity to a "commandant at Bergen Belsen" and "Uncle Joe Stalin.") To Blake and Shelley, Empson affirms, "the reason why the poem is so good is that it makes God so bad" (1961, 13). It was Blake who, surpassing both Shelley and Coleridge in attributing to Milton a Satanic sensibility, famously wrote that Milton "was a true Poet and of the Devils party without knowing it" (*The Marriage of Heaven and Hell* plate 6; Blake 35). But Blake, in formulating a kind of Freudian Milton *avante le letter*, foregrounds the fact that his Milton is also a product of his "imagination." "You might as well," Blake writes citing a contemporary's misquotation of Shakespeare, "quote Satan's blasphemies from Milton & give them as Milton's opinions" (Wittreich 34). Unlike those in the "Satanic camp" of critics ostensibly defined by him, Blake allows that his own wildly antinomian Milton, though powerful, remains of his own creation. In many ways a response to the Milton of eighteenth-century critics and editors, Blake's Milton provides a knowing counterimage to those of his predecessors.

The Scholarly Milton: Milton in the Twentieth Century

Against the contemporary figure of the "stiff Puritan," a response to the perceived excesses of the romantic Milton that had reappeared in the criticism of the late nineteenth century, by 1925, Denis Saurat emphasizes, in the century of the academic Milton, the poet's "triumphant individuality." With emphasis on "the unity of his private and literary life," Saurat's *Milton: Man and Thinker*, called "the most influential book on Milton in the twentieth century," is among the first to turn a form of distinctively scholarly attention to Milton the man (xi; Shoulson 200). Indeed Saurat provides a systematic and scholarly account of the romantic Milton, asserting the same divinity of matter to which Johnson protested and that Blake figured in his illustrations. Saurat also affirms, echoing Blake and Coleridge, that "Satan is not only a part of Milton's character, he is also part of Milton's mind" (183). Against the Milton of Christian "dogma," Saurat brings together the public and private Milton, resisted in earlier versions of Milton, by emphasizing *Paradise Lost*'s "connection" to the poet himself, his "character and emotional experience" (xi). That Miltonic self is defined, like his Satan, by both "passion" and "sensuality," and thus Saurat's implicitly Freudian reading echoes precedent romantic renderings of the poet: "Whereas inferior artists build their monsters artificially," Saurat writes of Milton's Satan, the poet takes his monster "living and warm with his own life, out of himself" (184). The passion and sensuality of *Paradise Lost*, Saurat suggests, following Blake, might be attributed to the corresponding nature of the poet. Saurat celebrated the image of Milton inherited from the romantics, with the wildness displaced by Addison intact, but he presented his heretical and passionate Milton within the critical contexts of twentieth-century scholarship.

T. S. Eliot and C. S. Lewis, both responding to Saurat's work, set the course for Milton Studies for the second half of the twentieth century. They both take as their starting point Saurat's celebration of Milton the man, as well as the centrality of the "personal" (Milton's heresies), to an understanding of the epic. Although Eliot, as Jeffrey Perl has observed, had a habit of returning to topics and revising his earlier perspectives, in both of his essays on Milton (1936 and 1960), he admits "an antipathy towards Milton the man" (138, 148; Perl 122–8). In the earlier of the two essays, Milton's poetry, Eliot writes as he makes "the case against Milton" (153), could "only be an influence for the worse, upon any poet whatever," and not only had an adverse effect on poets in the eighteenth century, but remains "an influence against which we still have to struggle" (139). Eliot blamed Milton for being a "*great* poet," and not just "a *good* one" (139), concurring with Saurat about the unavoidable centrality of Milton the man, not celebrating him however, but condemning his religion and politics, judging him finally as both "scandalous" and "perverse" (148, 153, 149). Perhaps identifying himself too much with the Puritan poet and "individual," Eliot excises Milton and his "personality" from the classical canon, the "Tradition" that he would construct. Notably, in the second half of the twentieth century, Harold Bloom would create a different version of literary history, with Eliot's classical canon demoted, and the distinctly romantic and "wild" Milton not excised or repressed, but at its center.

Like Eliot, C. S. Lewis responds to Saurat's presumption of the centrality of Milton the man, not condemning him as Eliot did, but claiming, the staple move of orthodox proponents of the poem, his irrelevance. Saurat's Milton, the twentieth-century version of Toland's Milton and the Milton of the Romantics (the Milton that Addison refused to see, and that Bentley and Johnson saw but didn't like), was heterodox in theology and radical in politics. In his *A Preface to Paradise Lost* (1942), however, Lewis dismisses what he calls Milton's "private thoughts," "idiosyncratic and accidental as they are," as well as the "heresies" that "reduce themselves to something very small" (89). Lewis's *Paradise Lost* rather is defined as "Augustinian and Hierarchical," and also, as he writes with a slight nudge and a wink, "Catholic" (although he does immediately acknowledge that he's using the term, in its ordinary sense, to mean "universal," not "Roman Catholic" [81]).

Paradise Lost manifests, according to Lewis, "order, proportion, measure, and control," and bases its poetry on conceptions not to be found in seventeenth-century radical politics, but in those that have been held "always and everywhere by all" (79). Criticism, "lost in misunderstanding" since Blake, should not be interested at all in connections to "Milton's private thinking" (129, 89). Rather, Lewis asserts, "we are to study what the poet, with his singing robes about him, has given," and not the "private theological whimsies" that he "laid aside" during "his working hours as an epic poet" (90). Lewis's Milton hearkens back to the attempts of Bentley and Johnson to separate the private radical, heterodox, and "wild" man from the putatively orthodox achievement of the poem. To the extent that Lewis attacks, like Eliot, "personality," he is attacking a Milton attached to "revolutionary politics, antinomian ethics, and the worship of Man by Man," but also a conception of criticism that focuses more on "psychology" than on the "best of Milton which is in his epic" (129, 90). "Why," he writes, with a jibe at Saurat's emphasis on passion and sensuality, "must Noah *always* figure in our minds drunk and naked, never building the Ark?" (90). Saurat, through his reading of the romantics, had brought not only the individual but the "unconscious" into *Paradise Lost* (184); Lewis, the figure of Anglican orthodoxy, for whom "Decorum" is the "grand masterpiece," prefers Milton the "very disciplined artist" to the admittedly "undisciplined man" of passion (90).

Like orthodox readers before him, Lewis comes to clean up some of the more "embarrassing" aspects of the epic, although as with Bentley's, his effort to render the poem orthodox reveals the heretical energies that inform it. The controversial issue, for example, of Milton's angels who eat and enjoy other physical pleasures gets treated by Lewis with not inconsiderable alarm. Even though Lewis claims to avoid "critical prudery," he insists that Raphael's angelic proclamation of enjoyment of angelic intermingling, induced by Adam's blush-inducing question in Book 8, should not be confused with "sensuality," and that angels share nothing of the human "desire for pleasure." In order to suggest that readers not attribute to the angels a "homosexual promiscuity," Lewis bizarrely attributes to Milton's angels what he says "might be called" – one can almost see *him* blushing – "transexuality" (109). Lewis's insistence on an orthodox Milton, like Bentley's before him, can't help but reveal the heretical perspectives, even the passionate and sensual energies, it attempts to repress.

Milton Today

The last half-century of Milton criticism has been enormously rich and complex, with Stanley Fish's *Surprised by Sin* (1967) placing Milton back into the center of the critical canon after Eliot's hostility and what F. R. Leavis described in 1936 as Milton's "dislodgement" (42). An avowedly angelic and orthodox reading of the epic, Fish's book in some sense pursues the tradition of interpretation set forth by Lewis. Fish sees *Paradise Lost* as finally elaborating a singular and monolithic vision, and the heresies it elicits are there as temptations to the reader *only*. From Fish's perspective, the Milton of *Paradise Lost* prefers "final certainty" to the "ambiguity of the poetic moment" (Fish 43), and he suggests that passages of Satanic sublimity, like the description of Satan as a tower, are designed to reveal the perversity of the fallen reader.

By 1987, the Milton of *Surprised by Sin*, John Rumrich writes, had become the "corporate, almost institutionalized, vision of Milton and his work" (1996, 2). Rumrich's "Uninventing Milton" (1990) and his later *Milton Unbound* (1996), attempt to move away from what he identifies as the "paradigm" that had become "foundational" to contemporary Milton scholarship (1996, 4). In his *Destablizing Milton* (2008), Peter Herman, following Rumrich (as well as William Kerrigan's "Milton's Place in Intellectual History" [1989]), decries the detrimental influence of both Fish and Lewis. The "Milton as a poet of certainty," Herman argues, has "very wide, very deep roots" (19). Citing the continuing and "current hegemony of the angelic Milton," Herman proposes his own "paradigm shift," encouraging a new breed of "guerilla Miltonists" (the term was used first by Douglas Bush against Eliot), a "New Milton Criticism" that will eschew certainty and coherence, for a Milton who "does not," in Herman's words, "come to a conclusion" (19, 21). Similar to Saurat's Milton who, we are told, "intellectually was very near to not believing," the Milton of Herman's volume not only does not embrace orthodoxy, but questions, if not undermines, it (171).

Herman, although surely identifying a persistent strand in Milton criticism, might be seen as part of a recent critical history focusing on Milton's radicalism and heresy, suggesting a perhaps not so solid angelic hegemony of critical responses. John Rumrich's first book, *The Matter of Glory* (1987), Stephen Fallon's *Milton among the Philosophers* (1991), John Rogers *The Matter of Revolution* (1998), as well as the essays in Rumrich's and Stephen Dobranski's collection *Milton and Heresy* (1998), have all contributed to a growing body of literature on the nature and origins of Milton's heterodox beliefs. The extent to which the orthodox Milton of theology has not been, as Herman claims, singularly dominant is also registered in an historical turn to Milton's political contexts, signaled in the publication of the collection of essays coedited by the Cambridge historian Quentin Skinner *Milton and Republicanism* (1993), a return in some sense to the Milton who Toland celebrated. Sharon Achinstein's *Milton and the Revolutionary Reader* (1994), elaborating the contexts for Milton's political and poetic interventions, is part of the general move to see Milton and other figures of the seventeenth century in their radical political contexts. In this regard, Nigel Smith's *Literature and Revolution in England* (1997) and David Norbrook's *Writing the English Republic* (2007), although not devoted exclusively to Milton, have been crucial in contributing to the current moment in Milton Studies. Blair Worden's *Literature and Politics in Cromwellian England* (2008), focusing on Milton and his contemporaries, has been said to exemplify this "New Model Criticism," which "subjects literary works to more and more intensive contextualization" (Burrow 25). The emphasis on "highly specialized contextual labors" (Burrow 25), very often political, among recent Milton scholars culminates in the biography by Corns and Campbell *Milton: Life, Work and Thought* (2008). Milton's most recent biographers suggest that the stages of Milton's "radicalization are the spine that runs" through their study, and self-avowedly present a Milton who is "self-serving, arrogant, passionate, ruthless, ambitious and cunning" (3).

So dominant were political paradigms and Milton's radicalism to the study of *Paradise Lost* already in 2001, that David Loewenstein felt prompted to qualify the move "to politicize and historicize" with renewed emphasis on "religious ideologies and beliefs" (2). To offset, protest, even refuse the explicitly political, rationalist, or radical Milton, there is the persistently orthodox Milton of Fish's *How Milton Works* (2001), the "ironic" but orthodox (Lutheran) Milton of Victoria Silver's *Imperfect Sense* (2001), and the hallucinatory and "delirious Milton" of Gordon Teskey's account (2009). Jeffery Shoulson's *Milton and the Rabbis* (2001) and Douglas Brooks' collection *Milton and the Jews* (2008) also provide an unexpected perspective on the epic, helping to elaborate rabbinic contexts for *Paradise Lost*.

Interest in gender in *Paradise Lost* arose in the late seventies with the rise of feminism and feminist criticism. Christine Froula's "When Eve Reads Milton" (1983), Diane McColley's *Milton's Eve* (1983), and Joseph Wittreich's *Feminist Milton* (1988) helped define the issues of importance for the coming decades. Milton's relationship to the feminine is also explored in a set of important essays published by Mary Nyquist in the late eighties and in the essays by various authors included in Judith Walker's collection, *Milton and the Idea of Woman* (1988). Recent books such as *Milton and Gender*, edited by Catherine Gimelli Martin (2004), Shannon Miller's *Engendering the Fall* (2008), and Louis Schwartz's *Milton and Maternal Morality* (2009), have further complicated our sense of Milton's conceptions of gender relations and hierarchy.

That *Paradise Lost* allows for so many contextualizations and that Milton does not "come to a conclusion" may not relegate him to "incertitude," but show, as Freud did of Michelangelo's Moses, that *Paradise Lost* surpasses the multiple and sometimes divergent interpretive perspectives that it elicits. The battle between Milton's warring angels of critical camps need not end with the Milton of orthodox certainty or radical heresy finally triumphing. To accede to one of these versions of Milton is the equivalent of succumbing to what Blake was warned of in his "imagination:" to be "misled" by one definitive and final conception of the poem. The manifold, contradictory, and often equally compelling versions of *Paradise Lost* testify to a poem often arguing through paradox, a "wild work" resisting any single set of readings.

To the extent that, as Paul Stevens writes, all Milton criticism conceives of itself as "the New Milton criticism," every generation may find itself dissatisfied with or exhausted by the partial renderings bequeathed to it (790). That a particular version of *Paradise Lost* may seem polemical may already reveal a need for new approaches (the need, as Herman affirms, to say, "enough!"), or that indeed a New Milton criticism is already on the horizon (25). At the current moment in Milton Studies, so conscious of the reception of *Paradise Lost*, the possibility of seeing the defensive functions of earlier aggressive interpretations, how they often come to conquer uncertainty or exclude other voices, may more likely allow for new experiences and readings of the poem. Almost a half a century ago, A. J. Waldock conceded that although "we may never feel Milton's classicism as strongly as Addison could," there are nonetheless "a great many other things to feel that Addison never dreamt of." "We are," Waldock concludes, in some ways, in a better position for estimating *Paradise Lost* than ever Addison was" (145). And this, finally, may be true for every generation of readers, ours especially, of Milton's great epic.

Further Reading

Editions and Early Commentaries

Addison, Joseph, *Criticism on Milton's "Paradise Lost,"* ed. Edward Arber (London, 1868).

Baron, William, *Regicides No Saints, nor Martyrs* (London, 1700).

Bentley, Richard, *Milton's Paradise Lost* (London, 1732).

Blake, William, *The Complete Poetry and Prose of William Blake*, ed. David V. Erdman (Garden City, NY, 1982).

H[ume], P[atrick], *Annotations on Milton's "Paradise Lost"* (London, 1695).

Johnson, Samuel, *The Yale Edition of the Works of Samuel Johnson*, vol. 21 (New Haven, CT, 2010).

Milton, John, *Paradise Lost* (London, 1688).

Richardson, Jonathan (father and son), *Explanatory Notes and Remarks on Milton's "Paradise Lost"* (London, 1734).

Shawcross, John, ed., *Milton: The Critical Heritage: 1732–1801* (London, 1972).

Milton: The Critical Heritage (London, 1970).

Toland, John, *Amyntor: or, A Defence of Milton's Life* (London, 1699).

A Complete Collection of the Historical, Political and Miscellaneous Works of John Milton (Amsterdam, 1698).

Wittreich, Joseph, *The Romantics on Milton* (Cleveland, OH, 1970).

Secondary Material

Achinstein, Sharon, *Milton and the Revolutionary Reader* (Princeton, NJ, 1994).

Armitage, David, Armand Himy, Quentin Skinner, eds., *Milton and Republicanism* (Cambridge, UK, 1995).

Bloom, Harold, *Modern Critical Views: John Milton*, ed. Harold Bloom (Philadelphia, 2004).

Brooks, Douglas A., ed., *Milton and the Jews* (Cambridge, UK, 2008).

Budick, Sanford, *Milton and the Sublime* (Cambridge, MA, 2010).

Burrow, Colin, "New Model Criticism," *London Review of Books*, 19 June 2008, 25.

Campbell, Gordon, Thomas N. Corns, John K. Hale, and Fiona J. Tweedie, *Milton and the Manuscript of De Doctrina Christiana* (Oxford, 2007).

Campbell, Gordon and Thomas N. Corns, *John Milton: Life, Work and Thought* (Oxford, 2008).

Dobranski, Stephen, *Milton in Context* (Cambridge, UK, 2010).

Eliot, T. S., *On Poetry and Poets* (London, 1965).

Empson, William, *Milton's God* (Cambridge, UK, 1961).

Some Versions of Pastoral (New York, 1974).

Fallon, Stephen, *Milton among the Philosophers* (Ithaca, NY, 2001).

Fish, Stanley, *Surprised by Sin* (New York, 1967).

How Milton Works (Cambridge, MA, 2001).

Freud, Sigmund, *On Creativity and the Unconscious* (New York, 1958).

Froula, Christine, "When Eve Reads Milton: Undoing the Canonical Economy," *Critical Inquiry* 10,2 (1983), 321–47.

Griffin, Dustin, *Regaining Paradise: Milton and the Eighteenth Century* (Cambridge, UK, 1986).

Grossman, Marshall, *Authors to Themselves: Milton and the Revelation of History* (Cambridge, UK, 1988).

Herman, Peter, *Destablizing Milton: "Paradise Lost" and the Poetics of Incertitude* (London, 2008).

Herman, Peter and Elizabeth Sauer, eds., *The New Milton Criticism* (New York, 2011).

Hill, Christopher, *Milton and the English Revolution* (London, 1978).

Kerrigan, William, "Milton's Place in Intellectual History" in *The Cambridge Companion to Milton*, ed. Dennis Danielson (Cambridge, UK, 1989), 253–67.

Kolbrener, William, *Milton's Warring Angels* (Cambridge, UK, 1996).

Leavis, F. R., *Revaluation: Tradition and Development in English Poetry* (London, 1936).

Leonard, John, *Faithful Labourers: A Reception History of "Paradise Lost," 1667–1970*, 2 vols. (Oxford, 2013).

Lewis, C. S., *A Preface to Paradise Lost* (London, 1942).

Lewis, C. S. and E. M. W. Tillyard, *The Personal Heresy* (London, 1939).

Loewenstein, David, *Representing Revolution in Milton and His Contemporaries* (Cambridge, UK, 2001).

Marcus, Steven and Charles Taylor, "Calls for Papers," *Common Knowledge* 1.2 (1992), 6.

Martin, Catherine Gimelli, ed., *Milton and Gender* (Cambridge, UK, 2004).

McColley, Diane Kelsey, *Milton's Eve* (Urbana, IL, 1983).

Miller, Shannon, *Engendering the Fall: John Milton and Seventeenth-Century Women Writers* (Philadelphia, 2008).

Moore, Leslie E., *Beautiful Sublime: The Making of Paradise Lost: 1701–1734* (Stanford, CA, 1990).

Newlyn, Lucy, *"Paradise Lost" and the Romantic Reader* (Oxford, 1993).

Norbrook, David, *Writing the English Republic* (Cambridge, UK, 2000).

Nyquist, Mary and Margaret W. Ferguson, eds., *Re-membering Milton* (London, 1987).

Perl, Jeffrey, *Skepticism and Modern Enmity* (Baltimore, MD, 1989).

Rogers, John, *Matter of Revolution: Science, Poetry and Politics in the Age of Milton* (Ithaca, NY, 1996).

Rumrich, John, *Matter of Glory: A New Preface to Paradise Lost* (Pittsburgh, PA, 1987).

    Milton Unbound (Cambridge, UK, 1996).

    "Uninventing Milton," *Modern Philology* 87.3 (1990), 249–65.

Rumrich, John and Steven Dobranski, eds., *Milton and Heresy* (Cambridge, UK, 1998).

Saurat, Denis, *Milton: Man and Thinker* (London, 1925).

Schwartz, Louis, *Milton and Maternal Morality* (Cambridge, UK, 2009).

Sharratt, Bernard, "The Appropriation of Milton," *Essays and Studies* 35 (1982), 30–44.

Shoulson, Jeffrey, *Milton and the Rabbis: Hebraism, Hellenism and Christianity* (New York, 2001).

Silver, Victoria, *Imperfect Sense* (Princeton, NJ, 2001).

Smith, Nigel, *Is Milton Better than Shakespeare?* (Cambridge, MA, 2008).

    Literature and Revolution in England (New Haven, CT, 1997).

Stevens, Paul, "Milton in America," *University of Toronto Quarterly* 77.3 (2008), 789–800.

Tayler, Edward, *Milton's Poetry: It's Development in Time* (Pittsburgh, PA, 1978).

Teskey, Gordon, *Delirious Milton* (Cambridge, MA, 2006).

Thorpe, James, ed., *Milton Criticism: Selections from Four Centuries* (London, 1951).

Waldock, A. J. A., *Paradise Lost and Its Critics* (Cambridge, UK, 1947).

Walker, Judith, ed., *Milton and the Idea of a Woman* (Urbana, IL, 1988).

Walsh, Marcus, *Shakespeare, Milton and Eighteenth-Century Literary Editing* (Cambridge, UK, 2008).

Wittreich, Joseph, *Feminist Milton* (Ithaca, NY, 1988).

Woodhouse, A. S. P, "Notes on Milton's Views on the Creation: The Initial Phases," *Philological Quarterly* 28 (1949), 211–236.

Worden, Blair, *Literature and Politics in Cromwellian England* (Oxford, 2008).

INDEX

Cambridge Companions to...

AUTHORS

TOPICS